I did not have to join, but I did! Anything must be better than being cooped up in a dreary drawing office from 8-00 am, to 5-00 pm, each day. There was the added threat, my red headed workmate, David Williams, and I, would be declared exempt by our employer, in the exigencies of essential war work. Joining HMF on 17 October 1939, six weeks after the outbreak of war, my loyal oath was shattered on day three, and from then on, I owed nothing to any King or Country.

Commissioned in November 1940, I was posted, as a cast-out, from Northern Ireland; – "To a tropical peace station in the east!" on 4 December 1941 boarded a ship to, wherever? It was to be a very rough ride. Arriving at Rangoon on 5 March 1942, two days before its closure, I met with the remorseless Japanese Eastern military rampage in Burma.

Lacking Command, and every possible item of provisioning; – Ammunition, Food, Medical, to the point of discard, I found it necessary to assert myself. Releasing the true story in 1984, Prime Minister Thatcher used Scotland Yard Serious Crime Squad to stultify my attempts, to release the apparent 'unsavoury' truths contained in this book. They illustrate the raw philosophical application of the highest level of man management, and the disciplined conducting of executions, at a time of military abandonment, and sheer desperation.

Discarded at the time, by Prime Minister Churchill, and his Generals; – men confused, flustered, and indifferent, towards the 1941/42 Eastern War Command: – It's not that Parliamentary successors do no want to know, it is rather that they will not admit, the damnable situation into which the British Army in Burma was placed.

Seventy years later, with deep scepticism turned to incredulity, Captain Fitzpatrick recalls his feelings of betrayal, and disillusionment, towards those in authority over him and his proud regiment, as they struggled and fought with incredible success in appalling conditions through Burma's torrid and hostile plains, and jungles, towards the Indian border. Few survived, and this book seeks to lay bare the flawed and incompetent decisions of those in military command, and in Whitehall, resulting in this most catastrophic of all British army withdrawals.

This story is of the forlorn and desperate army discarded by Churchill, in which survival required assertion of outstanding initiative and determination, superseding seniority in military rank, whenever necessary.

Unable, or unwilling, in 2001, the editorial Committee, of the Burma Star Association magazin, 'Dekho!' under the Presidency of, The Viscount Slim OBE DL, declined the offer of review of the first publication of this book. The Royal Engineers Assocation, in which I served, replied; – "I don't have a reviewer". Sad!

DITCHED IN BURMA

NO MANDALAY, NO MAYMYO

(79 SURVIVE)

DITCHED IN BURMA

NO MANDALAY, NO MAYMYO

(79 SURVIVE)

Captain Gerald Fitzpatrick

A CIP catalogue record for this book is available from the British Library.

ISBN 978-0-9572783-0-1

Prepared and printed by:

York Publishing Services Ltd
64 Hallfield Road
Layerthorpe
York YO31 7ZQ

Tel: 01904 431213

Website: www.yps-publishing.co.uk

CONTENTS

INTRODUCTION

CHAOTIC CHICANERY –
PARLIAMENTARY AND MILITARY

World War Two – 1941. Piecemeal! The year in which the fate of the Far Eastern theatre of operations was sealed

With the war on the 'door-step', and on accepting two shillings, (2s/0d), 'commitment' money, a young man, or girl, with no hope of ever meeting the King, joined, 'His Imperial Majesties Armed Forces.' All became immediately, under the influence of other remote men; – Luminaries; Parliamentarians and Military Generals, controlling affairs; all of whom were considered competent, and highly proficient, in their responsibilities of co-ordinating events.

In lower functions, there were long established Navy, Army, and Air Force, Unit Commanders, trusted, and considered proven in the diligence of their duties. They were, however, seldom introduced to new entrants, except to reprimand as necessary; – although, in the event of their coming from, selective, and formative educational establishments, they became cosseted.

Voluntarily enlisting into the Army, along with my friend and works colleague, on 17th October 1939, six week after the outbreak of war, I was shattered, and disillusioned, by a foul act that I have never forgiven. No longer was I serving King and Country! All further effort was to be centred on Me! And Me Alone!

1941 was the worst of years for Britain, the nation stood alone against the might of the Nazi hordes occupying a submissive Europe, and threatening invasion of Britain. Any thoughts of conflict, or reinforcement, in the remote Far East were suppressed, a year of denials and shortcomings by Churchill and the warlords, in which were shaped many tragedies, and disasters throughout the eastern world.

In early 1942, British armed forces were in turmoil, as they re-mustered and trained, following the evacuation at Dunkirk. Industry was desperately short of supplies, and food rationing was biting hard, with coupons controlling all purchases. It was the longest, busiest, and most depressing year.

Following twelve months service as a sapper in the Royal Engineers, I was commissioned, in November 1940. Developed as a specialist infantry platoon commander, and aware that I must have active involvement in the near future, with not the slightest inkling of where this might be. Transferred between three King's Own Yorkshire Light Infantry Battalions; – the 7th, 1st, and 2nd. It was with the 2nd battalion that I had all the active involvement one may wish for.

I include this introduction in order to detail the actions of governments and military chiefs, and their failure to plan adequately for an inevitable eastern conflict. The indifference and incompetence in dealing with early warnings resulted in the unnecessary loss of thousands of lives, and in many more thousands spending long youthful years in tropical prison camps.

Starving and thirsting, I was involved in the longest ever withdrawal undertaken by any British army force, with men dying on the line of march. We were castigated, rather than praised, for the effort. Actions of resistance in the early months of 1942 halted the progress of the Japanese, it so exhausted them that they terminated their devastating advance at the Indian border, and were thus, denied contact with hostile nationalist revolutionaries, in India and Ceylon.

Nothing in wartime compares with the treachery of Prime Minister, Winston Churchill. He discarded the British Army in Burma, and betrayed China, at the critical and pivotal time that Chinese forces were releasing British troops from captivity.

Members of the armed forces, soldiers, sailors or airmen, were never in position from which to appreciate the dubious machinations of the government. Politicians and military chiefs had the screen of secrecy behind which to hide their blunders. The cloak of silence covered much political muddling, indifference, and some downright treachery. Under the Secrecy Act, sensitive information was conveniently withheld from the public for thirty years following the war: − For example, in 1942, exasperated by a series of reverses, Churchill withheld news of the destruction of the Cunard Steamship Company liner, S.S. *Lancastrian,* by German bomber aircraft. To this day, the tragedy remains the greatest loss of life ever in a sea tragedy, with five thousand drowned. This convenient cloak of secrecy, also covered Churchill's most treacherous aberration, one in which my colleagues and I suffered. It was subsequently revealed in a, 'for your eyes only', message to President Roosevelt.

In late 1941, after two years of war, the world had been changed by the global ambitions of Hitler and the German nation. Earlier warning of this outcome was Hitler's denouncement of the Treaty of Versailles as early as 17th March 1935, the precipitate action ignored by all countries except France, which reacted by increasing military conscription. Belatedly, Britain introduced conscription, on 26 April 1939, all males reaching the age of twenty, were required to serve for eighteen months in either His Majesty's Forces or down coal mines. Following a short initial training, the first conscripted intake in July 1939 was overtaken by the outbreak of hostilities between England and Germany.

With the Emergency Powers Bill 1940 introducing conscription for women, in 1941, it placed 33 million, men and women, under the order.

Britain knew exactly where it stood. It stood alone, with its Empire, against the all conquering Axis powers. Germany and Italy, were occupying continental Europe, and brutally ill-treating observers of different creeds and customs.

As the long year of 1941 drew to a close, the British people knew that they were not going to remain undefeated without a titanic struggle. It was the year of closer bonding between the countries of the Empire; − India, New Zealand, South Africa, Canada, and Australia. There were also the dependencies, including Nepal, which already having given much, were further strengthening their resolve to defeat the Nazis, recruiting, training, and striving to 'Come to the aid of the mother country'. German forces overran Europe with little opposition, Panzer tanks crashing through the much vaunted Maginot line, caused early capitulation of the French government. They chose to preserve Paris from attack and destruction.

Unoccupied Spain remained devastated, recovering from its recent civil war. Neutral Portugal's capital, Lisbon, became a base for international espionage. Switzerland's questionable neutrality was honoured. Ireland stood by, feeling that it owed Britain nothing; – though regardless of the national policy, many thousands of Irishmen so abhorred the Nazi doctrine that they joined the British Armed Forces.

From 1935 to 1939 there had been a relentless build-up of German forces, and in the first two years of war, from 1939 to 1941, Britain witnessed the effectiveness and efficiency of detailed planning. Mainland Europe was occupied, German forces overran Scandinavia, (with spirited opposition in Norway). Panzer tank divisions swept through North Africa, German aircraft attempted to bomb Malta into oblivion, and U-boats scoured the Atlantic shipping lanes in wolf-like packs, sinking massive tonnages of allied shipping, conveying supplies to Britain.

Germans and Italians domiciled in Britain were arrested as potential enemy agents, and incarcerated in specially prepared camps. They were eventually employed in agriculture and other less security sensitive pursuits. London, underground railway platforms were tightly packed each night with men, women and those children too young to be evacuated away from the city, all taking what little they could of sleep and shelter, from the incessant nightly bombing by the Luftwaffe.

Churchill was a political chameleon and opportunist. In some form of chagrin, and in order to further his own ends, he tetchily changed political parties twice, from Tory to Liberal, and back. Liberal to Tory. However, at the point of his lowest standing, in June 1941, when criticism of his many failures in the conduct of war, to date, was strongest, his fortunes changed in the most ironic manner.

Outside his knowledge or planning, the shaky Prime Minister had the luckiest of breaks. It was truly, 'The fluke of the century'. It came about from governmental misjudgement of international affairs back in August 1939.

Britain had tried, and failed, to make an alliance with Soviet Russia, in order to co-operate against the emergent and aggressive Germany. In the event, the scales were turned against Britain on 23 August 1939: – Russia elected to make a pact with Germany, and on 1 September 1939, German armed forces invaded Poland. Two days later, on 3 September 1939, Britain declared war on Germany.

Russia and Germany, the mighty powers with efficient mobilised forces, saw Britain as a weak and vulnerable nation. However, it was Hitler's treachery that brought about rapid change, and Churchill was delighted to see differences arising between Russia's, President Stalin, and Hitler. Feeling that this vindicated Britain's earlier failure to complete the 1939 pact with Russia: – In an anti-Russian publicity campaign, and attempting to deflect British minds from home front problems, Churchill declared: -

"Many illusions about Soviet Russia have been dispelled in these few fierce weeks of fighting in the Arctic Circle. Everyone can see how Communism rots the soul of a nation, how is makes it abject and hungry in peace and proves it base and abominable in war".

All was to change within days of this damnable utterance: – Following Russia's failure in the war with Finland, Hitler came to regard Russia as a weak and struggling force, and sought to exploit the situation. Turning his army from Western Europe, and delaying the imminent invasion of Britain, Hitler turned to the East, launching a massive attack on Russia.

Finding a new set of circumstances, Churchill, as was his practice, 'turned his coat!' Russia now became the ready-made, though possibly reluctant, ally of Britain. The Prime Minister expressed undisguised relief when, in June 1941, the long-anticipated invasion of England was diverted. Hitler sought a rapid victory, in an all out assault on what he considered an inadequate, dilapidated and much over-rated Russian Army, hoping thereby to silence increasing discontent within Germany.

Supervised by KGB officers, Russian merchant vessels loaded at British ports. Churchill's wife Clementine gave much publicity and support to campaigns supplying Russian needs. Stalin's insatiable demands for arms, tanks, aircraft and food were enormous. Royal Navy and merchant shipping convoys to Russian ports suffered losses to German U-boats operating in the northern waters of the Barents Sea. Fortunately, by this time, Britain's armed forces were strengthened and reorganised, as munitions, aircraft, tanks, and agriculture production, became government-directed, with increasingly high efficiency.

As the year of 1941 moved towards winter, Britain stood alone against the Axis powers, with Russia a remote and struggling new found friend. Germany was the all-conquering power. The Italian army was considered comical and inconsequential, following its recent struggles against Ethiopian tribesmen.

One undeclared enemy was in France, where the Vichy French were consorting with Axis occupying forces. Manipulating and profiting from the parlous situation of the British, was the United States of America, which bore out Churchill's pre-war forecast: – "In the event of hostilities in Europe, the Americans will remain remote and indifferent".

President Roosevelt and Churchill met at Placentia Bay in August 1941 in order to sign the Atlantic Charter. From here on, Churchill was on a begging mission. His plea; – "Give me the tools and we'll finish the job", fell on deaf ears, as merciless, Roosevelt extracted payment, and sought profit, where-ever possible, as in American eyes, Britain was losing the European war.

This was not the time for charity or credit. Recovering from the famine period, when thousands queued at Soup Kitchens in every American town, they were now showing newsreels from mid-1940; – the desperate period of the Dunkirk evacuation. The films indicated the parlous condition of Britain, and an early surrender to Germany was anticipated. Britain as a power was finished and gains could be made! American factories flourished as they geared for profit. Immigrants from Germany and Italy made the case for supplying to the Axis powers as well as to Britain. The Irish, remembering Churchill's treachery over the Home Rule Bill, had no wish to support a struggling Britain. Let them struggle!

Within the U.S.A. over fifty difficult years, had developed a suspicion of the British Empire, and had no scruples about supplying commodities it found convenient to produce; – Britain was grateful for anything. At the same time, doubts arose about whether America might, through neutral ports, be supplying the Axis powers. America would favour whichever power proved victorious in the European contest.

The carefully drafted Lend-Lease bill, with no formal account system, was not good business for Britain; the price was high and the quality of the aid suspect. Roosevelt's conditions were; − First, there must be a realisation of all British dollar assets; Second, America was permanently to take over the long established British naval and military bases in the Caribbean; otherwise, no help. In return for these undertakings, Britain received 51 obsolete American warships, of which no less than 41 remained unserviceable at the close of 1941. Britain received ten floating wrecks; a few of the remainder were eventually made serviceable.

Elsewhere, further 'blood money" was extracted by the Americans. When returning through the Barents Sea in 1941, after escort duty to a Russian seaport, 88 British officers and men aboard the Royal Navy cruiser H.M.S. *Edinburgh,* lost their lives in an attack by German submarines. *Edinburgh* was carrying 432 bars of Russian gold, worth £45,000,000, (45 Million Pounds). This money was advance payment for American supplies to a struggling Russia. The loss of British lives, and the gold, was never mentioned in America: -

In October 1981, Yorkshire-man, Keith Jessop, and his team, dived into the inhospitable depths of the Barents Sea in order to recover the booty, and the murky American deal was revealed.

To the American west, across the Pacific Ocean, Roosevelt's diplomats gave him cause to question Japanese intentions. Churchill's interest in the Far East, on the other hand, was about as deep as that of the Brigade of Guards: − (There was a saying among British soldiers stationed in hot foreign climes, 'The rarest commodity east of Suez is a Guardsman's shit'.)

For Churchill, as with the Guards' Brigade, the east terminated at the Suez Canal, and there can be no wonder at his failure to read the omens correctly, when Roosevelt asked his opinion of Japanese intentions. Churchill could not have been more wrong. He advised that Japan would lie quiet for a while, and that, 'Japan was more likely to drift into war rather than plunge'. Roosevelt commented; − "That in Japan's present mood, remonstration might have an opposite effect to warning them off".

Curiously, the extensive American intelligence organisation had no alternative advice to offer Roosevelt. Unaware that Japan was not to lie quiet for much longer; -It was a case of the blind leading the blind, and in the event he accepted the guidance given by the struggling British Prime Minister. These confidences were exchanged in late November, 1941. The treacherous day of December 7 was drawing close, and Uncle Sam was about to be toppled from the fence on which he had sat, for two and a quarter long and prosperous years.

U.S. isolationism had not, however, been well-received by the British public. They remembered World War I, when a similar situation existed, and America, – 'sat it out for three years'. With German forces fully occupied against Russia, Churchill was given a little time to consider new options, and turned his mind to other theatres of operation. Although, it was as though no danger existed beyond Suez, when on 17 September 1941,he became hell-bent on getting two further infantry divisions, plus tanks, into the Middle East, and justified the diversion of a troopship, destined for a Far Eastern posting, by saying, – "Malaya can wait and West Africa can be fitted in, or not, as convenient. The problem we have is one of priority". On the following day, 18 September 1941, Churchill stated; – "There should be no serious fighting until March 1942, except in the Western Desert".

This accorded with the judgement he had given Roosevelt on the Japanese 'lying quiet'. On the basis of this, Churchill considered as minor, the role undertaken by forces beyond Suez. He caused a delay in dispatching five British infantry battalions to India, and British and Indian troops (including Ghurkas) were sent as reinforcements to the Middle East. Churchill's comment on the troop situation in India was that; – "Although it was no doubt very thin, India was to be assured that the delay in reinforcement was only a brief one".

Paramount in Churchill's thinking at this time was North Africa; – every effort was directed towards supplying and reinforcing the Desert Army. For all matters east of Suez, the good old maxim applied, – 'Show them a British man-of-war. That will settle matters'. This maxim was scuppered, when it became opportune to 'show a British man-of-war'. Because of the lack of sea power, and the British Admiralty proposing to dispatch a flotilla to eastern waters, the proposal was vetoed by the Commander in Chief, British Home Fleet.

In the early spring of 1942, the C in C, protested against the deployment to Singapore, of seven capital ships, one aircraft carrier, ten cruisers, and twenty-four destroyers; – a catastrophically incompetent decision in view of the activity about to overtake the East. Churchill declared his support for the Lord High Admiral.

Later, in attempting to justify his catastrophic error, Churchill wrote of Roosevelt: – (sic)

"I was in charge of a struggling country, beset by a deadly foe. He was aloft, august, at the head of a mighty neutral power whom he desired above all things to bring into the fight for freedom. But he could not as yet see how to do it".

Churchill realised; – Britain had to plan her own scheme of war. He was in no doubt of the American president's priority; it was to maintain isolationism.

Roosevelt's political opponents were many. He had strong opposition from immigrant Italians and Germans, and greater opposition from the Irish, who were unable to forget hundreds of years of British oppression. In short, American immigrant sentiment strenuously resisted helping in any British conflict.

With the privilege of sixty years hindsight and the release of long hidden confidential papers, it is possible to identify failings within British command and between nations. Agreements were made and broken. Incompetence, and at times cowardice, was to be seen in commanders on the field of conflict. Diversion of ammunition, food, and reserve troops, between areas of conflict may seem insignificant to those far away; – but one biscuit going to a soldier meant one less available to civilians at home; – a bullet, a tank, or tin of 'bully', going to one theatre or regiment, meant denying it to another.

News of happenings in the Far East, where Japan had already been at war for four years with China, was scant, and considered irrelevant, it was overshadowed by happenings in the western world. Attempting desperately to overcome the effects of sanctions, applied by Britain and America, particularly on oil supplies, Japan was becoming increasingly active. Previous Japanese pacts, made with both Britain and Germany were over-ridden by desperate circumstances. In seeking to end all controls applied by foreign powers, the Japanese secretly, and in great detail, planned to occupy the Far Eastern possessions, of France, Holland, and Britain, and go farther into French Indo-China, the Dutch East Indies, Malaya, the Philippines and New Guinea. Japanese spies were trained to occupy a variety of jobs throughout the whole of the east. They were engaged in any capacity affording espionage, or the recruitment of dissidents.

British intelligence reports on Japan indicated that the previously isolated nation had further interest than the war with China. Churchill gave the matter scant consideration, and commented that if Japanese aggression drew in America, he would be content to have it. "It may be no bad thing if it brought America off the fence". "They have plundered Britain long enough!" His priorities were; -

First, – the defence of the British Isles, including the threat of invasion and the U-boat war;

Second, – the struggle in the Middle East and Mediterranean;

Third, – supplies to Russia;

Last, – resistance to Japanese assault;

Showing a measure of apprehension, Roosevelt commented that it would be serious to underestimate the gravity of the threat from Japan; but nevertheless, with his eye on the main chance, he contemplated offering a Lend-Lease agreement to China.

Although Roosevelt, unlike the British, was equipped with the most expensive intelligence network in the world, he rather liked Churchill to think that it was he advising him. It appears that F.D.R. wished not to know the truth, so long as he could avoid committing the US forces to active service, and causing unrest at home.

In the meantime, improved production in Britain, throughout 1941, had caused a change of attitude in Churchill. There was a less dependence on America for aid. On 9 November 1941; – (four weeks before the fateful 7 December), Churchill said; –

"I would rather have an American declaration of war now, and no supplies for six months than double the supplies and no declaration".

Roosevelt! Disregarding the interests of Australia and New Zealand, and of British, Dutch, and French nationals in the Far East; – on 25 November, made a futile agreement with Japan: –

'No armed advancement in North East Asia, and the Southern Pacific', valid for a period of three months. This was, 'Pending further negotiations on an agreed basis'.

What did Roosevelt hope to achieve by the short-term pact?

Why make a pact for so short a time?

On 30 November 1941, the Japanese government telegrammed to Hitler: - "War may suddenly break out between Anglo-Saxon and Japan nations, quicker than anyone dreams."

Japanese military planners were making a fool of Roosevelt; – The Japanese fleet was already under sail for Pearl Harbour. They had isolated Roosevelt, getting him to operate behind the back of Churchill and other world leaders, and to buy a phoney three month pact.

Three weeks before the Japanese bombing of Pearl Harbour, possibly the most bizarre naval encounter of the war took place in the Indian Ocean, off the coast of Western Australia. On 19 November 1941, Battle Cruiser H.M.A.S. Sydney, on normal patrol duty, chanced upon a merchant vessel and approached. The vessel proved to be an armed merchantman, and taking Sydney by surprise, revealing heavy armament, opened fire and mortally wounded Sydney. Before her sinking, Sydney managed to return devastating fire, and both vessels journeyed to the seabed. It was normal in shipwrecks that lifeboats, or rafts, would save some crew, yet very surprisingly, in this case the search revealed no Australian survivors.

The truth about the action was revealed in recent years, by an elderly German, a survivor of the wreck, now a naturalised Australian. Sydney had 'come upon Kormoran, a German armed merchantman, it was awaiting a scheduled rendezvous with a Japanese submarine. Having witnessed the short sea battle, the Japanese submarine surfaced, rescued all German survivors, and then set to machine-gunning all Australians, to a man.

News of the sinking of Allied craft in eastern waters was sensitive, and Churchill did not want to be seen scaremongering Roosevelt into taking precipitate action, so, with the co-operation of Australian Prime Minister, John Curtin, copies of signals were withheld from Roosevelt.*

Even at so late a stage, anyone could fight, so long as it was not America. On 24 November Churchill advised his Foreign Secretary that Japan might attack Dutch possessions, – "But it was best to leave this as a direct issue between America and Japan". He continued: -

"If, after a reasonable interval, the United States is found incapable of any decisive action, even with our immediate support, we will nevertheless, although alone, make common cause with the Dutch". "Any Japanese attack on British possessions, carries with it, war with Great Britain as a matter of course".

On 6 December Britain and America, although aware of Japanese fleet movements, failed to appreciate their significance. Churchill had a theory, that in order to bluff an enemy, "one should cause a mass of manoeuvre". On the morning of 4 December, whilst awaiting my posting

---

* Hudson – Document on Australian Foreign Policy 1937-49, pages 232-3

Signal 131 Churchill to John Curtin, sent London, 28 November 1941 1.00 am.

Cablegramme Winch 6 Para (3) accept my deepest sympathy in the feared loss *of Sydney* so close to Australian shores.

We also have had a grievous blow this week in the loss of the Barham. Which blew up as a Result of a U-boat torpedo, involving the death of about 700 men. This is being kept strictly Secret at present as the enemy do not seem to know and the event would only encourage Japan.

Page 238

Signal 134 Curtin to Churchill

Cablegramme Johcu4, sent Canberra 29 Nov 41 6.45 pm. Received 29 Nov,. 1.15pm.,

I greatly appreciate your expression of sympathy in the loss of H.M.A.S. *Sydney*. It is a heavy Blow to us. (cont) sinking *of Barham* and secrecy.

from Glasgow, I did not know that I was to become part of Churchill's 'mass of manoeuvre,' in little more than forty-eight hours.

Within three weeks of the secret Japanese-American pact, on 7 December, the Japanese fleet, and air force, attacked and demolished the American Navy, based on the coast of Hawaii's, Oahu Island, at Pearl Harbour.

In 1937, changes in the sovereignty of Burma had caused friction in the government, and Burma was declared no longer part of the Indian Empire. It was now a separate territory, with partial self government, and Reginald Dorman-Smith, a former Labour politician, as British Governor. He was stationed near the Maymyo military base in northern Burma. There were two residential regular British infantry battalions, 1st Gloucesters, stationed at Mingladon, near Rangoon, and 2nd KOYLI at Maymyo, a pleasant up country hill station. There was also, the locally recruited Burma Frontier Force. Reluctantly tolerating these forces were many tribes and local warlords, in their respective territories; – Kachins, Chins, Shins, Burmans and others, they were incessantly in conflict.

Fifty years after these events, access is available to documents denied during wartime, and reveal blunders of the western leaders who ignored clear signs of Japanese hostility, and the forthcoming war in the eastern hemisphere. It was impossible to envisage that, from a draft of thirteen officers I would lose four fine colleagues, and be most fortunate to escape the hell of Burma, one of only nine Officers and seventy Other Ranks to survive from a 550-strong British infantry battalion. The conditions in which the KOYLI Battalion were required to serve, in December 1941, and early 1942, was beyond anything previously encountered, particularly in training. British forces were assaulted with such aggression and speed, that our limited preparations were wholly inadequate. There was no time in which to organise reinforcements, or supplies of any kind.

Over Christmas 1941, Churchill set sail for America. He was unsure whether the Americans now intended to restrict their war effort to defeating Japan, their immediate adversary, and then withdraw, leaving Britain and Russia to fight it out with Germany and Italy. Furthermore, he could not be sure whether American munitions, and service supplies to Britain, would be permanently stopped. An embargo had been placed on all U.S. supplies to Britain, immediately Japan attacked Pearl Harbour. Churchill was determined to make it clear that Britain would continue to withstand the bombing, rationing, and other problems, but its people had to eat. He pointed out that the Allies were certain to be heavily attacked in Malaya, and in the Far East.

On board ship, on his voyage across the U-boat patrolled Atlantic, Churchill was preparing papers outlining the development of the war. These focussed mainly on air attacks, and forthcoming military assaults into Europe, along with proposals for North Africa, although with no consideration for the Far East. He fully expected early success for the British army in North Africa. Churchill did not need a further setback, to make him appear weak in Roosevelt's eyes.

Churchill met Roosevelt knowing that he must tread carefully. He and his government were afraid of a blank refusal. America was exploiting the situation to the full. Churchill was warned by Roosevelt that there must be no attempts at agreements with Stalin and, 'no secret or special pacts'. The US President never mentioned his secret, short-term pact with Japan. Failing to give assurance on any subject, F.D.R. revealed nothing of his plans. He controlled Britain's supplies, and Churchill got no satisfactory answers to his repeated requests for further aid.

General Auchinleck appeared to be doing well, commanding the British Eighth Army in the Libyan Desert. His forces*, were soon to be attacked by Rommel's experienced tank divisions, and Auchinleck was to become another one of the 'Churchill' disgraced generals. General Bernard Montgomery assumed Middle East command.

The German U-boat menace was gradually being overcome. British munitions output was at its highest. Morale in Britain was increasing in the eighteen months since the evacuation of Dunkirk: – Troops were better trained and equipped. There was little likelihood of a German invasion, as the feared Russian Front was taking its terrible toll on German forces.

- 7th Armoured Division; 4th Armoured Brigade and Support Group;
  4th British Infantry Division; Guards Brigade (motorised);
  5th New Zealand Brigade; Polish Brigade Group 1;
  32nd Army Tank Brigade.

Persisting in his practice of, 'control from afar'; – On 21 December 1941, as Japanese forces began assaulting Hong Kong territory, Churchill signalled the Commander: –

"Continue vigorous fighting in inner defences, house to house if need be, maintain resistance, help allied cause, prolong resistance. Obtain lasting honour".

Throughout December 1941, and January 1942, Japanese landings were taking place on many fronts, spreading outwards like a fan throughout south-east Asia, including Malaya. Their forces continued to attack the U.S. Pacific Fleet, based on the Philippines, leaving no more than a small force of submarines. American Air Force planes were destroyed in battle and on the ground, as well as in air and naval bases. The consequence of this was that Australia and New Zealand were immediately exposed to possible Japanese attack.

Completely unaware of Japanese intentions, the two greatly loved Antipodeans countries had long deployed the best of their trained forces to the war in the west.

Based in Singapore, in December 1941, were the two capital ships, H.M.S. *Prince of Wales* (35,000 tons), (Admiral Phillips), and Battle Cruiser, H.M.S. *Repulse* (Captain Tennant). These were the only British Navy surface vessels in Asian waters. Commander in Chief, Home Fleet, begrudged them. Churchill regarded the deployment of the two ships, in order to meet the inevitable Japanese threat, as a matter of no great urgency; he also; – "Wanted time to think about it".

Time was a luxury the Japanese did not allow. The efficiency of Japanese aerial warfare was greatly underestimated. The range of their torpedo bombers, based at Saigon, approximately 400 miles from Singapore, was considered impossible. News of their performance came as a surprise and shock, to both British and American experts.

On Wednesday, 10 December 1941, the two warships, thought to be so formidable, were obliterated. They were attacked by 85 Japanese planes off Singapore, and sunk. Admiral Phillips was killed. Captain Tennant and 40 per cent of the *Repulse* crew survived. In all, 840 sailors lost their lives, and 2,000 were saved.

There was no protective R.A.F. support. One Royal Australian Air Force squadron was available, on an 'as needed' basis. In the circumstances, this unit was never troubled. The Japanese lost three planes and 18 airmen. This single action ripped the heart out of British naval power in the Far East.

Within four days of Japan's entry into the war, there were no Allied capital ships remaining in the Indian and Pacific Oceans. Japan had full battle-fleet command of Pacific and Asiatic waters, about 5,000 sea miles in all directions. No previous attack, assault or onslaught in the war, had been successful to this extent. About one fifth of the world's population was under threat.

Churchill was shocked on hearing reports of the sinking of the two ships. By this time, of course, Churchill, and the Commander in Chief, Home Fleet, had conveniently forgotten their opposition to the proposed deployment to Singapore of capital ships, aircraft carrier, cruisers and destroyers. Adequate support from sea and air power might well have halted Japanese advances. The astonishing speed of Japanese action spared Churchill and the Admiralty the necessity of explaining the absence of standard protection, by aircraft carrier or otherwise, for the capital ships and their crews. The ongoing ferocity of the Japanese assault saved Churchill's blushes: – It allowed no time for parliamentary questioning, or discussion. Churchill frantically signalled the Singapore Commander, -

"Nothing compares in importance with fortress Singapore ".

Churchill's priorities were changed in less than one week. He immediately promised reinforcements to C. in C. Wavell; – Including the 18th Army Division, four fighter squadrons, anti-aircraft and anti-tank guns, and numerous aircraft, – 'when Libya was won'. The 18th Division, however, contained very few experienced men; they were mostly newly-conscripted, and had hardly completed basic training. The ships were at least two or three weeks' sailing time from Singapore. On arrival, the men would require at least six to eight weeks for tropical acclimatisation. The promised aircraft from Libya were 'pie in the sky'. They had to fight, win, repair, re-arm and travel; – time was not on their side.

It was accepted that Japan, having overall domination of Asian and Pacific territories, would continue 'mopping up' British, French, and Dutch possessions. Little thought was given to prospects beyond these territories; – Australia and New Zealand, as with Burma and India, were not considered to be at risk.

In the period of Wavell's ill-fated earlier command, in the Middle East, in addition to many British casualties, the Allies lost about 9,000 Anzac troops. Following their initially succeeding in repulsing German paratrooper assaults, good men collapsed for want of food and ammunition, and were butchered for want of supplies. Many considered that it was Wavell at fault, although Churchill had played a part in diverting provisions. Australian Premier, John Curtin, was greatly displeased with Churchill, while Churchill put the blame on Wavell, the man whom he had transferred, 'out of sight, out of mind', – Beyond Suez!

Churchill's appointment of Wavell as Commander in Chief, Far East, indicated his low priority for the region. Governor, Dorman-Smith, of Burma, questioned the Churchill appointment of Sir Robert Brooke-Popham, as General Officer Commanding Far East, based at Singapore. Dorman-Smith considered the situation required, 'a more dynamic personality'.

Hereabouts we have some shilly-shallying. Wavell, having been appointed Commander, Far East Command, on 11 December 1941, caused some questioning. It was not until two days later, Churchill advised Dorman-Smith that Wavell was in charge of Military, and Air defence of Burma. Wavell assumed command of Burma four days after the outbreak of the Japanese war. Putting Burma under Far East Command he considered a cardinal mistake. At a 'senior staff appreciation of the Burma situation', Wavell reported: –

"All considerations, political, and geographical, combined to prevent the defence problem being taken sufficiently seriously ".
From mid December 1941 Burma was, therefore, a lost cause.

Wavell was lacking in initiative, and Curtin blamed him for the loss of Australian troops on Crete: – He did not, at this point, consider the fact that Churchill had denied supplies to Wavell, and Wavell made no issue of his differences with Churchill.

Dorman-Smith, in his Maymyo office, was for five days, in ignorance of the invasion of Burma, at Tenasserim, the long southern finger of the country; – whereas local people knew of it on the day of the attack.

The War Office in London was preoccupied with problems nearer home. Wavell was the man on the spot, and he had recently established that Burma 'need not be taken seriously'; – whilst Middle East commanders, Montgomery in particular, demanded that he should be given prior consideration on all supplies.

The sheer size of the task! Wavell's limited knowledge of Burma! This, along with the little time available, made effective defensive deployment impossible. The carefully prepared and rehearsed plans, of the rapidly approaching Japanese assault force, had been made over a number of years.

Wavell was doubly engaged and watching two fronts, 'PI-Force', in Persia and Iraq, to the West. As though of no significance, he now had the commitment in Burma, to the East, with the Indian sub-continent intervening. He appeared to tackle each task as a tactical exercise on which to report, rather than a job to be done. He reports of this time: –

"We were not prepared to fight a full-scale war against a first class armed power in the Far East".

The Japanese entered Burma, and rapidly captured the southern airstrip at Victoria Point. Sir Kenneth McLeod, as General Officer Commanding, Burma, gave the, 'Order of the Day': – *"On land, sea and air, we will repulse the foe "*. He forgot to say with what?

On 11 December 1941, Germany officially declared war on America. Three days earlier. Hitler ordered: –

"The German Navy must attack American ships, wherever found".

America showed her true colours. All supplies to Britain were immediately 'frozen and embargoed'. At this stage, the Americans did not know where their front line of defence was. Their western shoreline trembled lest it feel a Japanese onslaught.

Manufacturing plants, recently established to exploit the European war, were now turned to meet American needs.

Japan was exploiting its spectacular successes, brought about in part by collaborators, trained and planted in occupied countries, long before the bombing of Pearl Harbour. The British had been blind, or indifferent, to developments taking place under their noses in Burma, where strong nationalist movements had developed, similar to those in British India. Within hours of the Japanese bombing Rangoon, there was an outbreak of murder and looting. Nationalist U-Saw's brutal 'Galon Army' attacked political and commercial targets, in particular Indian merchants and shopkeepers.

24 year-old Thakin tribal leader, Aung-San, who had previously fled Burma, for sanctuary in Japan, now accompanied the Japanese forces. He was leading a small army of 30 native Burmese, called 'The Thirty', and seeking collaboration with villager headmen. The serene exterior of Burmese individuals could hide a murdering Dacoit, capable of using his *dah,* or matchet, to carve the unsuspecting to death.

Through the offices of both, Premier U-Saw, and the Thakin Leader, Aung-San, Burma was riddled with Japanese informers and fifth columnists, long before 1939. The British authorities chose to minimise their significance. There was never going to be war in Burma?

Wealthier Indians began the general exodus, fleeing the country by sea through Rangoon, the main exit, if they were quick enough. The alternative was the tortuous 'Burma Road' to Chungking, in China.

With no opposition, Japanese planes began dropping leaflets over southern Burma. Prepared by Aung-San, they urged the Burmese to welcome the Japanese, and get ready for their offensive. The British authorities took no notice. Japan was to benefit enormously from the Burmese public relations exercise. Guided in their advance, without the need of map or compass, travelling through safe routes, and knowing the ground to be unoccupied, they used spies to select vantage points from which to engage the British, who never suspected the degree of local co-operation.

Britain hoped to conduct the war in textbook style strategy, with constructed defences, and impractical pre-planned 'trench warfare'. The invading Japanese did not operate in that manner, yet any suggestion of alternative tactics was stamped upon by British Commanders, who regarded it unacceptable to have Burmese recruits trained in counter-espionage, or to consider what assistance the 'simple' Burmese might give to insurgents.

Churchill, in America over Christmas 1941, reminded senators of his two years' start in war operations, and pointed out that, had America abandoned its isolationism some years earlier, the German war machine might not have been launched.

Roosevelt, and the Senate, agreed to Churchill's proposal that Wavell should be appointed Supreme Allied Commander in South East Asia; and, owing to the rapidly developing situation in the Far East, Churchill, 'patronising and graciously', accepted the appointment on behalf of Wavell. He continued to outline the organisation and operational plans for all forces coming under Wavell's command. As the man on the spot. and confident of Senate approval, Churchill assumed unquestioned support from other members of the British Empire, and with inadequate time for exchange of communications, agreed by proxy to the Wavell appointment,: -For the Dutch, Canadian, Australian, and New Zealand Governments. At the same time, he warned that forces to be made available would be destroyed by the Japanese onslaught. This comment condemned Wavell.

Ozzie Prime Minister, Curtin, was no Churchill-lover. On 20 February he demanded Eastern cover. Requesting reinforcements for Singapore, Curtin signalled:

> *"We want Divisions not Brigades. Anything that is not powerful, modern and immediate is futile".**

Expressing disenchantment with Churchill, Curtin published a letter in the Melbourne Herald, denouncing Britain, and asking the approval of the Australian people to join with the U.S.A., as, *"having more common interests"*. The decline of the British Empire, so distrusted by U.S. Senators, was now well advanced.

---

*Churchill to Roosevelt. *The Complete Correspondence Warren F Kimball* (p 365)

During his visit to Washington, Churchill observed that: –

"Americans considered that war could be conducted throughout to a pre-determined plan, whereas the British do not think that, 'logic and clear-cut principles', are necessarily the sole keys to what ought to be done in swiftly-changing and indefinable situations. In war particularly, we assign a larger importance to opportunism and improvisation, seeking rather to live and conquer in accordance with the unfolding event than to aspire to dominate it, often by fundamental decisions. There is much argument about both views. The difference is one of emphasis, but it is deep-seated".

The problem with the Japanese had been the shock of simultaneous widespread action, their audacity and precision. Japanese tactics caught the western world unawares. But why did Britain not practice what Churchill preached? –

"The flexibility and initiative, devised to meet unfolding events ".

Churchill in Washington, and later in Ottawa, spoke in confidence of an eventual victory, whilst at the same time confirming that he had not anticipated,

"The long marvellously prepared assault of Japan".
"I could feel in anticipation the lashes which were soon to score our naked flesh".

Servicemen and civilian, prisoners of the Japanese, were to feel those lashes, throughout four long years.

Addressing the Canadian House of Commons in Ottawa, Churchill spoke of the treacherous Vichy French Government, with whom Canada was still in relations. He told of Vichy collaboration with the Nazis, and their not evacuating France in 1940, to join with the British in North Africa. He called the Vichy French General Staff, *"Cowardly traitors"*. When I warned them that Britain would fight on alone whatever they did, their generals told their Prime Minister, and his divided cabinet: -

"In three weeks, England will have her neck wrung like a chicken'.

Churchill's reply was: –

"Some chicken! Some neck!'

To complete Churchill's epic year of 1941,he was informed of the situation in North Africa, where Auchinleck's forces were suffering defeat. The British 1st Armoured Division, and the Guards' Armoured Brigade, were being out manoeuvred. Rommell's forces were about the capture the vital port of Benghazi, and push eastwards, towards Tobruk and possibly on, to Cairo, Port Said, and the Suez Canal. This was the last straw for Churchill; it overshadowed anything happening elsewhere.

The considerable loss of men and arms prevented any thought of resources being diverted to the Far East. Auchinleck was relieved of Command, banished from the Middle East, and 'posted', beyond Suez, to remote India.

Following Wavell's appointment as Supreme Allied Commander of the American, British, Dutch and Australian Command (A.B.D.A.), to be based on Java, he flew to Batavia, on 7 January 1942, acting on receipt of a policy document drawn up by the Combined Chiefs of Staff in London and Washington: -

> *"Hold the island chain, Malaya, Sumatra, Java, to Northern*
> *Australia, as essential support positions; re-establish*
> *communications with the Philippines through the Netherlands*
> *East Indies, and maintain essential communications within the*
> *area generally".*

Before Wavell received the demanding message, it was outdated and impossible to execute, with Japanese forces ravaging the whole zone. Wavell was a soldier trained to carry out orders, and he wasted precious days attempting to oblige; -attending useless conferences, establishing forlorn Command Headquarters, in Java.

It took Wavell to 15 January to organise and co-ordinate the headquarters. Meanwhile, in this vital period, the Japanese were undermining his plans, before the ink dried, so rapid was their progress on every front.

Sickened by the numerous calamitous, persistent, and disruptive interventions to his Command, the tense and frustrated Wavell, signalled Churchill. He fallaciously requested confirmation of his duties, with the cynical rejoinder: -

"Was it effective operational control?"

With no immediate reply to the sarcasm: – Churchill reserved his venom!

Wavell's only possible reinforcements were the 18th Division. None acclimatised troops, still at sea, and intended for Burma. However, with no notification to Wavell, Churchill diverted the ship, and the Division, to Singapore.

In the New Year of 1942 the Army Council, in London, took stock of the war situation in the Far East, and decided there was need for urgent action. They realised that Churchill must do something to impress the ally across the Atlantic. By being seen to do something in the Eastern Zone, and pleasing Roosevelt, they felt they might prevent him from embargoing the Lend-Lease programme.

With the loss of the two British Capital Ships, *Prince of Wales* and *Repulse,* off Singapore, there was now nothing to impede Japanese assaults on land, sea, or in the air. British morale was shaken to the core.

The serving man remained in ignorance of the shilly-shallying of Prime Ministers, Presidents, and desk-bound Admirals, Generals, and Air Marshals. They would give an order in London and return home to sleep. The same order, received in that remote tropical land, meant going out to march, to starve, to thirst, or to die.

Singapore had never had a need for air defence, and its small token air force was rapidly in trouble; – without maintenance or spare parts the number of aircraft was soon down to single figures. Lacking air support, the contribution from the limited naval craft available was ineffectual. Wavell's appreciation of the Japanese potential for landing troops in Malaya was woefully wrong. He had not contemplated the multiplicity of Japanese attacks. He expected the Japanese to use conventional tactics, and he planned accordingly.

Churchill accepted no blame for the setbacks at Singapore, and scolded his First Sea Lord: -

"This is really not good enough. Here we have been absolutely outmanoeuvred, and apparently outfought, on the west coast of Malaya by an enemy who has no -warship in the neighbourhood. Consequently our forces are made to retire from successive positions, precious time is gained by the enemy, and a general state of insecurity engendered in our fighting troops. The shortcomings are only too evident. Why were the enemy allowed to obtain all these craft? We apparently have none, or very few, although these were waters we, until recently, controlled. Secondly, when mention is made of heavy machine-gun fire from the banks, how is it the enemy hold these banks? They cannot be manning with machine-gun points commanding every part of the sea down which these barges must come. You should surely call for much more precise reports. This command of the western shores of Malaya by the Japanese, without the possession of a single ship of war, must be reckoned as one of the most astonishing British lapses recorded in naval history. I am sorry to be disagreeable, but I look for a further report of a far more searching enquiry".

'The further report of a far more searching enquiry', must have been a serious discussion point in the next few years, amongst the troops of the ill-fated 18 Division. The troops Churchill deflected into Singapore, slaving on the dreaded Burma Railway, and in Changy Prison Camp.

Notwithstanding the logistical impossibility of doing so, Wavell reported to the Combined Chiefs of Staff that he would try to hold Singapore, if he got his promised number of aircraft. He continued planning on the forlorn assumption that he would receive a body of reinforcements.

By the end of January 1942, the causeway from the Malay Peninsula, to Singapore, was blown up. The Japanese had landed five divisions of men, all trained for specific tasks; – they had support tanks and superiority in air power. The Australians were thrust in, along with the untrained 45th Brigade of 18th Division, and inflicted heavy losses on the enemy, who continued to drive forward regardless, absorbing units and brigades in their assault. Japanese fifth columnists had made arrangements for guidance, food supplies, arms, and bicycles, to help the insurgents on their way.

As defenders pushed forward, attempting to secure the mainland, they were virtually eaten up by the Japanese in their approach to Singapore Fortress, which they entered by the landward side. Once the causeway to the mainland was demolished, all that was left in Singapore was a large number of people, mostly non-combatants, male and female. The two remaining Brigades of the newly arrived 18th Indian Division, were in strange surroundings, of little use in defence, and certainly not ready for attack.

On 10 February, Wavell paid a brief visit to Singapore for the last time, saying to his officers, *"I look to you and your men to fight on to the end, to prove that the fighting spirit that won our Empire still exists, to enable us to defend it".*

The Japanese landed unopposed, and by 12 February had established an occupying force of three divisions, along with tanks. Churchill sent a message on the day Wavell was at Singapore, suggesting that 33,000 British, and 17,000 Australian troops, greatly outnumbered the Japanese. Once again he was playing the 'numbers game', forgetting his own intrusion into Wavell's command, and his diversion of the untrained 18th Division into Singapore. The Australians were good, well-trained units, but the British Indian Divisions were almost totally ineffective. Yet Churchill's message continued: -

"The 18th Division has a chance to make its name in history, Commanders and Senior Officers should die with their troops. The honour of the British Empire and of the British Army is at stake. I rely on you to show no mercy or weakness in any form".

Three days later, on 13 February, from 2,000 miles away in Java,Wavell signalled General Percival, at Singapore: -

"Continued action essential, house to house if need be. It may have a vital influence in other theatres".

He was unaware of the influence other theatres were to have, on starving his troops, in the near future.

At 8.30 p.m. on Sunday, 15 February 1942, Singapore Fortress ceased hostilities, with unconditional surrender to the Japanese.

By land, sea and air, the Japanese had proved British strategy on defence to be outdated and ineffective. Japan had used the native populace, the possible ally that Britain had so neglected. One million people in Singapore were in grave danger, with supplies and water seriously affected; – troops were overrun and short of ammunition. In all, some 85,000 men surrendered, of whom 70,000 were combatants. Wavell had previously lost 8,000 Australians on Crete, and now a further 17,000 at Singapore.

By 16 February, the Japanese were occupying territory at Bali, Makassar, and Timor, and it could not be long before they attacked Java. On the night of 25 February, Wavell departed his short-lived Java headquarters. He was now operating over an area the size of which no other commander in history had contemplated.

Responsibility for operations in Burma was now passed to India Command, and Wavell signalled Churchill that the A.B.D.A. defence area was dismantled, and that he would now go back to India, as Commander in Chief.

On 28 February, the Japanese invaded Java. They killed, or captured, 15,000 British, Australian, and American staff of A.B.D.A, Headquarters. Few of those captured were to survive Japanese prisoner of war camps. Although the man on the ground was in trouble, he neither knew of his perilous situation, nor realised the indifference shown by the War Cabinet. The draft of Officers I was with heard nothing of significance as we journeyed for three months, from December 1941, to March 1942. Cocooned within the environment of eastbound ship, and train, we were in total ignorance of the enormous success of the Japanese advances.

London newspapers, of 19 January 1942, carried the story of the arrest, in Haifa, of Burmese Premier, U-Saw. He had previously visited both, the Japanese Ambassador in neutral Lisbon, and the Japanese Consul General in America, seeking, as he claimed, assurance about Burmese students studying in Japan. These individuals, however, were being trained in espionage and sabotage. British Intelligence intercepted and decoded a signal, indicating that U-Saw had given the Japanese assurances that he would give them all help possible if they attacked the British in Burma. He would ensure a Burmese rising, and join with them in driving the British out of Burma.

U-Saw's opponent, the Thakin leader, Aung San, along with his small independent force, 'The Thirty', was guiding Japanese troops through the jungles of the southern Burmese border, in late January and February 1942. They captured the small towns of Mergui, and Tavoy, and at the same time, were recruiting and expanding the Burmese Independent Army. British Politicians, and Military, greatly underestimated the effectiveness of the zealous young Thakin leader, although warnings were clearly given in the relentless assaults conducted in nearby Malaya and Singapore. British Forces in the Far East were unaware of the development of a new kind of enemy.

With the banishment of Auchinleck from the Middle East, Montgomery was appointed G.O.C. British Forces in North Africa. He was to become, 'the enemy within', to British forces beyond Suez. Supported by Churchill, he ensured that reinforcements, arms and rations, were restricted in distribution, going no further than Suez.

On Australia's doorstep, Japanese forces were striking into New Guinea. Australia could give no more; – their best troops had suffered greatly under Wavell's command. Survivors were now stranded in the west, with little opportunity to return to the homeland.

Following his recent fruitless visit to the USA and Canada, the British press and Parliament, expressed growing speculation over Churchill's competence. Daily news of unopposed Japanese devastation throughout the Far East further undermined his position, and Churchill was rattled by the hostility shown towards him. Seeking confirmation of his authority, he called for a vote of confidence in Parliament. The vote was carried by the astonishing majority of 464 to 1. With this huge vote of confidence, Churchill became a little cocksure. He misread the signs, wrongfully assuming that he also had the support of Australia, and New Zealand, for his policies.

Premier Curtin realised his immediate problem was to the north of Australia, in New Guinea, and it was urgent. At Curtin's request, two Australian divisions were dispatched by sea from the Middle East, to return to the defence of the homeland, with units intermixed through three ships, according to the space available. On 20 February 1942, unaware of the ad hoc loading of the two divisions on three ships, Churchill requested Curtin to divert one of the two ships, now rounding Ceylon, into Burma, to arrive about 26 or 27 February.

Curtin was adamant. He wanted his army returned to meet the adverse situation developing in Australia. In an attempt to pressurise Curtin, Churchill *involved Roosevelt, and on 22 February, Attlee, the Secretary of State, sent the following cablegram to Curtin: -*

> *"We could not contemplate that you would refuse our request and that of the President of the United States for the diversion of the leading division to save the situation in Burma. We knew that if our ships proceeded on their normal course to Australia while we were waiting for your formal approval they would either arrive too late at Rangoon, or even be without enough fuel to go there at all. We therefore decided that the convoy should be temporarily diverted northward. The convoy is now too far north for some of the ships in it to reach Australia without refuelling. These physical considerations give a few days for the situation to develop and for you to review the position should you wish to do so. Otherwise the leading Australian Division will be returned to Australia as quickly as possible in accordance with your wishes".*

Churchill was committing an Australian force, in ships under British Command, to certain doom. It was impossible for the force to have steamed from Ceylon to Rangoon, disembarked, acclimatise, and be deployed, before the Japanese captured Rangoon on 6 March. With a 24-hour sailing space between each of the three ships, it was unlikely that even one of them would penetrate the Japanese sea and air screen.

With no American troops involved, (Where had they been?), it was easy for Roosevelt to support this plan. On Roosevelt's behalf, (Believe it, or not!), R.G. Casey, Australian Minister to the United States, despatched a cablegram to Curtin: -

> *"I fully understand your position in spite of the fact that I cannot wholly agree as to immediate need of first returning divisions in*

Australia. I think that the principal threat as against the main bases of Australia, and Burma, both of which must be held at all costs, is against Burma or the left flank, and that we can safely hold the Australian or right flank. Additional American fully equipped reinforcements are getting ready to leave for your area. In view of all this and depending of course on developments of next few weeks I hope you will consider the possibility of diverting second returning division to some place in India or Burma to help hold that line so that it can become a fixed defence. Under any circumstances you can depend upon our fullest support: – Roosevelt".

Churchill and Roosevelt were once again intervening, and disregarding, the man appointed Supreme Commander. In the event, Curtin was courageous enough to stand his ground. He was not to be intimidated or pressured by Churchill and Roosevelt. On 23 February, Curtin sent a cablegram (139), to Attlee: – reiterating the reasons for his decision: -

"In your previous message it was clearly implied that the convoy was not proceeding to the northward, From 241 it appears that you have diverted the convoy towards Rangoon, and treated our approval to this vital diversion as merely a matter of form. By doing so you have established a physical situation which adds to the dangers of the convoy, and the responsibility of the consequences of such diversion, rests upon you".

"We have already informed the President, (Roosevelt), of the reasons for our decision and, having regard to the terms of his communications to me, we are quite satisfied from his sympathetic reply that he fully understands and appreciates the reasons/or our decision".

"Wavell's message, considered by Pacific War Council on Saturday, reveals that Java faces imminent invasion. Australia's outer defences are now quickly vanishing and our vulnerability is completely exposed. With A.I.F. troops we sought to save Malaya and Singapore, falling back on Netherlands East Indies. All these

northern defences are gone or going. Now you contemplate using A.I.F. to save Burma. All this had been done, as in Greece, without adequate air support".

"We feel a primary obligation to save Australia not only for itself, but preserve it as a base for the development of the war against Japan. In the circumstances it is quite impossible to reverse a decision which we made with the utmost care, and which we have affirmed and re-affirmed".

"Our General Staff, (General Sturdee), advises; – 'although your 241 refers to the leading division only, the fact is that owing to the loading of the flights it is impossible at the present time to separate the two divisions, and the destination of all the flights will be governed by that of the first flight'. This fact reinforces our decision".

It was almost inevitable that, had the convoy diverted, it would have met Japanese planes, or ships, in any approach towards Rangoon. It was fortuitous that the temporary diversion, when rounding Ceylon, saved the Australian convoy. At the time of the diversion, Japanese planes were concentrated on bombing Ceylon, and the Japanese navy had complete command of the seas. Had Churchill succeeded in shanghaiing the convoy, it would have perished as did 18th British Division, diverted by Churchill into Singapore.

Churchill represented the fall of Singapore, to Roosevelt, as the greatest disaster in British history. Wavell, at this late stage, considered Burma to be of greater importance, in view of the access to Eastern India, and the industrial and commercial centre of Calcutta. He seemed, however, to be totally unaware of the support that dissident elements in India were preparing to offer Japan, in order to assist in ridding India of the British.

Later, throughout the following two years, and with the Japanese held at the borders of Assam, numerous riots and civil disturbances demonstrated India's reaction to Japan being halted in Burma. Mahatma Ghandi's Congress Party favoured passive resistance, although the Indian Revolutionary Army, led by Gupta Ramm, a known fifth columnist, caused numerous disruptions of trains, mail, and communications, thus deflecting military forces from the Burma front.

WITH THIS CHICANERY, I WAS ABOUT TO SOLDIER!

From the chaos that was Burma 1942, I was to serve later, in India, with my Regiment, and with General Bill Slim. Fortunately, missing the conflict in Europe, I visited numerous interesting locations, the depth and breadth of the country. The American bombing of Japan, in 1945, as I was on leave in England, caused my diversion into Germany, and I became central in the post-war activities, through which the Cold War developed.

1

THE LONG JOURNEY TO HELL

Joining and training

"What the hell am I doing here, and where the hell am I supposed to be going?"

It was not the cold and damp of the hoar frost from the river Clyde that bothered me. Standing outside the imposing portals of the Great Eastern Hotel, on Glasgow's famous Sauchiehall Street, one of a small tense group of junior army officers. The outer show of stoicism belied inner feelings; unwanted, humiliated, and rejected. Nothing was said, yet all shared the same emotion.

Thursday 4 December 1941: It was impossible to envisage the catastrophic event to come, within little more than forty-eight hours. The result of which, I was to be cast into a tropical hell, treacherously abandoned by a British Prime Minister. A Hell of a place, where one in three of the group would die, of wounds, desease, starvation and thirst.

A quiet dissent reverberated throughout, having joined the army to fight Nazis in Europe, all were now perplexed and thoroughly disillusioned, kicking our heels around Glasgow for the previous two weeks, awaiting orders.

Disillusioned, from 14 November, all prospects of fighting Nazis in Europe vanished. With the words; –

"I must advise you that all nine of you are to leave the battalion. You are being posted overseas; I cannot tell you exactly where, except that it is to join a battalion stationed at a peace station in the tropics".

Lieutenant Colonel E.E.E. Cass, Officer Commanding, 1st Battalion, The King's Own Yorkshire Light Infantry, addressed nine of us, subalterns, lined up in his office.

Wishing us well, we were dismissed. That was that! No handshake, no "Thank you", and no expression of regret, at having to part with so many young, keen junior officers, (Emergency Commissioned Officers).

Throughout the twenty inter-war years of peace, seniority in the military was achieved simply, 'by being there', and conforming. Cass was a product of the system. I was his one trained, and qualified, mortar officer (Netheravon, Small Arms School). As the only Roman Catholic officer in the battalion, I proved handy for R.C. church parades. The regiment had no declared policy on recruitment, although it was surreptitiously, from other than Catholic sources. A more important handicap to my remaining in favour with the C.O. He knew of my younger sister being evacuated to the family homestead in County Mayo, on the West Coast of Ireland. This might have proved embarrassing, in the event of the battalion being required to operate in its secondary, 'most secret', emergency role: 'To invade neutral Ireland and occupy the city of Limerick, in the event of a German assault'. I could be a security risk, and as such, I must go.

The Regimental Quartermaster measured each of the draft, for tropical khaki uniform, and topee headgear. Informed that regimental tailors, Messrs Conway Williams, of London's Savile Row, would forward the uniforms to our home address. Travel documents issued, nine disgruntled 'discards' mounted a three-ton truck, for the Larne-Stranraer ferry, and home embarkation leave for seven days; – Report to Glasgow, and await orders.

Designated draft Z-26, we consisted of 33 junior officers, 15 from the Gloucestershire Regiment, and 18 from the KOYLI. Lieutenant Watkin-Williams of the Gloucesters was senior officer and nominated Draft Commander. Realising that both regiments had regular battalions stationed in Burma, 1st Bn Gloucesters and 2nd Bn KOYLI, the mystery tropical station became less obscure. Burma was indeed a peace station, with no hint of war.

On the 17 October 1939, six weeks after the declaration of war, my colleague David Williams and I had enlisted into The Royal Engineers, hoping to serve together, 'for the duration'.

We became, respectively, Number 1882721, Sapper Gerald Fitzpatrick, and Number 1882722, Sapper David Williams. I was immediately senior to at least one man. The significance of seniority was about to be brought home to me with some force in the near future. David and I were mortified, after only three days of serving together, to be parted and posted to different units. My destination was Chelsea Barracks, London; David was posted to Wales. We were to meet but once more in our lives, and that was coincidental, later that year, both being on Christmas leave.

Transferred, in late 1941, to an undisclosed destination was a shock to my feelings. A sense of being banished into oblivion, after two years of hard training. The tradition of peacetime tropical postings was, for a standard period of nine years. In the present circumstances, an overseas posting could be until the end of hostilities, whenever that might be. It meant that I was never going to be tried, and tested, in action against an enemy; yet, knowing I could soldier with the best of them, I felt a need to prove myself. Now, it appeared to be all over.

To abscond, and 'jump' the overseas draft, was one option, maybe to rejoin another unit at a later date, where my experience would be appreciated and used. It would have been a simple matter to cross the border into the Irish Republic to join with my sister, and farm on the family homestead. The hard background of my early days, coupled with the discipline of commissioned rank, ruled out this option. I had trained in the disciplines of a sapper, and mastered the skills of explosives, demolitions, trenching, and rivetting, night and day map reading, all forms of bridging and river crossings.

P & O Cruise to Bombay

Throughout our Glasgow stay we heard diverse rumours, suggesting destinations; U.S.A. Canada, the Western Desert, Moscow, and Persia, amongst others, and every possible port of embarkation. Transports arrived, and after a short journey through slush and fog, we came to a halt on a narrow road in a gathering of small buildings. Scotsmen in the draft rapidly declared the place to be Gourock, a small town by the mouth of the River Clyde. To one side, in the cold swirling mist were small houses. Opposite stood a huge blank wall, the two ends of which vanished into the mist, grey and dirty, with no windows or doors. It was the side of a huge ocean going liner, under the best possible camouflage, a blanket of freezing fog, and moored alongside the town quay.

Ascending the gangplank, the transformation from the dull Clydebank scene was staggering. The dim, damp, and dismal, became a spectacular wonderland, a warm illuminated palace of lush deep pile carpets, fine decoration, leather upholstered furniture, and paintings, surrounding a huge ornate staircase. The men of the crew were dressed in immaculate white uniforms, and overseeing all was Captain J.H. Biggs.

The wartime situation, and the horrific dangers at sea, appeared to have changed nothing for Captain Biggs and his crew. Their job was to convey nurses, military, and civilians, wherever the government decreed. This was a proud ship, S.S. *Strathallan,* a liner of the Peninsular and Oriental Steam Navigation Company. Loading continued throughout the day, a variety of large and small parties. Last of all, came 50 women of, Queen Alexandra's Military Nursing Service (Q.A.I.M.N.S.) Generally referred to as QAs. A diverse Services collection, totalling 3449, to be disposed as follows:

West Africa	45
South Africa	4
Aden	14
Middle East	184
Iraq	960
India	1663
Burma	112
Ceylon	386
Malaya	81

Each group were allocated their piece of the ship for the journey, until discharged at a port of disembarkation.

The dull feeling of rejection vanished. Friendships developed, on boarding *Strathallan*. We unified, and somehow, strengthened, into a purposeful bunch, from what had been no more than a number of insecure individuals.

Unaware that the circumstances, and timing of our journey was about to become central, to some of the greatest events in world history, and we were en-route to shape some of it. William (Bill) Lauder Riddell, and I were fortunate in being paired to share an upper deck cabin, number B-29, normally a single cabin, now converted into two berths. The cabin was immediately next to the string of cabins allocated to the fifty QAs. Other members of our draft were less fortunate, and allocated larger cabins, down below on E deck, with seven or eight sharing. It took a little time to settle in, look around, and find that we had the luxury of a deck steward, (more in the interest of preserving P&O assets, than for the comfort of common soldiers).

Strathallan set sail the following morning, – 5 December 1941, casting off slowly through the mist, and out, down The Firth of Clyde, into the North Channel of the Irish Sea. As the fog lifted a little, we saw the sea covered with ships of all shapes and sizes, moving around adopting allocated stations. Possibly, between 50 or 60 vessels formed Convoy WS-14. The move off was steady, on a sea calm as a millpond. Royal Navy battleship H.M.S. *Ramillies,* accompanied by escorting destroyers, took station alongside the convoy. We gave no thought to our changed circumstances, leaving the security of land, for the perils of the sea.

The shattering truth about Britain's sea losses, when subsequently released, was that in 22 months of war, to December 1941, British and Allied shipping losses totalled 1141 vessels, with a gross of 4,190,281 tons (averaging 52 ships, and 200,000 tons monthly); – 429 sunk by German U-boats. 108 to mines, 113 to surface craft, 324 to aircraft, and boats, 167 to other causes. P&O Lines suffered greatly in this catastrophic treatment. We knew nothing of these perilous statistics, and the dangers we might expect.

On *Strathallan,* therefore, we were entering into a precarious theatre of operation by simply being at sea. In the event of attack, we could make no contribution to influence the outcome. Convoy WS-14 was entirely in the hands of the Royal Navy, and British Merchant Navy. Lurking in shipping lanes, German U-boats hunted in packs. However, sheltered by atrocious weather conditions, we sailed westward. Convoy speed was slow, regulated by the speed of the slowest ship. All having to hold station meant that ships capable of high performance, suffered buffeting as seas began to roughen. This was foreign to *Strathallan* and her normal peacetime smooth seamanship, even in rough weather.

Awestruck, I absorbed *Strathallan's* splendour, it presented a completely new way of life to that of rationed Britain. Provisioned in South Africa, she had an abundance, food of all descriptions, with menus of peacetime P&O luxury standard. Bill Riddell and I, fed down below on F deck, at long tables set for twenty, and the delicious food was plentiful, beyond anything I had previously known, and of a variety that was no more than a dream throughout beleaguered Britain.

Heading out into the Atlantic Ocean, it became a matter of wonder that there were no collisions between the mass of shipping as seas began to roughen considerably. On the fourth day of sailing, 8 December 1941, a message posted on the notice-boards informed of a happening on the previous day:

> *"On 7 December 1941, Japanese aircraft attacked American forces in the Pacific".*

Had we been aware of the damage sustained in this most unexpected assault, we would have found it incredulous, but rapturous delight rang through *Strathallan,* at the news that the U.S.A. was now, at last, at war. All credit for bringing about the U.S.A. intervention went to the Japanese.

We sailed on, observing the night sky, and that the North Star was constantly seen over to the right. The sun arose each morning from behind the ship, and each evening, it dropped over the front end. Navigating in this crude manner, established that we were sailing east to west, and guessing our speed, estimated *Strathallan* to be moving in a north-westerly direction, heading towards Newfoundland, and passing close by Greenland.

On the evenings of both the third, and fourth day at sea, destroyers were dropping mines, and moving at speed to the rear of the convoy. Nothing of this was reported on-board *Strathallan,* security within the enclosed floating community being as close as ever; although as night fell, the sky to the rear glowed red, and flames were seen rising from two of our ships.

Seas became rougher and the weather fouler with each coming day. By the fifth day, they were running with 80-to 100-foot waves, like a fairground switchback, with crests half a mile apart. *Strathallan* climbed, and glided, from crest to trough; at other times, the sea was a maelstrom, throwing the ship like a cork, forward, sideways, and in every direction. H.M.S. *Ramillies,* a 70,000-ton battleship, was tossed high on the crest of one wave, to plunge downwards like a stone, out of sight, as waves disintegrated. The 23,722 ton Strathallan was like a rubber duck on these waters. In the restricted speed conditions, there was no allowance for avoidance, and the Captain's skill in navigation was of no avail. The ship throbbed and vibrated as the propellers lifted from the sea, shuddering as she balanced on the crests.

Ramillies advanced suddenly and at speed, taking station close by, starboard of *Strathallan,* and at what appeared to be a dangerously close distance; – less than 150 yards, and for a few minutes occupied this station. Instantly, in those bubbling waters, a submarine conning tower surfaced, and submerged as rapidly. So brief was the sighting, that I had no time to identify, – was it British, or enemy? Surely, no British submarine would surface in those dangerous circumstances, when it might quite easily have 'bottomed' *Ramillies*. The intruder must have been German. This threat caused a chase by destroyers, and the dropping of depth charges. A constant cloud of fog, rain, and snow, ensured no danger of harassment by aircraft.

In these treacherous seas, there were many casualties. Nine out of every ten, passengers and crew, suffered seasickness to some extent; from mild, to total incapacitation. Racking the body with every movement, the vomiting and retching continued, when the brain and body surrendered. Nights and days have no end so long as the sea remains rough, and it remained rough. Captain Biggs was seasick, and confirmed this to be the worst sea that he had known in his long career.

There were rumours of two or three soldiers, each night, absconding over the side. Men already in low spirits at being posted overseas were now further depressed, and with the relentless, uncontrollable sea-sickness, may have chosen to surrender to the sea; but nothing was confirmed.

Being the sole member of the draft to fight off sea-sickness, I ventured on deck two or three times each day, regardless of the weather. In the intense cold, with decks iced and snowed over, I sought a few deep breaths of fresh air, a welcome relief from the stench of sickness permeating the vessel. I stayed on deck less than one minute; a man could freeze to death in those temperatures.

Attributing my resistance to seasickness, to what happened to me as a ten-year-old, when visiting Ireland with my mother. I was not sick on the turbulent Holyhead—Dun Laoghaire ferry crossing, as were so many passengers, but I was violently overtaken during the seven-hour train journey across Ireland. Nothing at sea was to have the same effect on me as did that awful holiday experience.

Attending my cabin-mate, Bill Riddell, and seeing him comfortable, I went below to check how other members of the group were faring. All were laid up, completely helpless, washbasins full of spew; it was everywhere, on clothing, bedding, floor, and furniture. I cleaned up, washing some of them, carrying sheets and clothing to the laundry, to wash and to dry. Having undertaken this task for a second time, I went out on deck, and threw up. It was simply a matter of being sick of the stench of vomit.

Seen to be fit and attending meals, I was detailed Ship Duty Officer for two days. This meant visiting and inspecting all lounges, decks, bars and accommodation, as well as checking sentries on deck duty. Returning to my cabin from official duties, I came upon a figure slumped at the entrance to the nurses' showers, situated opposite my cabin. It was a nurse in a pitiable condition, − even worse than the troops. She could not speak, or move, by herself. Regardless of rules and decorum, I took her into the showers and cleaned her down, from top to toe, dried her off, and then did the unforgivable; − took her into my cabin. Moving Bill into the upper bunk, I wrapped the young lady in a warm blanket, and placed her on the lower bunk, before washing and drying her clothes in the laundry room. She returned to her quarters some time later, with no one the wiser.

It was a week before the North Star appeared over *Strathallan's* tail, and the sunrise came over the left side, and set over to the right, (soldier's licence). We were now travelling from North to South, as the ocean flattened out, much calmer, as gradually, my colleagues, and others, began creeping hesistantly down for meals. One or two more days and we were in warmer climes. Now was the time for 'peacocks and peahens', to start 'strutting their stuff', on *Strathallan's* warm wooden decks. Limited though it was, romance between male officers, and a few QA's did blossom. Four or five of the younger ladies, declared an interest in the hundreds of male officers on board. Other ranks had no chance, as the upper A, and B decks, were restricted 'for officers only', and strictly out of bounds to other ranks.

'Poppit', was a diminutive and rather plump member of the QA. On boarding ship, she had been heard to say, "There must be a man on here for me". Another, a beauty with the most gorgeous pair of legs, was readily tagged 'Legs', or 'S.A.' (for sex appeal). She became the dream girl of hundreds of officers on board. It was not only the weather that got hotter!

Calculating sailing times and directions, it was established that *Strathallan* had been very close to both, Greenland and Newfoundland. Turning south, many ships of the convoy disappeared, en-route to Canada, or America, and *Strathallan* left the convoy. From here on, she sailed unescorted at her normal cruise speed. Shipboard games appeared, and the swimming pool opened to make life more bearable.

In our own interest, we started taking Burmese lessons from an older officer, who had spent years in the country. He stressed one highly essential introductory question: *'Burmesega pa ba tat dala?'* (Do you speak Burmese?) We did, however, learn the prince of all words in Burma, *Ye* (water), – *Ye-lo* (bring me water).

Joseph, our Goanese waiter, admired the way I attended all meals; he made sure I got good food. As a token of respect, and, in defiance of ship regulations, Joseph showed me down below decks at the 'front end', where the ship was heavily reinforced with sandbags. Here, amongst the sandbags, were the Goanese crew quarters. The bags were sculptured as a grotto, a beautifully decorated shrine to 'Our Lady, Queen of the Seas'. They were all Christian, and I could only trust that the 'Queen', took special care of these loyal and excellent men, when, twelve months later, *Strathallan* was torpedoed off North Africa, and sunk in the Mediterranean Sea.

SS Strathallan

On Christmas morning 1941, *Strathallan* lay at anchor in a huge bay, with a steaming jungle background. Mist was rising as a hot tropical sun heated the land. It was Freetown Harbour, in Sierra Leone, and all hell was let loose around the ship. Dozens of 'bum-boats' with one or two occupants surrounded the ship, offering bananas, coconuts, oranges, sisters or mothers, carvings and trinkets, hats; all essential for the intrepid squaddy, or so they said. Those not making offers for sale dived for coins. This was our first sight of land since leaving Gourock three weeks beforehand, and there was no shore leave. In peacetime sailing, the journey would have taken less than five days. There was some movement of personnel, ship to shore, and vice versa. It was a case of 'up anchor', and away, that same afternoon.

Christmas dinner that evening was a truly grand affair, followed by a dance in the main restaurant. The Christmas party was my first visit into the sumptuous dining saloon, simply for a drink or two. There was no possible chance of a dance, owing to the disproportionate ratio of males to females. Naive, no more than a youth, and lacking the social skills to join in the ball, I made my way back to the cabin. I had been there no more than a few minutes when there was a knock at the door. Answering, it was one of the nurses, elegantly dressed in a ballgown. I did not immediately recognise her until she said, "I've come to thank you for being so kind to me when I was ill. I saw you upstairs at the dance".

"Oh, that's all right. I didn't recognise you; I see you're looking better now".

"It was very crowded at the dance...?.....?"

Perfume permeated the cabin; – a beautifully modulated voice, and an attractive woman: — I got the message! Cabin B-29 became very precious, and used regularly on the remainder of the cruise.

Occupied with Milly, I missed one of the informal afternoon gatherings of colleagues. It felled me when Jimmy Ableson approached to say he had been deputed to inform me that I had been selected unanimously, by all the draft, as the man each wanted beside him in the event of our going into action. I was floored! My eyes filled as I returned to the cabin, and quite unashamed, I cried. There could be no greater honour than to be selected by one's colleagues, some older and worldly-wise, and a few younger than me. There were men of substance, better educated, and from professional occupations; it was hard to accept their choosing me as the man they could die beside.

Our small draft of KOYLI, and Gloucesters officers, were virtually free agents, enjoying the sea, which looked fantastic by night, its phosphorescence glistening in deep velvet blue water; beautiful by day, with flying fish and leaping porpoises. Romance blossomed as *Strathallan* sailed south for two days. Crossing the equator, was accomplished with the essential ceremonies, games, and tomfoolery. Tropical seaboard nights are made for love, and, sure enough, Poppit found her man, as the fun and games of the day closed.

She escorted him to the lifeboat deck, viewing the moonlit aquatic illuminations, and to continue the fun and games. In the velvet dark of night, the twosome popped into one of the deck life-belt chests. For a measure of privacy, they closed the lid down upon themselves, although the deck was officially out of bounds by night, and patrolled only by sentries in stocking feet. Slipping quietly along the deck, The Seaforth Highlander sentry, on duty that night, was unaware of whom might be getting into the chest; – dropping the latch on the life-belt container, it could not be opened from the inside.

It was late at night, as matron in charge undertook roll call. Poppit was missing, and not accounted for. The Provost Marshall was sought, as the man to take responsibility for the search. But not only was Poppit missing, the big, 17-stone Provost Marshall, was nowhere to be found.

The enquiry was deferred until morning, as speculation ran wild, even to the point of thinking the two might have fallen overboard.

The sun was up, and people were about, as shouts from within the chest, brought Officer Commanding Troops onto the scene. Deeply embarrassed, Poppit, and the Provost Marshall, emerged. They married at Cape Town some days later, as *Strathallan* lay, awaiting instructions. 'Legs', having also found her man, married aboard ship. Once again, as at Freetown, shore leave was not permitted, and *Strathallan* now had two married couples aboard.

Hogmanay fell, as we departed Cape Town, for Durban. Where Bill Riddell procured the bottle of whisky from, I do not know. Bill was as Scottish as Scotsmen get, and for New Year's Eve, he had somehow ensured his supply of the 'magic water'. Bars on *Strathallan* opened for only thirty minutes each evening, and drinking was restricted to one, or possibly two, drinks per man in each session. Full bottles of spirit were not sold. Hearing that Bill was, 'pissed out of his mind', and that he had a bottle of whisky, I went in search of him. Indeed, he was fully intent upon having a Scots, 'first footing', around the deck. He was offering the bottle to one of the sentries, at the very moment, Colonel, Officer Commanding Troops, approached from the opposite direction.

"Come on! You silly old sod! Have a wee nip. It's Hogmanay!" It was too late. Bill was ordered to attend O.C. Troops office next morning. The cruellest punishment possible, particularly for a Scot, was handed out for this offence. Bill was 'gated', confined to the ship for the duration of *Strathallan*'s visit to Durban. He would willingly have scrubbed the ship from stem to stem for a few free hours ashore.

The first opportunity for exercise, after more than four weeks at sea, was the all-ranks, 'route march', around the attractive-looking town of Durban, – but Durban was closed! Shops, and bars, had shuttered windows; it was like a ghost town. We were not to know, three or four days beforehand, the previous convoy had been allowed shore leave; a division of 'Anzacs', Australian, and New Zealand troops. The town was torn to pieces in their three days' stay, and the locals, thinking they were in for a repeat dose, were taking no chances. Seeing, 'True blue Brits', however, the town soon came to life, and hospitality was universal; everybody in Durban wanted to meet somebody in uniform.

During the five days' Durban visit, we helped solve a mystery, puzzling nightclub musicians. They knew, and had practised, the tune of the latest British dance craze, having picked up the music from the wireless; but try as they might, they found the dance steps impossible. Doors were opened willingly, drinks flowed, as patrons were introduced to; -

Put your right arm OUT, your right arm IN, Your right arm OUT, and shake it all about. You do the hokey-cokey, and you turn about. That's what it's all about. Oh! Hokey! Cokey! Cokey!

Each night, Bill Riddell waiting at the top of the gangplank, demanded to hear every detail of my doings in Durban. It hurt him beyond measure to have to tolerate the penalty placed on him by the 'old crone' of a colonel. Bill was, God bless him, destined to be one of those who did not survive, or have the opportunity to visit the town again.

Daytime heat was almost unbearable, humid and sweaty; nights were pleasant and cool. I was enjoying this cruise and its opulence, after the limited expectations of my boyhood. King George was paying the fare, and there was time to read, think and talk. Milly's regular afternoon comforts helped each day along. Life was good for this twenty-two year old, Second Lieutenant, the eldest son of a loving Irish mother.

A British Naval cruiser filled the whole visible skyline, as Bombay loomed out of the mist. H.M.S. *Devonshire,* berthed along the dockside landmark, 'The Gateway to India'. *Strathallan* berthed nearby, as though from nowhere, a million coolies garbed in red robes filled the wharf. Within minutes, the party of QA's disembarked, and were gone. There was no looking back by Milly, not so much as a smile, or a wave. We were not to meet again.

Strathallan was torpedoed off the port of Oran, in North Africa, on 21 December 1942. Many members of the crew were saved. Throughout the three months of our transit, of the total British Merchant Navy losses, P&O Lines lost the following ships:

Viceroy of India (19,648 tons), torpedoed off Oran; *Cathay* (15,104 tons), bombed off Bougie; *Narkunda* (16,227 tons), bombed off Bougie; *Ettrick* (11,275 tons), torpedoed off Southern Spain; a total of 86,000 tons of shipping, along with many crew members. This lists the losses of but one company; many more good ships and men perished serving, King and Country, in the same short period of time.

Bombay to Madras

People! People! People! From the lofty decks *of Strathallan,* it appeared that one would have to walk over heads, so crowded was the Bombay dockside. Hundreds of coolies dressed in red dhotis, (head-dress), were being herded like cattle, men using sticks, controlling them. Bill Riddell and I were accommodated in the nearby, Railway Hotel. Others languished in the lush, Taj Mahal Hotel, all, supposedly, oblivious of the surrounding filth and squalor.

Once again, we spent time hanging around the town for twelve days, awaiting instructions and directions to our final destination. Seeking to impress, Bill and I attempted our first wearing of tropical kit: topee, with green regimental pom-pom; shirt, with collar and tie; bush-jacket, with Sam Browne belt; green lanyard around the neck, with two bobbins above, and two below the top button, and ends tucked into each top pocket; pressed shorts, socks with regimental green tops, and shoes, highly polished. We made our way to, Green's celebrated restaurant, for the daily social event, 'the tea dance', and whatever else might be on offer. 'Real good and smart', all set to be taken down a peg.

"Do you mind if I make a comment? You look like a pair of pox-doctor's clerks dressed like that. The C.O. would blow his top if he were to see you". It was one way for Regimental Quartermaster, Lieutenant Bill Stevenson, to establish rank.

Deflated, we hurried back to change into regulation dress, as worn by Steve. It meant discarding half the over-elaborate rig-out.

Swimming out at Breach Candy pool by day, we acquired tans, and enjoyed the much-needed exercise. Each night, we would muster at Madam Rita's brothel, a large spacious house, with extensive grounds, in a select quarter of Bombay. As many as fourteen, or fifteen, members of the draft assembled each night, not for the much-too-expensive array of girls Rita employed, simply because here, we could get a drink in prohibition-struck Bombay, and have a dance and chat with the assortment of girls; a mix of white French, black French, Chinese, black African, white Russian, and English. Jimmy Ableson was our lone French speaker, and he enjoyed conversation with Madam.

Small though he was, Abe was a man's man, who uplifted one with his spirit, general enthusiasm and exuberance. Having left a young wife behind in Scotland, he must have had periods of doubts and low feelings. They never showed. There was not one pennyworth of envy, or enmity, in him. So far as he was concerned, everything was for sharing.

Abe loved his banter with Rita. She had the face of an old prune, befitting her profession, but her figure and dress were immaculate. Abe ribbed her on her foul looks, job, game, and profession. Rita had all the answers; she enjoyed being jibed in such manner. The girls loved our party visits for the opportunity of a chat and a dance with lively men. It was a change from the seedy, furtive stream of businessmen, lawyers, senior civil and military officers, and pissed-up sailors.

Taking a taxi trip along the infamous Grant Road, we saw hundreds of captive girls, all offering themselves for sale, from what were no more than cages, and it was a sickening sight. We could not imagine soldiers using these unfortunates, but they did. Little wonder that lectures on board ship emphasised hygiene and the use of contraceptives. It was much later, at the Red Fort in Delhi, as platoons undertook guard duty, that two girls 'traded' around the gates each day, one wearing luminous red socks, and the other luminous blue. Any sentry slipping out for a few minutes was invariably asked, 'Which one did you have? Red socks, or blue socks?'

Colour prejudice was rife, particularly towards any officer seen with a coloured girl. With no individual prejudice, we began to appreciate the old maxim, 'The longer you're out, the whiter they become'. Many of the pompous old senior officers, those perpetuating the prejudice, were not averse to a bit on the side, with a bearer, a friendly clerk, or even a nice young junior. But woe betide the subaltern bringing a female 'chee-chee', 'chilli-cracker', or 'touch of the tar brush', into an officers' mess. He would be out on his neck in minutes, particularly as a member of one of the County Regiments. In Service Corps, Ordnance, and smaller support units, such matters were less rigid. It was a matter of discretion.

Plentiful though the attractive girls were at Green's, old-fashioned etiquette and courtesy prevailed. Itinerant officers were unwelcome, until formally introduced, to Mamma and Pappa; any show of familiarity before this was unacceptable. Fruity Allan Whittaker, big and chubby in the Billy Bunter mould, found fun in attempting the outlandish, but he got his come-uppance when a girl stopped in the middle of Green's dance floor and slapped his chubby face. "I only asked her at which end of the bath she sat?" Nothing even remotely suggestive was funny to these girls, intent upon that most serious of all Indian safaris; – The Anglo-Indian girl, in seeking a white husband.

A battalion of Royal Artillery accompanied us on the next leg of our journey. It was by troop train, south and across India to Madras. This was a completely new experience, with six officers to each spacious couchette compartment, one with drop-down bunks. A huge block of ice, placed in a tray on the floor, cooled the intense heat. Halting at sidings each night for cooking and ablutions, the rail journey was of three and a half days. This allowed time to enjoy diverse foods at the many stations, and the novelty of stacking mangoes, and bananas, around the ice block. Travelling in close proximity day by day, it gave me a vital opportunity to assess the mettle, and qualities, of each of my colleagues.

Delayed for a further ten days at Madras, we were allocated inferior accommodation, in an open-style military camp, with concrete bays. A warm welcome to the nearby cricket club was the highlight; offered their full facilities of equipment, bar, lounge, and games. Tim Watson, an ex-public schoolboy from Blackpool, Lancashire, was the star cricketer of our party. Tim loved the game, and might well have graced the County team, had he been fortunate enough to survive the war. Club members particularly welcomed him, when, without practice, he scored more than 70 runs in each of the two matches in which he played. Tim had a keen liking for booze, and he shook the squad one lunchtime, asking the barman for six dozen pink gins, one for each run he had scored in his innings that day. He insisted upon having them lined up on the bar, six rows of twelve, and he drank the lot, walked back to his *charpoy* (bed), and slept until next morning. Tim greatly missed his home and his family, saying little, until the squad had designated me 'the man they wanted next to them in action'. With some premonition, he confided to me that he dearly loved his family and home, and felt that, unlike many, he had much to return home for, but it was not to be. Along with Bill, Abe and others, he was on a one-way journey.

In February 1942, two months after the bombing of Pearl Harbour, we remained unaware of the drastically changed, and desperate state of the war in the east. The speed of Japanese assaults on so many countries, was relentless. The whole of South East Asia, and the islands of the Pacific Ocean, were under threat. Far from, 'a state of total peace throughout the East', it was now in turmoil; though, to the best of our knowledge, Burma remained a peace station.

Japan prepared well for war. Their forces on land, sea, and air, assaulting many fronts; attacking all territory north of Australia, and east of India, intent upon controlling the whole of the Far East. Japan had long experience of aggression; they had been at war with China for many years, with no more than token objection from the West. The West was giving no help to China, and the Chinese were to remember this.

French Leave as British Stay

We boarded what appeared, a floating gin palace, at Madras docks, the heat was intense. S.S. *President Doumer* was a French liner, acquired by Britain in 1940, after the fall of France. 11,899 tons, and 486 foot length, she was not a small ship, although much smaller than *Strathallan*. This French tub was a totally different proposition; walls decorated with large vulgar black and green tiles, filthy and foul smelling. Floors covered in grease, supporting a herd of noisy clattering cockroaches of all sizes, some of which, appeared to be known personally to members of the French crew.

Alongside *Doumer* was a small tramp steamer being fuelled by a stream of dusty, sari-clad, female coolies, all following in line, carrying saucer-shaped baskets filled with coal. They walked up one plank, tipped the coal, coming down another, as a conveyor belt. A taxi halted on the dockside, and two members of the *Doumer* crew, both dressed in white uniforms, and slightly the worse for wear, on booze, got out, argued with, and paid the driver. One of them had a brief word with the Indian coolie supervisor, and the two walked to a shed along the dock, followed shortly by a young coolie girl, still holding on to her basket. Behind the shed, though still in view, one of the matelots produced a sheet of paper, and made a hole in the centre. Both used the paper and both used the girl. Finished, still carrying the basket, she walked back and joined the conveyor chain, as though nothing had happened. The matelots boarded ship, unconcerned as hell, their uniform fronts no more than slightly dusted.

Fulfilment seldom matched anticipation. Following *Strathallan's* high standards, our hopes of French food were soon shattered. On the third day out, Big Gilbert, the largest of the cockroaches, vanished, and the soup that evening was a little thicker. The food was appalling, captain and crew hostile. It was evident, the crew of the ship were not happy, to be carrying British troops, in dangerous waters.

Crossing the Bay of Bengal, from Madras to Rangoon, was a seven-day trip of silence. Whatever wireless news of world events the French captain may have, he guarded, always sketchy and evasive. We had no intimation whatever, of the extraordinary, and successful Japanese assaults, on so many fronts.

It was obvious, the French skipper knew more than he was prepared to reveal, when, on arrival at the mouth of Rangoon River, he decided, *Doumer,* had developed engine trouble, and the ship was not capable of proceeding, the 80 or 90 miles up river, to Rangoon Town. He must turn about and go to Calcutta, a voyage of five days. We complained that if the ship was capable of five days sail to Calcutta, it could equally sail the 90 miles to Rangoon.

Now was the time for Jimmy Ableson to disclose, he spoke fluent French. With no further pretences, he abused the skipper for his cowardice in turning to run, for the general French cowardice of 1940, resulting in the Dunkirk evacuation, and for his uncertain parentage, as a Vichy French bastard. It was a mystery how the skipper knew, the ship would sail for five days northwest, and not five hours due north. The turnabout, and run to Calcutta, meant several extra days on Japanese-controlled seas, plus whatever time it might take to get a second ship, and sail back to Rangoon. As we transferred onto a tender at the mouth of the wide Hooghly River, the French were given a derisive vote of thanks.

Eight months later, on 30 October 1942, a German submarine torpedoed President Doumer, northeast of Madeira, with the loss of 260 lives. This was two months before the demise of Strathallan.

Accommodation in a large hotel, on Chowringee, the hub of Calcutta, was opulent. It was here, we heard 'the impossible', the fall of fortress Singapore, to the Japanese. We were also advised that enemy forces were making progress in South Burma. It did not look good.

Tropical kit, so ill-used in Bombay, and especially bought for smart occasions in the 'tropical peace station', was clearly a non-essential from here on. With a Scot on hand, disposal and storage of kit was no problem; Scots have friends in all corners of the world, and Bill Riddell was no exception. A phone call to family friend Dylis Gunn, and storage was taken care of, as well as her visiting, and standing a treat of teas all round.

Another ship was confirmed for the following day. With but one night to 'do the town', things became a little hectic following the French debacle. Maybe the sea journey had affected him, or maybe he had an aversion to fans, but when, in the exclusive Century Club, Leslie Wise, looking upwards at the rotating punkah fan, fell flat on his back, the club manager made it clear that our party was unwelcome.

The following morning it was moving time once again, and on a visit to the quartermaster, stocking up and collecting haversack rations, I found myself loaded with a large blue carton of vital equipment. It appeared there had been no supplies for some considerable time, and I was charged with 10,000 'French letters', (condoms), to deliver.

Boarding the tender on the river Hooghly, we thankfully transferred to a British ship, another member of P&O Line, the British India Steam Navigation Company Ltd. S.S. *Ellenga*. Built in Glasgow in 1911, at 5,196 tons she was half the size of the French ship we had departed. *Ellenga,* shallow and broad, had traded around the eastern oceans for thirty years. Transfering from the tender, to *Ellenga,* Watkin-Williams, our man in charge, was giving directions, waving his arms about, when he got a shock. A 'shite-hawk' snatched a large cheese sandwich clean out of his hand. Everybody scaled down to minimum kit, no time was wasted in loading. With the river pilot aboard, we were on our way in a comfortable old tub of a ship, one that seemed to know her own way around.

2

CHINESE 'CHECKERS'!

Military Command strength in Burma on 22 December 1941 consisted of:

2 British Infantry battalions (1st Bn Gloucestershire
    Regiment, 2nd Bn King's Own Yorkshire Light Infantry)
2 Indian Infantry Brigades
8 Battalions Burma Rifles & Frontier Force
4 Indian Mountain Batteries
1 Battery, obsolete field guns

totalling approximately 10,000 men. Of this number, no more than 2,500 troops were considered effective, combatant, and dependable. British and Gurkha units were experienced; many had previously served on the Indian northwest frontier. Indian infantry were fine on parade, and in support of the civic authority in the event of civil disturbance; few were battle trained. The Burma Rifles, and Frontier Force, were not anticipating enemy incursion, and many returned to their home villages at early signs of hostility. It was here, amongst their own people that they felt their allegiance lay. A number 'went native', and joined with either Premier U-Saw, and his 'Galon Army', or the Thakin leader, Aung-San and his force, 'The Thirty', taking with them the arms and ammunition, supplied by His Majesty, King George VI.

In one of Wavell's submissions to Chief's of Staff, London, he requested; – 'fighter and bomber aircraft, an air warning system, anti-aircraft guns, and two further Brigade Groups'. Wavell's request was ignored, as were his previous Middle East demands. In convoy, and rounding the Cape of Africa, intended for use by Wavell: – 18th British Infantry Division, two African Brigades. Reinforcements destined for Burma, or India. The two

African Brigades never materialised, and Churchill diverted 18th Division into Singapore, by-passing both India, and Wavell. Churchill, arbitrarily, directed the troops, to where he felt the need to be greatest. Wavell was not consulted. In diverting 18th Division into Singapore, numbers were all that mattered, to Churchill, and the Army Council. When counting the number of units, they took for granted their quality, which was seldom justified. The outcome of Churchill's whim of intervention, proved catastrophic, 18th Division was given no time in which to acclimatise, or deploy effectively. Captured within days, they spent four years in Japanese prison camps. Bitter though Wavell must have been at this treatment, and with the loss of so many men, he made no complaint.

Two regular British infantry battalions, 2nd Bn Duke of Wellington Regiment, and 2nd Bn Royal Inniskilling Fusiliers, were transferred by Wavell from India to Rangoon. The two battalions were regular troops, trained and equipped for open, western-type trench warfare, and not for jungle operations.

News unfolding around Churchill continued to depress; – with failure in the western desert, – heavy sea losses, – Russian losses, (in millions). Parliamentary hostility towards Churchill's abortive visit to America: – A stack of obsolete American ships, the fall of Singapore, and an imminent threat to Burma and India. The Prime Minister was on, 'sticky ground'.

Churchill, however, came up with a new strategy. He wired Wavell,

"Contact with China is the most important feature in the eastern theatre of war".

Churchill could hardly appreciate the difficulties involved, in implementing this important liaison, with the Supreme Chinese Military Commander, Chiang Kai-shek. Wavell flew to Chiang Kai-shek's control headquarters, at Chungking, quite unsuspecting the impending Chinese-cum-American treachery. The Chinese leader was, as ever, accompanied by his astute wife, Madam Chiang. Attempting to 'borrow' two Chinese Armies, was a difficult task, and Wavell departed with no assurance either way. He was, however, soon to feel the repercussions of carrying out the Churchill decree.

American General, 'Vinegar Joe' Stilwell, was attached to Chiang, ostensibly as Commander of Chinese Armies: — At least, Joe, and Roosevelt, were free to think this, while Chiang maintained absolute personal control, over and above Stilwell. There was no Chinese action, without approval by Chiang, although Stilwell had been appointed with supposedly 'control responsibility', in return for American aid. Stilwell was aggressive, and abusive, towards the British. It is difficult to know whether it was Madam Chiang, or Stilwell, who stirred Chiang into seeking political gain out of Wavell's visit.

Wavell was in complete ignorance of what followed. Chiang chose to have an argument with Roosevelt, the cause of which was, for some reason, attributed to Wavell's visit to Chungking. Upon hearing of the umbrage taken by Chiang, Churchill realised that he could not afford to have China and America at differences. Not caring about rights and wrongs, he put the blame on the unfortunate Wavell. Western leaders were unaware of the way Chiang could blow hot and cold over any matter, in order to put pressure on Roosevelt for additional American aid. The effect of this episode, was to distance Wavell further from favour with Churchill.

In view of the speed of Japanese assaults, the prospects of Wavell receiving his promised reinforcements were now, 'pie in the sky'. With no encouragement in China, Wavell returned to Burma with the realisation that he was stuck with the forces he had got. As a final misfortune, his plane mistakenly landed on the wrong airstrip, at Mulmein, and was lucky to avoid being bombed by Japanese planes. Fortunately, it moved off rapidly, to the Rangoon air base, at nearby Mingladon.

The news Wavell received on arrival at Rangoon, was that Rommel's German tanks, against all Churchill's expectations, were defeating Auchinleck, in the north Africa desert. This meant there could be no release of reinforcements from that theatre.

A force of one hundred Japanese bomber aircraft, and support fighters, were attacking Rangoon. The town suffered heavy casualties, estimated at approximately three thousand dead, and two thousand injured; there were many fires, and panic rapidly set in: – Dacoits, Burmans, and many deserting native Burmese troops, were looting and murdering Indian traders, and many wealthy Burmese, as their families were fleeing

Rangoon in terror. The police force disintegrated, many to join with the Nationalist insurgents; there was a complete break-down of civil order.

Movement in Burma

The small bustling hill town of Taunggyi, at 7,000 feet, in the Shan State of Central Burma, is situated on a pleasant, cool, rolling open plateau. Occupied in August 1941 as a training area, by 2nd Battalion KOYLI, a strong, well-trained, regular Battalion, fully anticipating early recall for active service in the European war, or possibly the Western Desert. Mobilised at Maymyo, before its move to Taunggyi, KOYLI had no reason to plan for jungle warfare. With a Royal Navy presence in the eastern oceans, and the fortress of Singapore, considered 'the impregnable bastion of the east', there was no thought of danger to Burma.

With hills, jungle, and mighty rivers on its eastern border, Burma had no reason to feel other than secure. It was most improbable that Burma might face attack through neighbouring Thailand. The only recognised entries into Burma were through the port of Rangoon, and alternatively, the rough 'Burma Road', running from Chungking in China, to Takaw, and Lashio townships, in Central Burma. The route was difficult, and easily defended, though the necessity of doing so was never given a thought.

The cool, 7,000-foot high terrain of the Taunggyi plain came near to simulating European conditions. Training was planned on the assumption of an early return to the European front. Officers, and Senior Non-commissioned Officers, had undertaken a never-ending series of T.E.W.T.s, (tactical exercises without troops); they had studied the ground, and walked over it several times. Senior commanders, generals and brigadiers, considered themselves, the supreme authority on warfare, criticised and contributed. Planning and training theory, made many assumptions; the enemy always attacks from the front; – slit trenches, and communication runs, must be well-prepared; – machine-guns sited to fire enfilade, across wide fronts. Back-up facilities, or B'echelon, would adequately provision; – food, – water, – ammunition, – medical facilities, – reserves and reinforcements, at all times, along with mail.

The unimaginable shock, of the bombing of the American base at Pearl Harbor, it transpired, was only the first of many Japanese strikes, in their campaign for dominance of the Far East. Japan had good and accurate information on territories attacked, with the added assurance of native support. Their speed, and unorthodox methods, confounded traditionalists. With no time for preparation, attempts to halt the onslaught were either non-existent, or ineffective. Any counter-blow was invariably, either too late, or at the wrong point of attack. Japanese philosophy appeared to be; – 'Why have frontal conflict, when defences can be outflanked?' The British authorities failed to appreciate the considerable influence of fifth columnists, all well-trained by the Japanese.

Churchill played the usual Whitehall 'numbers game'. Assuming troops in the field to be at full strength, fit, efficient, competent, and combat-trained, not for one moment did he consider the reality, of the untrained, Burmese, partly-trained Indians, or ill-equipped British troops. The recently-arrived Wavell, likewise, had little time to assess the quality and equipment of his Burma force, and accepted the fallacy of effective and efficient troops. Having prospered on paper exercises for twenty years, between the wars, he conducted campaigns by preparing, written, 'appreciations of the situations'. Later however, he complained that he was, – "Not made responsible for Burma, until it was too late". In view of the Japanese speed and surprise, would any time have been soon enough? Nobody in their wildest dreams could have envisaged the Japanese succeeding in so short a time. In three weeks of assault, they had total command of the seas, land, and air of Asia, except for China.

No Allied commander knew what was happening. Coinciding with Japanese troop landings north of Singapore, a force also landed even further north, at Malaya, in the Gulf of Siam. Crossing Thailand, it advanced into the Tenasserim Peninsula (the finger-like strip of Southern Burma, pointing towards Singapore). With virtually no opposition, all emergency air-landing strips were captured, and occupied.

Wavell's command situation was similar to that of Singapore. No one had considered the mode of enemy attack, other than by an orthodox frontal assault. For the Japanese, any frontal attack was to be accidental. Local guides, informers, and fifth columnists were trained to circumnavigate obstacles, troop concentrations, and defences. It was beyond the wit of existing British strategists to counter such tactics. Time-expired senior military officers were scattered throughout the east, incapable of adaptability, unable to anticipate the incisive guerrilla methods of the enemy, and their nationalist supporters.

It was 9 December 1941, before news of the attack on Pearl Harbor reached Officer Commanding, 2nd Bn KOYLI. He received the order; – 'Dismantle camp, and move east from the Taunggyi training area, to Takaw'. He was required to prepare defensive positions, covering the difficult Burma Road, from Chunking in China, to Takaw, a small town on the Salween River. This great river is a wide, and fast-flowing torrent, about four hundred yards across, hacking its way down through high mountains, with no habitation on its banks because of the heavily wooded hills, and dense vegetation on either side.

At Takaw, the battalion prepared a classic, in depth, British defensive formation, as practised on the training area. Five hundred locals were recruited to assist, in the 'digging-in'. One company was given the additional task of moving further east, into a spectacular gorge, in order to prepare a series of rearguard positions, over a depth of 8 miles. Plans were elaborate; the road was mined, trenches dug, and a section of overhanging rock demolished, in order to block a small tributary river. Men worked, dug, and sweated, in the mosquito-infested location for two weeks, until Christmas 1941.

For a Commanding Officer, with long command of troops in the tropics, it should have come as no surprise to Colonel Keegan, when he suddenly noticed his men were going down like flies, sick with malaria. The Salween gorge was a death trap. One man was already dead, dozens reporting sick daily, malaria incubating in untold numbers of the remainder. Although medical staff advised the C.O. that the battalion might be decimated, he felt he must uphold, 'The traditions, and history of the Regiment', particularly with nine years service experience in Burma. To continue the work, was a risk he stubbornly felt he must take.

One feels entitled to ask, "What the C.O. had learnt in those nine long years in Burma?" The Japanese could have simply left the battalion, along with the defences: – Mosquitoes, aided by an insensitive commander, would have eliminated the unit. The Japanese, however, having been warned by the Burmese of the prepared defences, elected not to enter Burma by the Salween River route. Informers, almost certainly from the hired diggers, ensured the insurgents sought a quieter route. In consequence, Japanese infiltration was carried out further south. To deal with this, KOYLI were ordered south, on 23 January 1942. The strains, and costs, of six weeks work, were left behind at Takaw, but not the malaria. There had been no sighting of the enemy, not one shot fired, with the battalion already debilitated.

Senior officers lacked initiative, to recognise Japanese were being advised by ethnic nationalists. Many British soldiers who had slept with Burmese girls, in Maymyo, and Rangoon, had better basic knowledge. They suspected the Japanese operation, long before the start of hostilities. However, no senior officer would condescend to listen to bizarre, bazaar rumours, or discuss strategy, with common soldiers. Nor would he stick out his neck, to revise textbook principles, and dogma.

For eight sweltering hot days, by train and truck, 2nd Bn KOYLI was in transit southwards. The objective was, – 'To meet new circumstances, and perceived increasing threats to the area'. Men falling ill en-route, were returned to hospital at Maymyo. As a consequence, over the eight days of transit, the battalion strength was reduced, from 500 to 400. Malaria was no respecter of rank, and many commissioned, and senior non-commissioned officers, were infected. The consequent restructuring of companies, and platoons, was not well received by all. There were many jealous rivalries, with scores to settle.

The small town of Moulmein, situated near the mouth of the Salween River, at the northern end of the Tenasserim peninsula, was the intended destination. Speed and efficiency of Japanese infiltration, coupled with a weak communications system, left officers and men of the KOYLI in total ignorance of day-by-day developments. The situation changed drastically during eight days of transit. Moulmein had already fallen to Japanese occupation, along with the whole of the South Burma, Tenasserim Peninsula; -. A change of plan was made; on 31 January, KOYLI disembarked from the troop train at Hninpale, a small railway station on the eastern side of the Gulf of Martaban. Here they had first news; – the bombing of Rangoon Town, the general chaos, and the mass evacuation of civilians.

Guided by Burmese nationalists, across the three-mile-wide Salween River mouth, and penetrating the near-impregnable natural barrier of hills and jungle, the Japanese faced little opposition in their advance into South Burma. The first Japanese encounter, was with a company of raw recruits of the Burma Frontier Force. Mostly young boys, with little interest in resistance, they turned and ran, streaming west, through Hninpale rail junction, towards Rangoon. Along with them came individuals of Indian units, some injured, and many, who had? – 'Lost their unit?'

In the thirty-six hours' wait at Hninpale, KOYLI had time to consider their individual domestic situations. Many officers, and men, had wives and families in married quarters at Maymyo. They were shattered on hearing that Rangoon, the one port of exit, could possibly close at short notice. These considerations put additional pressures on the battalion, as men pondered over the problems confronting their loved ones. Many soldiers had Burmese, or Anglo-Indian, girl-friends, and all were at risk.

In the period at Hninpale, malaria incubation became manifest to a greater degree, and no less than 200 officers and men succumbed to the fever. Within days, more than one third of the battalion was affected. The battalion strength was reduced to a little over 300. The battalion strength was further impaired in the next few days, as companies were split in order that detachments could be attached to Indian, and Gurkha units. Companies were being used as support, and strengthening units, to Indian Brigades. KOYLI was a strong, and mostly regular unit, all spoke English; few indeed spoke, or understood Urdu, the language of Indian units. The battalion was not, at this time, identified as part of any fixed Brigade, and came under direct control of the Divisional Commander. Through him, detachments were attached to whatever unit was most convenient, or in need. Much depleted though it was, companies and platoons were deployed as though at full strength, and made responsible for what, in European circumstances, would be battalion, or brigade, frontages. They became, immediately; – 'Everybody's stranger, and nobody's baby'. Segregation of a platoon, or section, of non-Urdu speaking individuals to an Indian unit, meant that they suffered from lack of communication, so vital under battle conditions.

To break, or disperse segments of a unit of this calibre, was a mistake in the guerrilla-style operations to follow. Strength lies in the commitment of the whole. On the night of 10 February, a detached KOYLI Company, operating in support of an Indian brigade, strangers to them, was the first to be engaged in hostile action. The Company was deployed into a formal defensive position, at what was considered the most vulnerable point. The task was; – 'To stop the anticipated crossing of the Salween River, by the Japanese'. The Baluch Regiment ordered to patrol the river bank, one company moving north, a second moving south, leaving the KOYLI company sited in the centre, the anticipated crossing section. The depleted company, spreading itself over a battalion-size frontage, was weakened further, in having to conduct patrol operations.

Informed and guided by Burmese, the Japanese had already completed the crossing of the Salween, long before the KOYLI company arrived. They had secured a bridgehead, as the weakened Baluchis fled the assault. Within hours, the slender KOYLI force was almost annihilated.

Japanese captured the transport section, consisting of 108 mules, along with Burmese muleteers. No doubt, they welcomed the additional transport assistance, complete with newly-found, friendly Burmese handlers. Dispersed companies of the Baluch Regiment were also heavily attacked, and lost many men, both killed and wounded. Few escaped to re-form later.

Throughout the campaign to follow, Japan appeared to have the happy knack of knowing where British forces were deployed, or on detachment. In this way, they could 'mop up' the bits, rather than impose assaults on a main force. There were occasions when the Japanese created detachments, at places of their own choosing, by erecting road blocks at well-sited vantage points, thus isolating part of a force. Another means of bringing about isolation, was through the Burmese vandalising communications, by cutting signal lines. Army signallers attempting to repair lines were caught in ambushes, and hacked to death by Burmans wielding *dahs*. It was not possible to identify friend, or foe, behind the placid inscrutable face, apparently carrying out the daily chores of a village. It is considered that as many as 50 KOYLI members suffered this fate, and remain in Burma, – 'Missing; believed killed'.

Within two days, the battalion lost almost one whole company, and the larger part of its transport. A few trucks and mules remained, also the tracked carrier section consisting of four vehicles. The survivors of the company, making a 30-mile trek in an effort to rejoin the battalion, moved at speed through jungle, streams, and paddy fields. The one remaining anti-tank rifle was in the hands of Private Cryer, a tough Yorkshireman from Shipley. Heavy and bulky though it was, he refused to abandon the weapon as he struggled on alone, attempting to follow the tracks of the main party. Cryer became the first of many to fall further and further behind, to become another of those; – 'missing, believed killed'.

In the same area, a similar fate overcame signaller Lance Corporal Connell, of Doncaster, who had repeatedly gone out to repair damaged signal lines. He failed to return that day. Signallers remained at all times highly dedicated and conscientious in performing their duties. It was never enough for a signaller in trouble to say, 'My set is not working'; it was always, 'and I'll have it going in a minute, sir'. At all times, and in all conditions, as a matter of honour, a signaller would carry, drag or somehow transport, 'His set', establishing communications within the shortest possible time.

Within four hectic days, KOYLI were seeing defeat staring them in the face. The Japanese had negotiated what was considered the most formidable of defence lines; they had crossed the Salween River, developed a strong bridgehead, and created chaos with well-sited roadblocks. KOYLI rapidly assessed the lack of dependable support units. They witnessed trains and trucks passing through the station at Hninpale, en route to Rangoon, all loaded with equipped Indian, and Burmese troops. Few were injured.

Moving back to a formal, in-depth, defensive position, the battalion was surprised to find Japanese, circumventing their efforts, advancing and maintaining strength. The Burmese, with full knowledge of British dispositions, were now openly guiding Japanese along uncharted tracks.

Much was made of how the Japanese had an ability to gather, silently and unseen in the jungle, as though there was magic in this. The British were equally silent, but the Japanese had the advantage of having guides to bring them into position, out of range of listening British ears. There was one neutral in the noise contest; no man can keep a harnessed mule silent, Japanese or British. No jungle is so silent as to allow sound to travel great distances; with insects, birds, monkeys and trees squealing, whistling, howling, or just rubbing together, the jungle is a noisy place.

Concern over the tactical deployment of army units, and lack of defence effectiveness, had British Commanders in turmoil. Continuing to ignore the rapidly dwindling strengths, they planned formations, with 'time honoured', 'fixed lines of defence', and forward defence positions, prepared for set piece confrontation, when the real need was; – For consolidation of a force, in order to hunt in strength, and to hammer the enemy before he could consolidate a position. Attacks in strength could have been effective in those earlier days, whilst troops available were strong, equipped, armed and fed. To permit the enemy to split and divide units was to make his consolidated attack easier by far. So long as the Japanese had guides and spies, they could search out the weaker formations, for destruction.

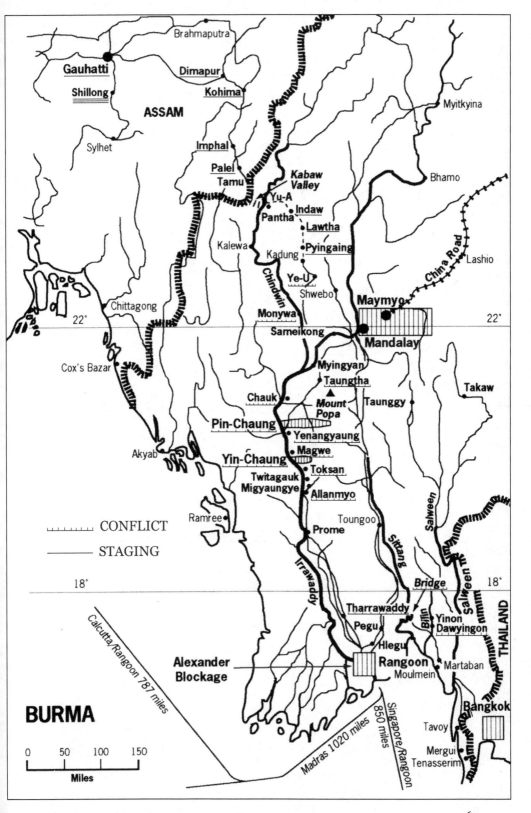

BURMA

CONFLICT
STAGING

Calcutta/Rangoon 787 miles
Madras 1020 miles
Singapore/Rangoon 850 miles

Alexander
Blockage

0   50   100   150
Miles

3

2ND BATTALION K.O.Y.L.I.
MUTILATION

In early February 1942, the conglomerate of military units in Southern Burma, were designated, 17th Indian Infantry Division, under Major General J.G. Smyth V.C. The depleted 2nd Bn K.O.Y.L.I., commanded by Lieutenant Colonel Keegan, joined with the division, and was posted to 16th Brigade (Brigadier J.K. Jones), and force marched 12 miles to the deployment area.

Countermanding the posting two days later, on 8 February, the unit was transferred to 48th Indian Infantry Brigade. Once again, urgency required a forced march of 20 miles, and rapid deployment.

St Valentine's Day, 14 February, was celebrated with real gusto. The order was once again countermanded, reversing the forced march, in order to rejoin Jones, at 16th Brigade. It did not make for happiness among the men, the least caustic description of the proceedings being, 'buggered about'.

One day later, on 15th February, 16th Brigade, less KOYLI, was withdrawn 20 miles to defend the line of the Bilin River, and the river bridge. By way of a change from running about, KOYLI were ordered to remain at Thaton Town, to receive a train, expected shortly, load the train with divisional rations and supplies. On completion, the battalion was to return on foot to Bilin.

Well into the night, long after the train was due, a dispatch rider arrived, saying that; "Owing to a misunderstanding, the train would not now be coming. – Abandon stores and return on foot forth- with". Joined by a small party of Indian sappers, charged with the task of destroying the road bridges, the battalion set forth in the black of night. As dawn was breaking, they heard the distant rattle of a train; it passed a few hundred yards away, moving in the direction of Thaton. Obviously, this was the train scheduled to arrive the previous evening. Sensing the unusual stillness of the normally bustling town, the Burmese train driver had panicked, and run off into the jungle, possibly to join the insurgents.

Thaton, however, was not entirely deserted. Two KOYLI 'squaddies', had fallen asleep, while mounting guard on the supplies. Awakening, they came upon the divisional beer ration. Enjoying the proverbial 'skinful', they had slept it off, as the battalion was footing it back to Bilin. The pair could have been killed or taken prisoner. Fortunately, they were not.

Private Bream, an Englishman, born in Burma, had worked for Burma railways before joining the army at Maymyo. He manoeuvred the engine to the correct end of the train. 'Jacko' Jackson, the second man, feverishly loaded the stores, and in a little time, the train, stores, and two lucky men were on their way to rejoin the battalion.

Back at Bilin, on the safer west bank of the river, General Smyth became apprehensive upon hearing the train's approach, and afraid the train might be full of Japanese, his first reaction was to consider destroying the rail bridge. Fortunately, he had second thoughts, and the train pulled into Hninpale station, with Bream and Jackson on board. Quartermaster Taffy Phillips welcomed rations that should have been destroyed the previous night, and Bream continued operating his 'private train', until its final destruction.

Deployed at Thaton, KOYLI eagerly awaited their first head-to-head encounter with the enemy. This was not to be. Intercepting Japanese assaults was like attempting to stop the flow of a stream; it will run around obstacles. Using local Burmese guides, the Japanese circumnavigated defences, and avoided Thaton. They were eager to make ground for their next objective, the crossing of the Bilin, a shallow river no more than 100 yards wide. Operating in this manner, they had brought about the isolation of the battalion of British troops, defending Thaton to no purpose, and cut them off from the main force.

On 16 February, withdrawn to west of the Bilin River, with the increasing toll of sick evacuating by the day, the battalion adopted a defensive position, along an extended front, on the riverbank. The West bank of the Bilin was a much variegated area of small straggling villages, surrounded by paddy fields, sugar plantations, and general agriculture. There were many trees around each village, and surrounding all was dense jungle.

Colonel Keegan, and Adjutant, Captain 'Rosebud' Doyle, went back to liaise with a Gurkha regiment, after first repeating the time honoured order, always given by 'higher command' (themselves safely away from all action); – "Hold the position, to the last man and the last round". The intention was that, as the Japanese crossed the Bilin River, they should be given one hell of a reception. The 'last man, last round' maxim, emanated from General Smyth, ignoring the fact, he had no other troops of quality, apart from his Gurkhas. As often happened with the 'old brigade of officers', it did not occur to him that he was going to need those troops, again and again, should he survive.

Major Wardleworth, given the defence of Dawyingon village, to the north of Bilin town, was mounted on a charger as he traversed the long main street of the straggling habitation, assessing requirments, in order to meet Smyth's plan; – 'to stop the Japanese crossing the Bilin'. Nothing looks better, or more prominent and inviting, than a British officer mounted on a charger, a most desirable target for any enemy. The locals of the village stood, or squatted, looking bland, chewing the inevitable betel nut, spitting out the red juice, and showing total indifference to the intrusion of a man on a horse, as they awaited developments. Wardleworth deployed his platoons in a spread of defensive positions.

Advancing through the village, and rounding a bend, one platoon was surprised to come upon a detachment of Japanese already across the river, and washing at a well in the street. They made a dash for cover, and to join up with their main force sited on a hill; shots were fired and further Japanese emerged. Unaware that the enemy was entrenched in large numbers, Wardleworth rallied two weak platoons to assault the village. Outnumbered, and ill-equipped, it became a hopeless task. It meant withdrawal.

Hopelessly beaten! This was the beginning of the longest ever withdrawal by a British Army force.

Stretched and vulnerable, over a frontage of almost 20 jungle miles, with no communications, meant total isolation of each small detachment. The situation was such that the enemy was in position to concentrate attacks on any detached British unit. It was impossible to assemble a force at speed, and in strength, sufficient to attack and destroy the numbers of Japanese ensconced in Dawyingon village. So well prepared were their defences, it was obvious much of the preparation was completed before their arrival. On his return, Keegan assembled what he could of an assault force, in order to enter the village, in an attempt to dislodge the Japanese.

With support from the 3-inch mortars, Keegan launched an attack; – in action for the first time. Sergeant Benny Mee of Leeds, along with the remaining fit, Benny Dransfield of Rotherham, Corporal Bareham, George Kibbler, Gigger Lee, Joss Isaacs, Ted Hewitt, and Mycock, pumped ten-pounder bombs as fast as they could go. Japanese were now well dug in, with their strength increased, to possibly 300 or more, they suffered many casualties from rifle, Bren-gun, and British bayonet. A number of Japanese officers were shot, while attempting to rouse troops already dead.

The mortars maintained a creeping barrage, adjusting the range, and driving the Japanese backwards. Retreating enemy made easy targets for a section of seven soldiers, situated in a bungalow, with Sergeant Howson. The mortars ceased when they became a danger to the seven. Japanese concentrated greater firepower onto Howson, and it became time to withdraw. Barnsley man, Lance Corporal R.G. Wood, wounded in the foot and unable to walk, was having no part in the withdrawal. Moving behind a tree, he gave the thumbs up sign, and was seen to be hitting Japanese until he himself slumped back, killed.

The Japanese made no attempt to advance into the defence system set along the road from the village. Keegan did not read any significance into this, nor did he consider the possible Japanese strategy. They were, however, doing as they had done throughout their series of successful assaults across Asia. They were being guided around the problem.

At nightfall, and fresh from the boat, the lst/4th Battalion Gurkha Rifles arrived, following service on the northwest frontier of India. Beloved soldiers and renowned fighters that they are, this unit was not trained, for scrub and jungle warfare. Without hesitation, (no Gurkha hesitates), and supported by Benny Mee and his mortars, they advanced the following morning, 18 February, attacking Dawyingon, only to be repulsed. Repeating the attack, they inflicted many casualties on the Japanese, and suffered heavily themselves in the conflict, until it became prudent to withdraw, no further attempt being made to capture the village.

Other Japanese continued the infiltration process, with troops moving around the weak southern flank of Jones' brigade. Although Japan had suffered many casualties at Dawyingon, they knew that with their defence arrangement, and strengthening forces, they were adequate for whatever attack the British might launch. Whenever necessary, the Japanese defended first, and then infiltrated, without wasting time on the consolidation of positions; it was the pattern used throughout.

Lacking wireless communication, KOYLI became entirely dependent upon company runners. In unfamiliar territory, a man had to find his way to a location, and once on site, there was the problem of finding the responsible officer to receive the message. This proved difficult, and fatally time-consuming, with the isolated A and B companies, detached as they were, up river, around the town of Yinon, some seven or eight miles north of Dawyingon. The two companies were unaware of the devastation inflicted further south. Lacking communication, from A and B companies, in the first twenty-four hours, General Smyth developed a rash of anxiety, causing Keegan to become concerned about his dispersed units. He sent carrier officer Goldthorpe, with no support, or cover carrier, to contact the two companies around Yinon.

Goldthorpe had no problem locating A company. On arrival, he found the Company Commander, concerned at the heavy enemy concentrations surrounding him. Appreciating the urgency, Goldthorpe turned the carrier in order to return, and report the situation; – immediately, Japanese opened up, firing from the jungle. Goldthorpe returned Bren-gun fire in the direction of the enemy, as he set to return to battalion

H.Q. Finding a road bridge blocked with stones, and the bridge itself burning, as the Japanese opened up, with further rifle and machine gun fire, Goldthorpe's driver, Private Parker, spun the carrier round and set off back, towards Yinon. Surviving a hail of fire from ranges of no more than a few yards, the carrier was pitted, and cut on front, sides and back.

Another road block, another trap. In his innocence, Smyth decided the blockage should be cleared, and a way made for tracked vehicles. Forty Indian sappers, with two trucks and carrier support, were sent forward to blow the bridge and make the gully fordable. Anticipating predictable British reaction, the Japanese set an ambush, covering the blockage. As sappers dismounted from the transport, Japanese opened fire with machine-gun, rifle and grenade. They mowed the Indians down, to a man, with mortars continuing to rain shells into the area. Two surviving carriers scuttled, one back to brigade HQ, and one forward towards Yinon. Parker and Goldthorpe remained, in order to shoot up Japanese machine-gun sections, although, within a short time, the carrier became a prime target. With limited manoeuverability in the jungle area, the carrier was fired on, almost every inch as it sped back to brigade H.Q.

'A' company, reduced drastically in strength, and desperate for ammunition, had three small platoons in separate actions of withdrawal, against superior numbers of enemy. Casualties increased, as overwhelming numbers of Japanese emerged from the jungle onto the road. Fighting became hand-to-hand, with bayonet and sword, rifle butts hammering many Japanese heads. Company Sergeant Major Houseley, a second row forward in the battalion rugger team, bent several skulls with his rifle-butt. Grabbing two Japanese by the scruff of the neck, he bashed their heads together, as he himself was hacked to pieces by several swords. Houseley's party accounted for many Japanese before they themselves were exterminated. The remainder of A company became a target, for mortars and machine guns. Major W.G.Haughton, the Company Commander, was killed by a direct hit.

Japanese remained hidden in the jungle, firing incessantly at the remains of Haughton's company, now reduced to less than two dozen men. It became virtually, a matter of, – 'every man for himself'. The mule section was stampeded down the road, in the hope of causing distraction;

it was not of much value, as the mules and men were wiped out, and only one driver got through. Private Chuck Collins of Bradford became tired of being pinned down under fire, without knowing by whom. Fixing his bayonet, he set out seeking Japanese to kill, knowing that he must also die.

Corporal Jim Rowley, of Sheffield, went in search of his son-in-law, Corporal Bill Macdonald, only to find him shot through the stomach. Macdonald made his final request, for as many full Bren-gun magazines as possible. With his gun in position, he stayed to shoot it out with whoever came, knowing that he was dying, yet, as a champion boxer, welcoming competition to the last. Eventually, fourteen or fifteen bedraggled, and surviving members of A company, found their way back to H.Q.

At Yinon, B company, under Captain Walter Baxter, found the area, 'teeming with Japanese', on both sides of the river. Receiving no orders, no news, and worst of all, no rations or friends, but plenty of enemy, they were isolated. Efforts at communication with headquarters were to no avail. The situation was to bring about one of the most heroic, individual feats of valour, in the whole war. Somebody had to get through to battalion H.Q. in order to advise them of the company predicament.

Goole man, Private Wallace, (Wally), Abbott, volunteered for the mission, determined he could get through on foot, and alone. Abbott filled his water bottle, and securing his equipment in order to minimise noise and rattle, he moved off quietly, at about eight in the morning, of Wednesday 18 February. Knowing he must move silently and avoid roads and tracks, he went straight into the dense jungle, where the undergrowth could have been sheltering enemy, as it sheltered him. Speed of movement, and maintaining direction, in these conditions, over cliffs, hills, rivers and dense undergrowth, without map or compass, is hard to achieve. To cover the eight or nine miles, before the early tropical nightfall, was a difficult target. Abbott enjoyed the challenge, and departed with the good wishes of his chums. All knew his chances to be slim, and few expected to see him again.

With no compass, Abbott's line of approach was towards distant gunfire, where the main body of the battalion was in combat. There were many obvious signs of enemy as he traversed and crossed tracks, until about mid-day, when the sun was at its highest. Halfway towards headquarters, he encountered a more prominent track with, in the distance, what appeared to be two broken-down British trucks. Abbott moved carefully down the track before approaching the vehicles.

With no warning, a machine-gun opened fire from the jungle, a bullet hitting Abbot in the thigh, knocking him to the ground; his rifle fell out of reach, knocking pieces off the vehicle. He took cover behind one of the wheels, and suffered no further injury. Abbott expected to be mutilated, in the time-honoured manner, the machine-gunner stopped firing, and the man departed. Abbott struggled back into the cover of the jungle, crawling along the roadside ditch, he came upon a heap of bodies covered in brushwood. The bodies were those of Indian sappers, killed in ambush the previous day. In Wally Abbot's own words; – "Whilst behind the truck, I noticed there had been fighting in the area, a dead mule, empty. 303 cases, and Bren mags. There were no rifles or ammo with the bodies, or at least, I didn't see any. My only water on the journey was my own water bottle filled before leaving 'B' Coy". He felt himself fortunate to be alive.

The high velocity quarter-inch Japanese bullet had made a small clean straight wound through the flesh of his leg, which meant Abbott could manage slow movement as, now indifferent to pain, he proceeded, limping and staggering rather than walking, He continued for an hour or two, before once again joining the track and halting, to listen and to check his wound. It was not bleeding too badly, and he felt confident of completing the mission, particularly so when he sighted four approaching Burmese. He moved to attract their attention.

The natives appeared friendly, and directed him towards British troops. As Abbott relaxed and prepared to take a drink from his water bottle, he saw one of the Burmese poised with his *dah,* (the long broad bladed knife carried by most Burmese), making to strike at his head. Abbott warded off the blade with his hand, as the others also started striking, hitting his protecting hands and arms. Summoning up superhuman strength, Abbott forced himself to his feet, scattering the men, and pulling a grenade from his pouch, removed the pin, and presented it to them from behind the cover of a tree, killing all four. Wally says; – "I like to think I got them, but I can't be sure. I didn't hang around to find out". The thigh wound was now the least of his worries; – the fingers of his left hand were almost detached, and those of the right severely damaged with a considerable loss of blood. Using his military first field dressing and a bandolier, Abbott applied a tourniquet on his left arm, tucking this into the neck of his shirt as a sling. He was aware that he still had a job to do for his mates.

Carrying a grenade in his right hand, and determined to complete the task by nightfall, Abbott set forth once again. Staggering and losing consciousness from time to time, he continued through the jungle, aware that he might collapse and die, if he failed to reach H.Q. before dark. On meeting the road once more, he realised that survival depended upon him staying on it, and making all speed. Arriving at a Gurkha sentry out-post, refusing evacuation until he had delivered his message, he was carried to receive medical attention.

Thirsty, hungry, and sore throughout the night, Abbott lay in a Gurkha slit trench, feeling a failure to his mates, as infiltrating Japanese fought with Gurkhas, over and around him; – he was the helpless observer in a night of conflict. Sleeping and waking to the sound of crossfire, a moan and then silence, he never lost sight of his main task, as the following morning, Gurkhas carried him to report to Keegan. Abbott had a drink and some food before being evacuated into oblivion: – The lot of the common British soldier, his bravery 'airbrushed out', and not rewarded.

In his 94th year, Wallace 'Wally' Abbott, died at Lincoln, on 27th April 2011. My wife and I attended his funeral.

Hearing from Abbott, Keegan arranged for a message to be dropped to Baxter from the air, saying, "Abandon all heavy equipment, withdraw to Kyaikto immediately". This was fine, except that on the same morning, two planes with British markings had strafed Baxter's company with machine-gun fire, no doubt mistaking them for Japanese. Whilst doing little damage, there was considerable suspicion when, three hours later, Keegan's plane circled as troops took cover, to drop a canister, which landed on a sandbank, out in the Bilin river. It was almost equidistant between Baxter's company, and the Japanese, seen moving around on the far bank. Sergeant Bob Steermint volunteered to recover the canister.

Every weapon was trained on the far bank, covering Steermint as he crossed the paddy fields, and waded in under Japanese noses, to retrieve the canister, with not one shot being fired. Equipment was dropped down wells, and the company vacated, in late afternoon. As Japanese were seen assembling on the far bank, for an assault on the village. It was the following night, over twenty-four hours later, before Baxter's thirsty, hungry, and sick company arrived at Kyaikto, the battalion was scheduled to re-form. Not that the day, date or month mattered, but it was Thursday 19 February; the battalion having been frontline operational for only one week, it had been reduced in strength from about 500 to little more than, a variable 200, officers and men. Orders were given for 2nd KOYLI to move out along a route, one that might have appeared sensible on a map, but meant marching south and immediately across the front, within easy rifle range of the enemy, and continuing to the Bilin bridge area. This order was received three hours after the withdrawal of the defence troops, and resulted in 30 miles of haphazard, marching and skirmishing.

Baxter's company, withdrawing to Kyaikto, became segregated from the main force. There was a series of feats of heroism en route, similar to those of the other companies, and where many brave men perished inflicting maximum damage to the enemy.

Unswerving in achieving their objectives, the main force of Japanese was being hurriedly guided around a circuit to the north, in an attempt to reach and capture their next main objective; – the Sittang River Bridge.

The Sittang Bridge

Setbacks in conflicts around the villages of the Salween and Bilin rivers, where the battalion covered almost 300 miles on foot, through jungle, roads and tracks, were to become insignificant within the next few days. The battalion, now desperately short of water, food and ammunition, made its way back in the hope of crossing the next objective, the Sittang River Bridge.

The division was ordered back, as rapidly as possible, on a march of 20 miles over a newly-cut jungle track, three quarters of the track being hardly adequate for bullock-cart traffic. Troops were constantly aware of the proximity of the enemy, ever probing with advance parties, and infiltrating wherever they found a weakness. The main Japanese force was to the east, and northern side, away from the Gulf of Martaban, and in a race to reach the Sittang, ahead of the British.

The Sittang River, almost three quarters of a mile across, and spanned by the huge rail bridge, had been previously adapted by Indian sappers for road operation. Apart from the defence value of the river obstacle, the bridge was vital; it must be held if the remnants of 17th Division were to be extricated, in order to defend Rangoon, and South Burma. There were no further reserves, and no defence in depth, to the west of the Sittang. This was the unimagined – a totally impossible situation.

Troops were in a fix, and they knew it. They were prepared to fight a defensive action to the Sittang, on the basis of cut and thrust, as conducted in the past two weeks, and in the hope that the bridge would be held for them to cross on arrival. KOYLI officers were aghast at Kyaikto, to find a freshly arrived British unit, the 2nd Battalion Duke of Wellington Regiment, in a forward situation, in the 17th Division melange. The 'Dukes', withdrawn from civil defence duties in India, disembarked at Rangoon, with no induction, were sent forward, direct from the ship into the melee. They should, more logically, have been sent to defend the bridge, and maintain the west bank of the Sittang.

No fool, let alone a British general, should have committed a newly arrived unit into this maelstrom. KOYLI would have welcomed news that the 'Dukes' were defending the Sittang Bridge, rather than have them thrust into the melting pot and added to the numbers infesting the single, overloaded jungle track. Pleased as they were to see new British troops, they wished them anywhere, except at Kyaikto.

Arriving with the Dukes were the 2nd Royal Tank Regiment, and 7th Hussars, of the 7th Armoured Brigade. Sensibly, for once, they were dispersed into the more open ground of central Burma, to prove their worth in later action. The Royal Inniskilling Fusiliers, also newly disembarked, went to a northern situation, and joined with the 1st Burma Division.

Orders were given: – 'Kyaitko to be held until the morning of 22 February. One brigade to undertake rearguard duty on the town. A second brigade, (depleted as they were), with KOYLI, to move back six miles or so, and prepare a defence on both sides of the road. The third brigade to move off immediately, straight back to the Sittang'. (Each brigade, now hardly the strength of a battalion, was Brigade, in name only).

Aware of Japanese outflanking tactics, British officers disliked the idea of holding and delaying, at Kyaikto; – Seeking to get back to the vital bridge, as rapidly as possible. The atrocious condition of the newly cut jungle track, did not permit the density of personnel, without some measure of planned control. The narrow track was hot, with fine powdery dust, and stumps of newly cut trees, and protruding brushwood, hindering movement. Japanese aircraft, with freedom of flight, had one single column of moving troops for a target. For two hours, they bombed and machine-gunned the moving column, inflicting few casualties on KOYLI. Many from following Indian units, were killed or wounded. Unhindered; the Japanese attacked with successive flights; – strafing the ground with machine-gun fire.

As Japanese aircraft departed, a further ignominy was inflicted on the troops; another four or five planes appeared, to repeat the bombing and machine-gunning. The second force were 'friendly' aircraft, the remnants of the Royal Air Force, and a Mercenary American Volunteer Group, attempting to stem the Japanese onslaught, only mistakenly, to use British troops as targets, and maintain the dust cloud. Throughout a day of repeated attacks, by both enemy, and 'friendly' aircraft, the two never managed to meet over the target. Uncomfortable though the KOYLI defensive situation was, sited in a rubber plantation, the casualty list was modest, particularly considering the amount of lead and explosives delivered from the skies, by friend and foe.

KOYLI Adjutant, Major 'Rosebud' Doyle, accompanied by a small escort, was ordered to the Sittang, with the task of preparing a reception area for the battalion on their withdrawal. Moving along the dusty jungle track, the party was aware of hostile observers. For persons moving by night, it was standard to carry a grenade in one hand, and as all in this party were so equipped, they were not molested.

After a brief night halt with a Gurkha unit, the party arrived at 5 a.m. at the village of Mokpalin, two miles from the bridge. Within one hour of Doyle's arrival, and with no warning, Smyth, the General, and his Divisional H.Q, along with a Gurkha Battalion, 'upped-sticks', and vanished. Crossing to the safer west bank of the Sittang, the only troops of 17th Division to cross the intact bridge.

Within the next hour, the Japanese attacked, destroying vehicles, and blocked the narrow road, in an attempt to isolate Divisional HQ by creating a strategically defended roadblock. With the greater part of 17th division stranded on the vulnerable eastern side of the river, the ambush was set, less than one mile from the bridge. Although not physically capturing the eastern end of the bridge, the enemy had most of 17th Division trapped, bottled up on a track, littered with dead men and animals. Firing became heavy, and further vehicles damaged, from heavy machine-gun and mortar fire.

With British committed, at Bilin and Kyaikto, the Japanese used locals, guiding them along lesser-known village tracks, setting the trap for 17th Division. The futility of sending the Dukes into a forward offensive situation, was all too clear. They should have been held in reserve, to fulfil the more positive role of defending the bridge. In the event, the Japanese pinned down the Dukes; they suffered many casualties before extricating themselves. The blockage created instant panic, and a new situation; it had to be cleared. Troops trapped along the track remained unaware of the danger.

Senior officers of Division, and Brigade, were not conspicuous. There was no question of waiting for orders or directions. It was essential to attempt extrication, to secure and defend the eastern end of the bridge, and preserve the crossing point. In the turmoil, many men became detached from units. Small groups of British, Indian, Gurkha, and the few loyal Burmese, formed together in resistance, as news of their plight spread.

KOYLI had difficulty in disengaging; the action involved a heavy rearguard battle throughout the journey along the track, until late afternoon, and it used up precious ammunition, and heard news of the road blockage; also, of attempts by the motley collection of troops denying the bridge to the Japanese. Occupying higher ground south-east of the bridge, two much-reduced brigades formed a perimeter, in order to defend an anticipated attack from the south, and cover possible approaches along the railway embankment, which ran parallel to the river. The brigades had considerable activity throughout the night, as the Japanese sought to capture the bridge intact. It was pure luck that the defence positions were well-sited, as the Japanese were concentrating their attack from this direction. The Japanese attacked and probed, in an attempt to infiltrate; there was no giving way, despite the incessant assault.. The British were 'obstacles' that had to be moved, but as guides could find no way around this defence, they stayed, killing Japanese at a steady rate. There was a feeling of containment.

A shattering noise, heard above all others, left nobody in doubt of what had happened. At 4 a.m. on the morning of 23 February, there was one enormous explosion, followed rapidly by another; then, absolute silence.

What seemed like an interminable silence, had lasted only seconds, but the significance of those explosions penetrated numbed brains, and no man was in doubt that the great bridge, now on the river bottom, had been denied the enemy. But at what cost? Heavy hearted, 17th Division returned to the task in hand, and shooting continued, every bit as intense as before, except that the expletives grew stronger. Shooting Japanese, while at the same time, cursing the individual ordering the demolition of the vital Sittang Bridge.

A short time earlier at Bilin, General Smyth had panicked, and had been about to demolish the bridge on the approach of a train. Here, at the Sittang, he had once again panicked. Survival meant crossing the huge expanse of river; – every man considering ways and means of attacking the monster. Few had training sufficient to swim the distance; indeed, many had a dread of water. The Japanese problem must be solved before any move could be made towards the riverbank.

General Smyth, ensconced on the safer west bank, did absolutely nothing to assist those he stranded. Quite apart from the troops involved, there were vehicles, arms, ammunition, mules and supplies. Further reserves within Burma were few indeed.

The sole reason for the Sittang Bridge blowing, was that Smyth was ensconced on the safe west bank. A Japanese assault was not imminent. Troops of the division knew that so long as the bridge remained, there was a means of crossing. If ever there was a case of 'wait until you see the whites of their eyes', this was it.

The massive bridge destruction was the ruination of the British Army in Burma, and eventual cause of the ignominious abandonment of the country. There was to be no recovery. The country was gone in two weeks, and British forces decimated. From this point on, it was withdrawal. The world was closed to Burma, communications, command, and reports were sketchy, no more than guesswork.

With meticulous preparation, planning, and equipment, Japan knew precicely what they were about, in attacking throughout the East, and pressed their advantage. British Parliamentarians, and Military Command, living on World War One memory, and a belief of superiority, under a blustering Prime Minister, floundered at every juncture.

Yorkshiremen do not suffer fools gladly. There were no apologies for calling whoever ordered demolition of the bridge 'a stupid bastard', and much worse than that. It was a route, the British were beaten! There was panic, in securing a boat to cross the river. However, all boats had already been taken to the west bank, holed and sunk.

17th Division remained in one hell of a fix. The only lull in the sound of firing had been the silence, following the bridge explosions. As dawn broke, Japanese troops were seen, entrenched in numbers around the defence perimeter. For the hungry troops, short of ammunition, sick at heart, and gagging for a simple drink of water, it became 'cabaret time'.

In France, during World War I, a Scottish Colonel was awarded the Victoria Cross for gallantry; he walked on the parapet of trenches as a piper played the bagpipes. Germans were not fools; they knew that to shoot him would only relieve his suffering. The Marines in North Africa had a Colonel, renowned for repeating the feat of stupidity.

Colonel Keegan saw this situation as his opportunity to establish immortality: – KOYLI must have a feat of similar valour. He decided to walk about in the open, as though endowed with a charmed life; defying gunfire, moving between companies, he crossed the paddy fields. Was he thinking, to be shot, might be one way out of his predicament? For some reason, possibly to identify the points he visited, the Japanese ignored him throughout the morning. It was only when he came out for an encore in the afternoon, they bothered to shoot at him. If one must be so stupid as to walk about in front of machine-guns, and mortar fire, one should at least ensure that one has a Scottish piper putting on the agony. Keegan was relieved of his problems, and evacuated; – he survived to a great age.

Containing the riverbank, south-east of the bridge, KOYLI and the Dukes, along with Gurkha units, came under heavier fire. Scattered individuals nearer the bridge were busying themselves collecting anything floatable, in order to make a raft to cross the river. As the collecting commenced, Japanese aircraft arrived, flying to and fro, shooting freely at anything moving on the river.

Back in the 'stockade', Sergeant Benny Dransfield, from Rotherham, and Dewsbury's 'Gigger' Lee, moved the one remaining three-inch mortar as far forward as possible. Attempting to get on terms with the superior range of Japanese mortars, they added extra charges to the standard six on the bomb tails, and rapid-fired on the enemy until all ammunition was exhausted. There was no respite, and many instances of courage. Rosebud Doyle was shot in the thigh, and though twice the size of Dransfield, Dransfield picked him up, and carried him to the river crossing.

The Japanese attack eased, possibly short of ammunition following the long hours of fighting. It was sufficient for KOYLI to send their sick and walking wounded to make the best they could of crossing the river; they would have welcomed the intact bridge. Later in the day, the withdrawal order was given and companies vacated defences, taking with them the remaining wounded.

It was impossible under the circumstances to consider coordinating a crossing of the three-quarter mile river. 'Every man for himself' was the order. It was now swim, sink or the unthinkable, become prisoner, all possible combinations of effort resulted. Some were capable of swimming; others rafted on wood plundered from the village, or crossed with a raft party; a few bravely returning the raft or boat, to help others. Rosebud, with a damaged leg, crossed using one bamboo pole. The hour long crossing was too much for some, as, hungry and exhausted, they gave up the ghost, and drowned.

Weapons, for which there was no ammunition, were stripped down before flinging them into the river in disgust. One resourceful team of non-swimmers used the sunken bridge to string themselves across on ropes.

The situation of the non-swimmers was tragic, and as for those frightened of water, there was no saving them, they could only sit on the riverbank to await their fate; several sealed their own fate with the final shot from their rifle. Mortar Officer, Captain Howden, my immediate predecessor, had a leg shattered in the defences and, with help, struggled to the riverside. Captain Douglas Wardleworth, though wounded in the shoulder, swam across the river, collected a sunken boat, and plugged the bottom, swimming the boat back across the river for Howden. He then re-crossed the river in an attempt to organise, a 'west bank collection point'. Single men, or two alone, were easy targets for roaming Burmese Dacoits.

Quartermaster Sergeant Harry Darby, of Sheffield, was an old soldier who thought he knew exactly what to do. He lifted Howden into the boat returned by Wardleworth, filling it carefully with wounded and non-swimmers, before guiding it from the bank. The weight in the boat was, however, too much for the grass, earth, and wood plug, inserted by Wardleworth. Within a few yards, the boat sank, and the wounded were disgorged into the river, to swim, drown, or be helped back to the shore. Re-plugging the boat, only the critically wounded were put inside, whilst others, and non-swimmers, held on to the outside, with instructions to kick their legs if they could. It was a long, tedious, two-hour crossing for these men.

Harry Darby was nobody's sweetheart, although he had a wife back in Maymyo; he was a rough beggar who knew what morale was all about. 'Sing, you bastards! Sing!' He started, 'River, stay way from my door', and 'By E-Oh-Go!' until he had everybody singing, including Howden. Howden, and others in the boat, sweat pouring from their bodies, maintained a rhythm, as, using their bush hats, they baled water from the leaky boat. With a few songs, ribald jokes and jibes, at others swimming in the water, the hour of crossing soon passed; every yard seemed easier as the west bank appeared, and the immediate menace receded.

Once across the river, Howden was carried along the railway line, using a bamboo door as a stretcher. Arriving at a train, he was placed on top of the coal in the tender, and carried back the few miles to the village of Wah. He managed to talk himself onto a refugee train and three days later, with his wound still undressed, arrived at Mandalay. His leg, now festering with gangrene, required immediate amputation, and within a few days he was moved, and flown out of North Burma to India. Howden later considered himself to be a lucky man in view of the conditions yet to come in Burma.

General Officer Commanding had squandered the possibility of security, when ordering forward his unprepared troops, ones capable of defending the vital bridge. This Victoria Cross holding officer, commanding a British Army Division, had been concerned only in getting himself, and a small party, across to safety, before ordering the demolition of the means of escape for all his troops.

Semi-naked, or with soaking boots around their necks and no more than shirts and shorts, individuals emerged all along the western bank of the river. Many spent well over two hours in the water, and landed as far as three miles downstream, returning up the river bank to the railway line, and gathering point for the exhausted and hungry men. There they formed into protective groups before walking the 25 miles along the railway line, many barefooted, to the small rail station at Wah. The wounded and sick survivors were helped, and carried six miles to a small ambulance train; the remainder struggled on, attempting to stay with a group. Many were much too exhausted to keep the pace, and, once isolated, became easy prey for enemy gangs of Dacoits, who managed to keep their distance, and be out of sight as a main party approached.

One party of four, desperate for water, followed a small track that crossed the railway towards a village, only to find the place deserted, except for one or two cattle and poultry, a few wary elders, and one attractive young woman, whom they thought might be a decoy or trap. Taking drinking water from earthenware chatties at the houses, they decided to take a chance with her. As night began to fall they left the village, satisfied, and, carrying a full chatty-pot of water, each discussed their performance with the girl, having raped her twice each.

Unlike the much vaunted Dunkirk evacuation, there was no media interest in the few hundred men crossing the Sittang. Not one war correspondent, or film camera. Individuals arriving at the riverbank met with no helping hands, or ready cups of tea, and sandwiches. Instead they were required to summon up further energy, to survive to the next interminable stage of evacuation. Prime Minister Churchill made no stirring speech, on the destruction of a British Army force in Burma; and made no apology for his casting of 18th Division into Japanese prison camps at Singapore. He was not a man to admit his own shortcomings, or failures.

The surviving force, from diverse nations, was all that remained to defend south Burma and Rangoon, its capital. In two weeks of conflict, 2nd Battalion KOYLI was drastically reduced; – short of arms, food, clothing and most importantly, water. Eighty or so reasonably fit men survived to assemble at this point, from an original strength of over five hundred. The most insidious mass destroyer was the mosquito. Keegan had taken what he considered a 'justifiable risk' at mosquito-riddled Takaw. He was no longer there to see the result, as men went down in dozens. Depleted in strength, and intermingling as they trailed back from the Sittang, the 'Dukes', and KOYLI amalgamated, forming one undersized composite battalion. In order to maintain regimental identity, members of each battalion formed into two makeshift companies for a brief period. Drifters and stragglers continued to arrive, making their hungry and thirsty way over the 20 miles from Wah to Pegu, and then a further 30 miles to Hlegu, in order to join in the consolidation.

4

GOVERNOR AND GOVERNMENT
'ONLY A FEATURE'

Having fought day by day, and marched 300 miles in three weeks, without clothes, arms or commander, a battalion might well be despondent. Yet the rigours and trials of the past weeks were seen as achievements, and to have survived, as a measure of success. The men knew that they could beat the Japanese, given supplies, arms and better command.

At the Hlegu assembly point, Lieutenant Quartermaster Taffy Phillips, wasted no time in acquiring a truck and embarking on a scrounging expedition. He found hats, shirts, shorts, boots and arms of all kinds, including some almost prehistoric rifles; also small amounts of tinned soya sausages, beans, meat and vegetables, peaches, pears and jam. Of all Taffy's finds, the hats were to prove the most appreciated; Australian bush hats, versatile and utilitarian, protecting against the sun by day, and at night, moved to the back of the head, becoming a pillow. With something to eat, and a few hours of rest, morale recovered rapidly. The hungry, dishevelled men devoured food, including jam, straight from the large tins, eagerly opened with bayonets. They knew that the campaign was at, 'the end of the beginning'. Though beaten, there were further months of combat, and many hundreds of miles to traverse.

Amongst Burmese political groups, the Nationalist movement, headed by Premier U-Saw was developing. Having openly declared his intention; 'to rid Burma of the British', it appeared that a Burmese uprising was imminent; although British troops in Burma knew nothing of this officially. It was fortunate therefore, that Britain had intercepted U-Saw, and had him incarcerated outside the country; otherwise he would have been in a position to exploit the depleted British force, and cause loyal Burmese troops to turn against the British.

Anarchy reigned in Rangoon. Aware of the disarray amongst British forces, following the loss of the southern Kra Isthmus, and expecting the imminent arrival of Japanese invaders, Dacoit gangs and various Nationalist factions formed, and sought vengeance, killing, looting, burning shops, and homes, of their opponents. Refugees filled the one road north from the town. A few Indian traders chose to remain, in the hope of conducting business with the Japanese, and although there was a total breakdown of law and order throughout Rangoon, nuns remained at a leper hospital.

Following a series of meetings in Rangoon, Governor Dorman-Smith wired Foreign Secretary Amery at the Foreign Office in London. He advised him of the 'E' signal, the code ordering the evacuation of Rangoon, for 1 March 1942. It was arranged that only a demolition squad should remain, otherwise, as he put it; – "All would be in the bag if not evacuated immediately".

With the pronouncement of the order, Rangoon was placed under military law, and Dorman-Smith, ill-informed of Japanese successes, remained wholly confident of British military supremacy. He did not for one moment envisage British evacuation; it was unthinkable, as had been the fall of Singapore. Returning to Government House, at Maymyo, Dorman-Smith was accompanied by a few London newsmen. Of the original Government House staff, of 110 Burmese, only one cook and a butler remained, to provide the Governor and his guests with an evening meal. The party ended up drunk, in the Maymyo Gymkhana Club, with Dorman-Smith hurling billiard balls at photographs of former Governors. A former trades union official, out of his depth in this situation; his authority and pride had gone, along with his servants.

The British civil service in India, Burma and elsewhere, took its superiority over the 'natives' for granted. British officials and their wives, regardless of their status, expected to be elevated in the class structure; – Employing native *ayahs* to care for their offspring, *bearers* to attend to their every need, *kitmagars to* supervise the household, *bomangers* to do the cooking, *dhobis* to do the washing, and *sweepers* to carry away their rubbish. Civil and military officials learned rapidly, to conform to an unwritten code. With little tolerance of, and segregation from the Burmese, there can be little wonder that the Govenor, and the British in Burma, had no indigenous allegiance upon which to draw.

The British had lost civil control, and what remained of the depleted military force, was to operate for the next three months, in a hostile country. The Burma Rifles, and Burma Frontier Force, were absconding, almost to a man, taking with them arms and ammunition, as they returned to their families; Aung-San, and his associates, recruited many. Transport, mules, equipment, arms and ammunition lost at the Sittang River were impossible to replace. With the closure of Rangoon port, Burma became a sealed country. There was no way out, other than the long trek into India, except for a few families, and the injured, flown out from a northern airfield, already subject to bombing.

Govenor Dorman-Smith was badly informed, as were the military; – they knew nothing of the altercation taking place, between Churchill, and Australian Prime Minister, Curtin. It was in Dorman-Smith's mind, that one Australian division was being diverted to Rangoon. He panicked on hearing of the heavy losses of the British Army at the Sittang. His immediate reaction, on 25 February 1942 was to wire Churchill for confirmation;"Are we getting Australian reinforcements? yes, or no?" The reply was predictable: – "Australian Government refuses. Fight on!"

It must have been obvious to Churchill, as it was to Dorman-Smith, that there was nothing to 'fight on' with. The Sittang action, following Smyth's destruction of the river bridge, had completely negated the Army in Burma. It was not until after the fall of Singapore, Churchill gave Burma any serious consideration. He had plenty to occupy him elsewhere. In his notes on the war, Churchill wrote: -

"To the Australians, as to us, Burma was only a feature in the world war".

Yet, although he may have wished to, Churchill could not wholly ignore Burma. Its fall would create enormous problems; it would leave the way open to India, where the Japanese could expect the support from the many Indian factions, Ghandi, and other radicals, seeking to, – 'Rid India of the British'.

The prospect of Japan controlling Indian ports, was unthinkable, as it would give them control of the Indian Ocean, to the coasts of Africa. They would sever supply routes to the Middle East, obtain access to, 'the soft under-belly of Europe', and form a link with the Axis powers, Germany and Italy. Churchill appreciated that in Burma, it was no longer a matter of retaining a British possession. The problem was one of defending a vital strategic holding, and of such magnitude, as to be of world-wide concern.

Sheer desperation caused Churchill to press, even at this late hour, for an Australian division to be diverted into Rangoon; "As otherwise, Burma is wide open for the Japanese". He sent Curtin a further message: -

"President Roosevelt is in total agreement with the idea of diverting the Australian division into Rangoon".

However, the British link with Australia was fractured, and never to be the same again.

The plight of the remote army in Burma received scant attention. As though in his dreams; – Churchill had promised to reinforce and provide Burma with arms, aircraft, ships and food, but these were never forthcoming.

5

'SOME TALK OF ALEXANDER...'

Communications within Burma, did not allow Churchill a true picture of the physical condition of British forces east of Rangoon. He was, however, aware; officers in command were failing dismally. His memoirs describe his solution:

> *"No troops in our control could reach Rangoon in time to save it. But if we could not send an Army, we could, at any rate send a man".*

It must have been a shock to Irish guardsman, General Harold Alexander, to receive a call to report to the War Office, and meet the Chief of the Imperial General Staff. The call came, on 18 February 1942, Alex was on a routine visit, inspecting coastal defences on the Isle of Wight. He wasted no time reporting to Whitehall on the same day, with high hopes of appointment. He was, however, asked to proceed at once, and take command of the army in Burma. Alexander would not be informed of Churchill's many interventions, resulting, among other things, in the loss of the unfortunate 18th Division at Singapore. He would be told of Curtin's refusal to condemn his Australian division, to a similar fate in Burma, and how the Japanese had superiority and command of land, sea, and air, and that hopes of reinforcements were remote. His mandate was simple: – "Do what you can to hold Burma".

Weather conditions dictated Alexander's flying schedule. Day after day he waited, before the bomber carrying him could take off. Flying was dangerous, with German aircraft commanding the skies over Europe. With halts at Delhi, and Calcutta, Alexander arrived in India, for a briefing by Wavell and his staff, before flying on. Arriving at Mingladon airfield, near Rangoon, on 5 March 1942.

Alexander had been briefed in India on the forces which might, in extreme circumstances, be made available to him. In the event, because of civil unrest in the country, India-based units were retained for their existing role, support for the Civil Defence. The Burma operational force consisted of:

1   trained British division.
6   British Indian divisions, mostly untrained.
25   effective aircraft.
150 anti-aircraft guns, with untrained crews.

In directing Alexander, Wavell demonstrated his feeble grasp of the situation; he ordered:

> *"The army at Pegu must defend the town against the Japanese. Push the attacking Japanese back beyond the Sittang river".*

This order was conveyed to the deprived men of the composite Dukes, and KOYLI at Hlegu, 'not Pegu'. It is to their credit that, on the basis of promised Australian, and Gurkha reinforcements, the smitten force made to comply, and march the 25 miles to Pegu. Smyth, of Sittang Bridge infamy, redeemed himself somewhat, by intervening, and advised Alexander of the utter futility of the task. Alexander persuaded Wavell to change his mind. The result was just one more instance of 'buggering about', the changing of orders, so hated by soldiers, demonstrating to them the incompetence of their senior commanders. Within hours, the Japanese attacked and occupied Pegu town, and fortunately, spent time remustering and consolidating the bridgehead. It was the final action, east of Rangoon.

Alexander was lacking in eastern, or jungle warfare experience, and was rapidly to learn that he had come on no picnic. Advancing from Thailand on 16 January, it had taken the Japanese only six weeks, to be poised, ready to attack Rangoon, in early March 1942 In no more than three weeks they had, devastatingly, destroyed the defending British forces, and crossed in strength three major obstacles, the rivers, Salween, Bilin and Sittang. Civil authority was in panic, and those who thought they might remain, and deal with the Japanese, were now in flight. Dacoits knew traders to be carrying valuables, and they became prime targets. Those surviving the Dacoits joined in the 150-mile trek north, to Prome Town.

Civil and military officers, starved of information, could arrive at no conclusion to influence the course of the war, worsening day by day. It was rumoured that Thakins were organising an armed, mass rebellion, 80 miles north of Rangoon, at Tharrawaddy Town, and about halfway to the Prome river crossing. In the straggling districts of Rangoon, patrols had orders to shoot looters on sight, although the patrols themselves turned out to be the worst of the looters, rapists and murderers. Burmese soldiers raided the Gymkhana Club cellars and removed hundreds of cases of liquor. It was fatal, regardless of race, to occupy an isolated bungalow.

China offered the only possibility of military intervention. General Hutton flew to Lashio, in the hope of persuading Chiang Kai-shek to move his armies into Burma. The journey was wasted. General Stilwell, nominally liaison officer with Chiang Kai-shek, supported by Madam Chiang, resented Hutton's attempt at a direct approach to Chiang. She arranged for Chiang to travel to Chungking, thus avoiding the meeting with Hutton. Stilwell, intent upon asserting himself, sought to meet the British 'Number One', Wavell, in order to impress upon him that, 'Stillwell', commanded the Chinese armies. At this point, Wavell dispensed with the services of Hutton; he was relieved of command. Wavell, only partly aware of Rangoon's desperate situation, instructed Alexander: -

"Hold Rangoon as long as possible, the troops must live off the country to a much greater extent".

Hopeless words of a beaten commander! What he meant was, "I can't feed you", he did not realise how little there was left of the land to live off.

6

ARRIVE RANGOON

Confined within ships at sea, our small officer draft had no intimation of the immediate future. There were no Vichy French among the crew of British India ship S.S. *Ellenga,* to cause her to turn and run, as we approached the mouth of Rangoon River. It was 5 March 1942, the same day General Alexander arrived at Mingladon. *Ellenga* docked at Rangoon. Unaware of all that had gone beforehand: – We had arrived!

The columns of black smoke belching from the burning Syrian oil refinery on the east bank of Rangoon River were our first indication of trouble, and a few random rifle shots from the riverbank confirmed the hostility. We were too far out to have effect, as *Ellenga* sailed in mid-river, well out of range for accuracy.

At Rangoon Docks, the message was loud and clear; the scene was one of desolation and desertion. Heavy red dust, the result of Japanese bombing, covered everything along the quayside, and the straggling low warehouses. The devastation all around made one realise the courage of the skipper and crew of S.S. *Ellenga.* The ship had sailed up to a dockside that was itself a front line; delivering their cargo, they were within range of enemy rifle fire, and a sitting target, had Japanese aircraft come bombing.

We, humble draft of officers, cocooned in transit, in foreign climes, had been virtually incommunicado for three months, with no news, other than the limited daily shipboard bulletins, and language barriers to contend with, in India, and on the French ship. Nothing we might have heard could have prepared us for the state of things found in Rangoon. The Gloucestershire Regiment officers were first to disembark, and we wished them well. We did not see them again, although we were saddened from time to time to hear of one of them dying from wounds or sickness. So close to action, it was time for stocktaking. I knew that I was fit mentally and physically, with more stamina than most. I was highly trained and a specialist on the three-inch mortars. However, a bullet, bomb or mortar is no respecter of fitness. I had to live up to the honour bestowed upon me by the squad on *Strathallan* I would never fail them.

Captain Green arrived with instructions: -

"Strip down equipment to no more than absolute essentials capable of being carried on the person, no more than a small bedding roll".

Everything surplus was to be returned to Calcutta on *Ellenga,* and it was obvious there was no future for the 10,000 'French letters', issued to me in Calcutta, and carefully guarded on voyage. I started disposal of the light blue packages, scattering them into the Irrawaddy River. Thus absorbed, I saw my first dead man on the fast-flowing river, naked and face downwards, body swollen with the heat, his back burned black and blistered with the sun. As a swimmer, my first reaction was one of concern, to dive in and rescue him; it took little time to realise my effort would be to no avail, and the man was left to go his lonely way.

The moment one knows that action in war is imminent, is a test of manhood. There is no room for indecision, the remaining few moments on the deck of *Ellenga,* were the last opportunity for cowardice. As *Ellenga* made ready to return to Calcutta, many must have thought of sailing with her, yet not one man uttered the suggestion. From the deck of *Ellenga,* Maymyo seemed even further away than it had done when Copper Cass called me into his office in Northern Ireland, 10,000 miles away, to advise of the transfer to; –

"a peace station in the tropics".

The hazards of sea voyaging, and the dangers to the British Merchant Navy, in the three-month period from our boarding beautiful *Strathallan,* at Gourock, on 4 December 1941, to disembarking from *Ellenga,* on 5 March 1942, can be illustrated by the fact that, while we were in transit, the British Merchant Navy lost 500,000 tons of shipping, sunk by enemy action, most casualties occurring in the North Atlantic, the Mediterranean, or the dreaded run to the Russian ports of Murmansk and Archangel.

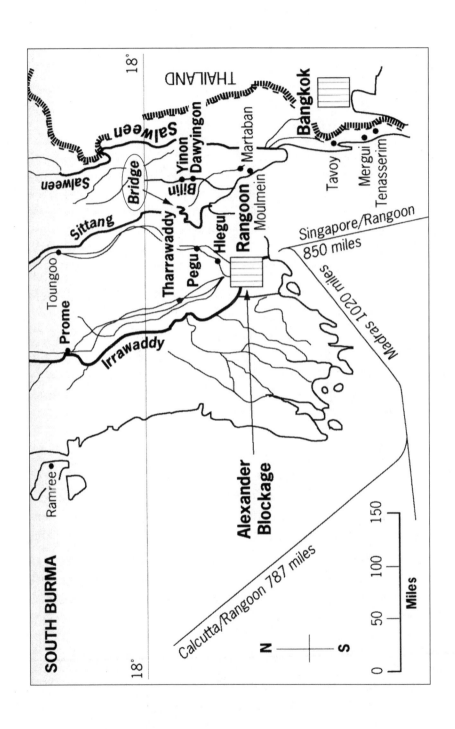

SOUTH BURMA

THAILAND

18°

18°

Salween

Salween

Bridge

Sittang

Yinon
Dawyingon

Bilin

Martaban

Bangkok

Tavoy

Mergui
Tenasserim

Tharrawaddy

Hlegu

Rangoon

Moulmein

Pegu

Toungoo

Prome

Irrawaddy

Ramree

Singapore/Rangoon
850 miles

Madras 1020 miles

Alexander
Blockage

Calcutta/Rangoon 787 miles

0   50   100   150

Miles

N

S

93

7

MOVING IN

Mounting the three-ton truck in mid-afternoon, we bade farewell to *Ellenga*, wishing her wonderful skipper and crew, good luck. *Ellenga* had good luck; she survived the war, and was condemned to a scrap-yard some years later, a true romantic beauty of the eastern seas.

Conveyed through the deserted, and hot dusty streets, of Rangoon, avoiding bomb craters, and passing many burning bungalows, we had one brief sighting of the golden dome of the Buddhist Shwe-Dagon pagoda. We travelled along deserted tracks, about 25 miles east from Rangoon, to the small village of Hlegu, situated about halfway towards Pegu, the town in which the Japanese were consolidating and re-mustering, following their successes in southern Burma.

Hlegu was the assembly point of the 'Dukes' and Yorkshire Light infantry, survivors of the Sittang crossing. Two fine units, each reduced in strength from four companies to less than one company. There was, however, a constant flow of sick and wounded adding to the gathering, most of those arriving being further weakened by having to make the hazardous trek up river, having been carried far downstream with the flow.

Forewarned as we were by Captain Green, about the desperate state of the war, the reality we met on arrival at Hlegu was a culture shock. The vision of our overseas battalion, 'in a peace station', was an illusion; here was a very different proposition. Nothing on earth could have prepared us for the unbelievable squalor before our eyes. What we saw was one thing, but when they spoke, what we heard was another. It was clear that these were not beaten men. The picture changed with every minute, and every spoken word. These were tough, desperate men, prepared to live as rough as needs be, anxious to get back and face an enemy who had taken so many of their comrades.

Here I met a rare military entity, a 'listening senior officer': a man of Field Officer rank, with true sensitivity, one prepared to 'talk about', rather than 'talk at', juniors. A man willing to accept assistance from me, a junior, on a matter about which he knew that I had better knowledge than he could have. Major Pip Moran, of the Dukes, was based in a fresh-looking bomb crater, sited within a rubber plantation, and acting adjutant, to the composite battalions. Calling forward the two senior members of the draft, Allan Ibbotson, a lieutenant, and myself; the senior second lieutenant, he explained the predicament resulting from the destruction of the Sittang Bridge, and the arrangements for mustering survivors. Pip Moran went straight to the point.

> *"There's no room here for anybody with doubts. I don't mind how senior, or how junior anybody is, I want officers placed in jobs they can do. I want your help in selecting those men you feel to be experienced enough to stay here, with the active units, and those you think should go back, to division and brigade".*

Not one member of the draft had experience enough, to relate to the conditions of the men and equipment around them. It was a matter of rough judgement, taking into account their ages and length of commissioned service. I was amazed when Ibbotson declared himself a non-fighting man, and not in a position to assess the squad capabilities. Ibbotson was an entomologist. I remain convinced that he travelled out; – 'to the peace station' and was allocated a military disguise, for travel, and in order to participate in a butterfly expedition. Seniority was mandatory, my authority came through my rank number, 160575; others were later. My assessment was based on my observations whilst in transit, and I nominated:

Battalion	Brigade/Division
Gerald Fitzpatrick	Allan Ibbotson
Andrew McLaren Young	Stuart S Renton

Robert 'Bob' E O Rimmer
Leslie P Wise
James 'Jim' Marsh
John A Welbourne
V L 'Steve' Stevens
Douglas C 'Dougie' Haigh
Arthur E Watts
James W 'Jimmy' Ableson
Douglas V Oakley

E H 'Tim' Watson
Alan Whittaker
William 'Bill' McKillop
William Lauder Riddle
George 'Chotta' Lawrence

Division and brigade nominees were despatched immediately on the truck bringing us to Hlegu. Those remaining were to meet the most astonishing men in the world, men of British 'Line, Infantry units'. In the adversity of war; men we were to come to know, in every bone of their bodies, who could joke and laugh in adversity; men to loathe for their brutality, and fear, to pity in sickness, and to admire for their tenderness, with animals, and with their chums, for their loyalty and love; men to astonish one with their naivity, men to love for ever, most of all, for being British.

Unaware of the mayhem of recent weeks, we joined the conglomerate only minutes after Alexander rescinded his futile order, 'to recapture Pegu'. For the unequipped force to return to action immediately, and try to do as Wavell ordered, 'attack Pegu and push the Japanese back beyond the Sittang', would have been a suicide mission; but with his precipitate reversal of the order, Alexander had got off on the wrong foot, so far as these troops were concerned.

Sergeant Benny Mee of Leeds, a trained and competent soldier, did not mince his words.

"We've been buggered about, we don't know whether we're coming or going. It's been "Come here! Run there!" Chasing our bloody tails till we don't know what the hell we're doing. They should come here and see the bloody state they've got us into!"

As mortar sergeant, Benny Mee was my immediate 'number one', and platoon sergeant, from here on. He knew, as much as one could know, of the treachery that often lay behind the inoffensive and inscrutable

Burmese face. I was pleased and privileged to gain Benny's confidence from the time of our first meeting.

Settling in, following the rescinding of Alexander's futile 'attack' order, and having met Benny Mee, I allowed myself the luxury of a brief moment for taking stock of my surroundings. Here it was, I backed the biggest winner of my life, in a meeting with two men busily 'drumming-up' tea in a dixie.

"Hello sir! Like some tea?"

"Yes please, I would if you can spare a mug".

"Are we muckers?" Asked the one with the 'lived in' face, like a stewed prune, the voice full of confidence, with a depth of meaning in those three short meaningful words.

"You've got the tea and I want some". "We're muckers!"

Fortunately, I had got it dead right, and the bond was sealed. That simple ceremony, and declaration of friendship, were to prove magic in the weeks to come. The privilege of meeting Private Danny Lobben of Bradford, and Private 'Jacko' Jackson of Barnsley, was well worth the three months' cruise. Danny had a long soulful face and doe eyes that belied the athlete, boxer, hurdler and long jumper, that he was. Jacko was a round man, with bright eyes, that twinkled starlike, from his years down the pit, before joining the Army. Being capable of 'mashing tea', the two had established themselves, battalion cooks.

"We've no mugs. It'll be an empty jam tin. All right?"

"That's fine, thanks".

Jim Marsh, seeing me with the tea, came across. "I'll have some tea!"

"Are we muckers?" asked Danny.

"Who the hell do you think you're talking to?" snapped back Marsh. He got his tea, but the damage was done. Hoyland Common, Barnsley Grammar, and Oxford University, had done nothing for Jim's social graces. Uppishness, and forgetting his origins, did not help his future in this crucial examination by two very human English soldiers. It was in a very cold silence that he got his tea, and with no further comment. He was simply 'noted'.

Pip Moran was attempting to shape two small companies from each of the two battalions, in order to compose a unit under Colonel Faithful, the Duke's Commanding Officer. The swift, arbitrary arrangement, established order, and some means of rapid communication.

Apprehensive about infiltration or an attack by assault forces, Pip Moran considered the Japanese might follow the railway line, in order to be in position to attack, before 'first light' the next day, and pressing home their successes to date. With Benny Mee and four men, I was detailed to proceed immediately on patrol, to observe the railway line approach, and to return one hour after dark. In the event of sighting the enemy I was instructed to open fire and withdraw, in order to give warning to the main party.

In the event, I saw nothing, and returned after a five-hour patrol. This small episode, within minutes of joining the battalion, gave me a feeling of early involvement, and control on my first operation. I had now commanded men in action and felt no inner fear. The men with me were an inspiration in everything they did; deployment, movement, silence, signals; – absolute confidence oozed from every one of them. It was a revelation and tremendous satisfaction to know that men could move in this manner, without the necessity for harangues and long explanations, without apprehension at every turn.

Lying in wait by the rail-line, gave me time to hear from these men, of the awful frustrations of the previous three weeks, and the many skirmishes with the Japanese. There had been many times when they felt they had the measure of the enemy, only to be ordered to withdraw from the position for some panic move, to dash and fill a gap being infiltrated by the enemy elsewhere. The main irritation was that the only instruction they ever received was, 'We're moving!' – Never any detail as to where, or how far, or for what purpose. Their disgust, and anger at Smyth's demolishing the Sittang Bridge, resulting in the loss of many of their chums, was beyond measure.

Early next morning, on 6 March, two trucks arrived; and along with several of my newly-arrived officer colleagues, plus 20 N.C.O.s and men, I was detailed to organise a move; to command an advance party, in a move of 60 or 70 miles, avoiding Rangoon, to the small agricultural village of Tharrawaddy, situated on the roadside, about forty miles north of Rangoon, close by the Irrawaddy River.

While awaiting embarkation onto the transports, I experienced what must be one of the oddest coincidences of the war. I watched as a Blenheim Bomber came down in flames, about one mile to the east, in the direction of Pegu. It crashed into the jungle, causing a huge explosion. This was the only operational British aircraft I was to see throughout my stay in Burma, and certainly the only one in the sky on that day. In India some time later, I received a letter from my cousin in Australia, in which she told me that her husband, 21-year-old pilot officer Ronald Llewellyn Rogers, and his observer navigator, Max Hickey, the crew of a Royal Australian Air Force plane, had been shot down over the Burmese jungle, on 6 March 1942. The location, and fact that it was a Blenheim Bomber, makes it quite certain that it was Rogers' and Hickey's plane that I saw. Subsequent enquiries indicated that no other British plane was operational at that time

8

WE'RE GETTING OUT

'Rangoon closed!' The fatal 'E' (Evacuate), signal was sent from Governor Dorman-Smith to Churchill on 6 March 1942. It was the unpalatable truth which Churchill had anticipated. Coincidentally, it was sent the day after Alexander's arrival, by air, and mine on *Ellenga*. The gallant ship had made a timely departure.

The dreaded signal meant that all within Burma were now at the mercy of the Japanese. The Japanese fleet sealed the mouth of Rangoon River. This was also the day that the Burma Independent Army landed, close by the Syrian Oil refinery. They were operating under Japanese supervision. The closure of Rangoon so soon after his arrival hurt Alexander greatly. He must have pondered over his wasted words in London, when saying farewell to Brooke, Chief of the Imperial General Staff, "I will do my duty. You must help me all you can". Rangoon was the only port of entry, and exit, into Burma, and there was now virtually no way out of the country. Civilians and military alike were in the trap.

The Burma Road through Takaw, leading towards Chungking in China, was infested with Japanese. A survey of the Assam-Burma frontier into India in the northwest was incomplete, and any pre-war plan for a road through this region was left 'decision deferred'. Churchill, Wavell, Dorman-Smith, and departing Army Commander Hutton were quite clear in their own minds. The army in Burma was beyond help; they were a beaten army, with no possibility of evacuation. They must be condemned to the jungle, as nothing could be done to assist. My officer draft were doomed! From this point on, whatever happened must be done without help from outside the country. Wavell's words, "the troops must live more off the country", betrayed his ignorance of the country. The months from January to May span the hot pre-monsoon season, in a scorched land where one blade of grass may be called an oasis.

The reversals facing Alexander in the hectic twenty-four hour period since his arrival at Mingladon airfield must have been shattering. The man sent by Churchill to get Burma off his back, and Wavell out of his nostrils, was now as close to his own doom as any army commander in the war. Ordered by Wavell to 'hold Rangoon, as a first objective', he arrived resolved to hold Rangoon, come what may. It was Wavell's further instruction, to 'push the enemy forces at Pegu back across the Sittang', which almost made Alexander the shortest-lived ever army commander. Alexander had no knowledge of the pathetic condition of the troops in his command. Not having seen them, Alexander assumed KOYLI and the Dukes to be two British Infantry Battalions, full strength, and fully equipped. It was fortunate for Alexander that Smyth confessed his mistakes, and advised him of the conditions created by the destruction of the Sittang Bridge. Credit must go to Alexander for countermanding the order to attack Pegu. Smyth was dismissed, and despatched out of Burma, along with Hutton.

The strength of the two Battalions, Dukes and KOYLI, totalled less than 250 men, many already wounded and sick, and all battle-fatigued. Looking around for support troops, Alexander found none. Realising the futility of attempting to hold Rangoon, Alexander signalled Wavell:

> "Retention of Rangoon impossible with small force at my disposal, some already encircled".

It is possible that Alexander was aware of his wireless communication being conveniently broken down. Delay in transmission let Wavell 'off the hook'. For him to have insisted on attempting the retention of Rangoon would have meant suicide for all.

From the visions of leading a mechanised, fully equipped fighting force into Europe, or the Western Desert, Alexander accepted his present predicament. He was commander in a country about which he knew nothing, of a spent and emaciated force, an army already defeated, and with little hope of survival. He had no idea how to extricate it from the landlocked confines. With Rangoon closed, and the China Road infested with Japanese, the alternative route out of the country was a colossal, 1,000-mile trek northwards, through central and north Burma, along the routes of the Irrawaddy and Chindwin Rivers; and one could only speculate about the plans of the Japanese, or the Burmese National Forces, to destroy the withdrawing columns.

Burmese, Gurkhas, Indians, British; all were sealed within the baking hot confines of a hostile land. We were prey on the run, Alexander was now commander of the greatest-ever withdrawal undertaken by British Army troops. For our small draft of officers, the ultimate in tests was about to begin. We were to join proven soldiers and assess their quality; – seniors and juniors alike. It had been made very clear to me that many of the men regarded several of the regular officers with scant respect.

The withdrawal of my small advance party from Hlegu was the start of a complete change of phase in the war. Up to the Sittang crossing, the British Army had been an ill-equipped and ill-armed force, conducting an 'offensive defence action', committed to stopping and opposing the Japanese whenever and wherever possible. The debacle at Sittang meant that there could be no further offensive action. Alexander and every officer now had a duty to extricate every man from Burma, by whatever means. At the outset, the size of the task, against a well-equipped pursuing enemy, was never envisaged.

By-passing Rangoon, and travelling northwards towards Tharrawaddy, my first phase of, 'extrication, withdrawal and survival', began. With no hope of further supplies, the emphasis was on survival. Extrication from Burma was to take four times as long as the Japanese, assisted by General Smyth, took to debilitate the British Army in southern Burma.

Much of the pre-war officer strength were killed or wounded, while of the remaining few, most had had short service with the battalion, and they had been rapidly promoted to senior responsibilities. Second lieutenants became captains overnight. A number of 'regular senior officers' were, 'extra-regimentally employed', in staff appointments throughout India.

9

ALEXANDER'S RAGTIME BAND

Siting the advance party camp near Tharrawaddy town was not difficult. I selected an area overlooking the road, and close by a small village, three or four miles north of the town, on open ground and backed by scrubland and woods, in order to have good visibility and convenient cover in the event of air attack. The space between the town and the base allowed for regular patrols and outposts in order to observe, as a prime objective, any indication of Japanese infiltration around the town.

Terrorist and National Independence organisations were known to flourish in this area; it bristled with hostility towards the British. Aware of this antagonism, we were alert from the outset, and patrols probed selected villages. Finding no immediate evidence of native opposition, it was reasonable to assume that, whatever strength of opposition there might have been, had moved; presumably to the south, in order to join with the Japanese in the assault on Rangoon. Not fully, 'in the picture', I had no reason to assume that Rangoon would be abandoned in the manner in which it was. Without prolonged and stubborn defence, in the time-honoured way, 'last man and last round'.

Transport returned to Hlegu to collect the main party. They were scheduled to join with us of the advance party on the following day, but only one jeep arrived, with newly promoted Captain Alan Chapman and his batman. Uneasy, I moved the base to the edge of the small copse of trees for better security and tightened the patrolling. My main concern was to ensure adequate diligence at the road junction in order to receive the main party, in the event of their arriving in darkness. In the long anxious hours under a velvet black sky, it was possible to rest when not on active patrol. There was no loosening of boot laces. Shoving the bush hat to the back of my head as a pillow, I got my back settled into a bit of soft warm earth. Millions of fireflies sped backwards and forwards against the background of the dark woods in a spectacular demonstration, a free ballet of beauty, in contrast to the drama that was taking place on the road over which we had travelled the previous day.

When the main party failed to arrive as scheduled, it became obvious that something was radically wrong, and it was with some surprise, I heard news of a Colonel Tynte, of the Cameronian Regiment. He had arrived to assume command of the battalion when I was absent for a brief period, and taking a wash at a well beyond the woods. Tynte had arrived and was gone within minutes, before I returned. I was never to meet with the man.

Alan Chapman had assumed command of the advance party, and gone back down the road to ascertain what might have happened to the remainder of the battalion. His search was to reveal absolute drama, and farce, the true pantomime of war.

The departure from Hlegu of the main party had taken place later than planned, and rather than travel speculatively into the dark, they halted by the roadside, north of Rangoon, and south of the small village of Hwambi, near the six-mile post on the Tharrawaddy road. Captain Geoffrey Baxter was sent with the few remaining men to guard the flank at a road junction in the village of Wanetchaung, a few miles east of the main road. On the main road, near this point, one of the most astonishing operations of the war was being conducted, and the Japanese were to miss a perfect opportunity of annihilating the bulk of the British force, including Alexander.

Anticipating that the British would uphold tradition, and stubbornly defend Rangoon Town in the time-honoured manner, 'to the last man and the last round', Japanese General Staff planned, with the assistance of Burmese leaders, to use village tracks with mules, elephants, and bullock carts to encircle the town and mount a surprise attack from the north-west. This operation would ensure a siege situation. Rangoon would be cut off by road, rail, and sea.

The insurgents were unaware that Alexander, with his staff, the Gloucestershire Regiment and remaining forces, were vacating Rangoon, and travelling north from the town along the Mandalay road. The British evacuation, coupled with the Japanese encirclement, brought tragedy for the 'Gloucesters', and I lost a wonderful colleague. In their encirclement of Rangoon, the Japanese needed to cross the Mandalay road. Closing six miles of it, they formed two roadblocks, one at the six-mile post, and one at the twelve-mile post. By a fluke of fortune, the Japanese had closed off the road to the KOYLI main party travelling north from Hlegu; they were stopped south of the six-mile block. The Japanese, expecting British troops to be consolidating in Rangoon, were unaware of their first stroke of luck. Fluke followed fluke for the Japanese, as, in forming the two blocks, they had cut off Alexander and his full band, along with the Gloucesters: – In fact, the entire army.

The closed section of main road runs briefly from east to west, and the Burmese-guided Japanese column was using this sector, in conjunction with village paths, as part of the encircling route. They passed without hindrance, and we of the advance party had no knowledge of the shenanigans happening "down the road". The KOYLI main party attacked the southern Japanese roadblock, sited only minutes from the overnight halt. The block was covered by Japanese machine-gun fire that ceased after a short period, and the Japanese withdrew.

Hearing of the predicament of the battalion, from 2nd Lieutenant Maclaren Young, of the Wanetchaung patrol, Tynte went south to investigate. He called for assistance from a few stragglers firing at the Japanese seen manning the northern blockage, consisting of logs and scrub wood, and sited near a bend in the road. Tynte ignored advice offered by experienced members of his escort, that the Japanese covered roadblocks with firepower. Defiant and foolhardy, he moved forward alone, and attempted removal of the obstacle. He was carved down the middle with machine-gun fire and died immediately. Tynte commanded for less than two hours; another commander to be lost in a show of unnecessary bravado.

In the short period of conflict around the roadblocks, the Japanese column, under Colonel Sakuma's command, entered and moved along the six miles of road, to vanish and complete the encircling movement along further tracks to the west of the main road.

Unaware of the existence of the Japanese force, Alexander and 17th Division H.Q. remained captive for some hours. He then followed the Japanese footsteps along the same piece of road, having not the slightest notion that he had been virtually captive, and at the mercy of Sakuma. Fortunately, the Japanese were equally oblivious. By choice or by accident, Sakuma and Alexander had each outmanoeuvred the other. Alexander had withdrawn from Rangoon, rather than put up the futile defence, expected by the Japanese. Sakuma had encircled rather than attacked, unaware that he had Alexander 'in the bag'. This was one predicament that Alexander was to ensure did not happen again.

Born in Burma, fluent in Burmese and Urdu, Corporal Howson accompanied Lieutenant Cranfield that dark night on a mission to observe the column passing along the jungle track. He could not recognise the language spoken; there was therefore little doubt that they were Japanese, and in very large numbers. They were moving confidently, with mules, elephants and bullock carts across the ill-defined village tracks. Howson confirmed that Burmese guides were assisting them. It must have been a great surprise for the Japanese to enter the town and to find Rangoon deserted. No 'last man and last round'.

10

COMMAND CHANGES

The situation at the Tharrawaddy base was grim as the fourth day dawned, and the story began to unfold, as in ones and twos, a steady stream of tired and exhausted stragglers arrived.

Reports indicated that heavy fighting had taken place, with many casualties, and nothing was known of the established officers of the battalion. Only that some were killed or missing, and that Tynte was gone. It was an ironical situation, one for which no man could be prepared, and for which no training manual provides. I was newly arrived and with no means of guidance in such a predicament. Vic Stevens approached me.

"Fitz! It seems that we're all there is, and as senior, you're the Officer Commanding. If you wish, I'll do Quartermaster".

"Right! O.K! Doug Oakley will do transport, Arthur Watts, Intelligence, and Dougie Hague, Animals".

This was ironical in the extreme. On leaving Glasgow, we were supposedly going 'to a peace station', where orderly rank and service predominate, and everybody knows everybody. We expected formal introductions, and to be made aware of the heirarchy. The only KOYLI officer any of us at the base were aware of was Green, who met with us at the ship. We had no idea of any others remaining, their ranks, responsibilities, or if there were any.

I found Steve's confidence astonishing. All that mattered in this situation was that my number, 160575, was senior to the remainder. I was mindful of the obligation placed upon me on board *Strathallan,* and to the best of my knowledge, I was Battalion Commander. Inwardly, I was shattered; this was one hell of a situation for a twenty-two year old. I knew my own job and limitations; although, with a few older men in the party, I had some reservations, but they soon vanished. With fewer than five days in this strange country, I appreciated that others had less experience than I. There was no map and apart from knowing that we were near the road to the north, I had no idea where we were; no knowledge of the country, its size or geography; no inkling of what remained of the organisation or command structure.

In my isolated situation, having seen the debilitated state of survivors at Hlegu, and hearing of the annihilation to the south, I could not be sure that any other British force existed in the country. All that could be seen were the oddments from various regiments as they mixed in with the stream of refugees, and caused congestion on the road. Bullock carts and handcarts carried Indians and Burmese of all classes and castes, panicking in their thousands in their desperate scramble to the north. Many unfortunates were falling by the wayside, and vultures attended the dead.

It was now that I called upon my training as a sportsman and my few years of engineering apprenticeship. These were roles in which I had met and overcome many problems. I assumed command of the small detachment, now totalling about 50 or 60 men. We were an isolated group facing many miles of marching to reach safety, and desperately short of food and ammunition. The idea of any support services was a joke, there were none. My exalted and reluctant command appointment lasted four days, and was willingly relinquished as two or three senior officers found their way back, and the exuberant Captain David Martin assumed command. It was from a member of the small party accompanying Martin that I heard the worst news I had heard in my life; that 'Abe' was dead.

'He got killed, sir, him and Sergeant Danford. He went straight at 'em, sir, straight into a machine-gun burst. He said, "Come on, these yellow-bellies aren't going to stop me", he had no chance, sir.'

Beloved Abe was dead, Second Lieutenant James Ableson 'killed in action'. I was shattered. Killed, after less than two days in the country, and though he died miles away, I had a feeling of guilt, of having let him down over his wish to have me near him in action. Sergeant Danford was killed attempting to recover Abe.

KOYLI attacked the two roadblocks, six miles apart on the same road, at the same time as the Japanese force was progressing along the enclosed sector. Abe was killed attacking the southern end, and Tynte, the northern. Both disregarded the advice of seasoned and experienced campaigners, both felt that they had something to prove. Tynte was a new commander. Abe was simply a fine new subaltern, a bloody good bloke. His fate could have befallen any of the draft of 18 officers; that none were at hand when he was killed emphasises the loneliness of the infantry field officer on active service. Commanding a platoon or company is a one-man operation, no matter how understanding and competent his N.C.O.s and men.

Initially, the Tharrawaddy area was considered to be the flashpoint, and more dangerous than Hwambi. Nationalistic uprisings were anticipated, as Burmans and Kachins were thought to be assembling in the area. My first meeting with hostility was when on patrol about two miles east of Tharrawaddy. I heard machine-gun fire 200 yards ahead, in the direction of a small open village. Moving cautiously closer, I saw a British tank slowly circling the village and firing into the houses, with a stationary tank standing nearby. It transpired that the stationary tank had arrived at the village first; the crew of two had dismounted and tried to trade cigarettes with the seemingly friendly locals, for eggs or a chicken. As the second tank approached, its crew witnessed their two colleagues in the process of being hacked to death by Burmans wielding *dahs*. Seeing the second tank approach, the villagers fled for cover, but were given no mercy; tank tracks ploughed through the houses and then circled the place, firing into the ruins, which were now aflame. Few could have survived.

Private 'Gigger' Lee, nosing around, peered into the stranded tank, to see a Burman taking cover inside. Fixing his bayonet, Gigger lifted the Burman out like a snail from a shell, before tossing him, like a bale of straw, into one of the blazing bungalows.

We were fortunate in getting a lift back to base on the tanks, the gunner of the second tank driving the stranded vehicle. The two dead men were buried in the copse of trees near to our base.

Taking a morning bath at a small well behind the copse, I noticed a man observing me from a tree across the clearing. It was obvious, in the current circumstances, that this man was up to no good. Ignoring him for the moment, I completed my ablutions and returned to base. Taking Sergeant Benny Mee and two men, we split up, two going each way, in order to encircle and capture the spy. Questioned by Burmese speakers, the man admitted that his village headman had detailed him to keep observation on the British troops. He would not, or could not, give any reason for spying, except to say that he had to report incidents.

Rules decreed that suspicious civilians should be handed over to the Civil Authorities for appropriate action. Arthur Watts, as Intelligence Officer, assumed responsibility for the miscreant. Bound and loaded onto the one and only jeep, Arthur conveyed the man to the police post at Tharrawaddy. There being nobody in attendance, he returned him to camp, where, having no means of lock-up, he manacled and ground-staked the man for the night. Watts conscientiously repeated the routine on the following day, with no better results, and the man was again secured overnight. By now it was clear that there were no civil police. Having returned from the Hwambi conflict, and aware of the hindrance and harassment carried out by Burmese, it did not take Captain Allan Chapman long to determine that petrol could not be wasted in carrying this miscreant backwards and forwards incessantly.

Before dawn on the following morning, along with Steve's batman, Private Ray Elsworth, Chapman marched the Burman out, dug a shallow grave, sat him in it, and shot him through the head with his revolver. The man sat up again and his scalp lifted, and Elsworth put another bullet through him before covering him.

The shots were heard in the camp, and Arthur Watts, on realising the man had gone, was livid. In spite of the complete breakdown in civil administration, Arthur was attempting to work by the book. From here on we were not to suffer fools gladly. Insurrection or dissent of any kind was punished instantly.

In his haste to occupy Rangoon, Colonel Sakuma continued his encirclement of the town. He had no time to investigate the British force that was so much at his mercy. Sakuma was determined to fulfil the planned 'surprise entry' into Rangoon by the 'back door' as rapidly as possible, in order to engage what he thought might be the defending British. Sakuma must have been astounded to find his 'surprise' to be of no avail, and the British withdrawn northwards. Hearing of the opportunity he had missed at Hwambi, he started north in pursuit of Alexander. Having followed for 30 miles, he realised that he was extending himself beyond his supplies, and that he and his force needed rest and provision in order to advance further. Sakuma returned to Rangoon in glory, to consolidate yet another prized objective.

Japanese General Iida joined Sakuma in Rangoon to plan reorganisation in the new situation, which required the pursuit of a weakened and depleted force. The few days of glory and planning spent by Iida and Sakuma in Rangoon gave Alexander precious time to withdraw to a new base and attempt reorganisation of what remained of British forces.

Alexander accepted some of the blame for Wavell's mistakes. He confesses in his memoirs that he ought to have ordered an earlier evacuation of Rangoon. He knew full well that this was the order Wavell should have made, long before his arrival. Alexander confirms in his memoirs that he, 'unwittingly gave the Japanese the chance to destroy the British as organised formations; yet they missed their chance.' It is clear that whatever information was available to Alexander in London and India, he was justified in arriving in Burma with every hope of holding Rangoon. It was not for Alexander to know that in the brief period of his journey, the errors of judgement made by others had dashed all hope.

Having spent less than twenty-four hours in Burma, it was impossible for Alexander to arrange evacuation through Rangoon. The Japanese fleet already occupied the Indian Ocean, and sailing from Rangoon to Calcutta required five days. There was no hope.

Abe and Tynte were two of twelve killed at the Hwambi blockage. The Japanese suffered many casualties; a reminder that the British were prepared to resist, and that much had yet to be done before they could claim victory.

Martin assumed command from me. He was a powerhouse of a man, not big, but strongly built, with good shoulders and legs. He was ordered to move the unit four miles south, to occupy a position in one of the smaller *chaungs* (dry river beds), close by the River Irrawaddy. Arriving after nightfall, it was steaming hot as outposts were posted to observe roads and river; the enemy was thought to be active.

The *chaung* was the nearest thing to a vision of Hell. There was no provision for water, or food, throughout the following day, and night. Intense heat, confined within the high sandy walls of the *chaung,* was oppressive beyond anything I had known before, and men were visibly wilting as sweat poured from them, their helplessness and inactivity an agony to them. We waited long hours, knowing nothing of any plan of action. It was easy to consider this the ideal spot for extermination.

The agony ended suddenly, in mid-morning after the second night. The order came: – 'With all speed to the river bank'. We were being ordered back, in the role of a reserve battalion, to the central Burma oilfield, at Yenangyaung. The reason for the suspense and uncertainty of the last two days hung on hopes that the Japanese would not bomb and sink boats continuing to ply their trade on the river. Had they done this, we would have been in real trouble. Survival chances moved from slim to possible as we moved down to the steep Tharrawaddy landing stage and aboard the ironically named paddle steamer, S.S. *Japan.*

11

YENANGYAUNG AND CHAUK OILFIELDS

Following the joys of cruising on *Strathallan* and *Ellenga*, the embarkation came as a surprise. After days of patrolling at Tharrawaddy, and long hours in the hot *chaung,* we were ordered back over 300 miles north, up the Irrawaddy River to the central Burma oil town of Yenangyaung. Release from the hell of the *chaung* changed everything; relief showed on every face as we boarded S.S. *Japan.* In some manner, this oddly named gem of a boat survived, plying its trade along the Irrawaddy.

With spacious cabins and large open deck areas, a true oriental, with Burmese skipper and crew, the steamer was crowded. It had, by some miracle, escaped bombing or machine-gunning by aircraft of one or other air force. Bren guns were erected on deck, and manned for use as anti-aircraft defence; also, as protection against hostile fire from the riverbanks.

Food supplies consisted of soya sausages and hard biscuits, obtained from a deserted depot, and cooking facilities were set up in the galley. There were no refinements, no padre, no doctor, no Regimental Aid Post, few wristwatches following the soakings in the Sittang. The only one working had been bought for me by my mother for my twenty-first birthday, eighteen months earlier. We were short of all essentials. There were no blue-and-white water-chlorinating tablets, no mosquito nets, no anti-mosquito cream, or the yellow mepachrine tablets for defence against malaria. It was a matter of surviving in the clothes on one's back, having a weapon with a limited amount of ammunition, and, most important of all, a water bottle and *chargul* (canvas water carrier).

Sharing a deck cabin with Jim Marsh, I was to see the benefit of my good early relationship with the Lobben-Jacko cooking combination. Early on each of the five mornings aboard S.S. *Japan*, Danny Lobben, or Jacko, would appear at the cabin before Marsh awoke, with an enamel mug of tea for me. The other one would follow within minutes with my shaving water, but they would not bother with Marsh. Following his refusal to be a 'mucker', his card was well and truly marked. He could expect no favours.

S.S. *Japan* was trading normally, as though no state of war existed; there were Burmese and Indian refugees on board, along with a large party of seventy-two identical-looking Chinese men. It was said they had been released from Rangoon gaol during the evacuation. They were unusual, in build and every respect, for men of their race, all standing five-feet ten or eleven inches in height, portly, and wearing identical light grey suits, white shirts and red ties. They were immaculately turned out, scrupulously clean, and impeccable in their manners. It remained a mystery how such a body of men should be in gaol together, and more so, why they should be travelling in mid-Burma, on a paddle steamer, up the Irrawaddy.

After two days on S.S. *Japan*, I began to feel movements between hair on my head, armpits, and crutch. I could see nothing and considered myself clean, probably one of the very few to take a wash each day whilst at Tharrawaddy. "Let's have a look", said Jim Marsh. I stripped off, and immediately, Marsh commented, "You've got crabs!"

I had never heard of the things before, but when Marsh showed me, I saw the freckle-like spots with six 'crab' legs digging into my skin. They would not pull out.

"What the hell do I do with these?"

"You want some blue unction ointment".

"Some chance of that! What else?"

"You'll have to shave off, all round, and try using carbolic soap".

There was carbolic soap on S.S. *Japan*, so shaving off, I managed to rid myself of the biggest animal to attack me throughout four years of tropical service.

Progress along the 300 twisting miles up the Irrawaddy was slow. There were frequent hold-ups, the steamer running aground on sandbanks, where either the crew jumped off the ship to pull it free, or the anchor was dug into the sandbank or the bank of the river, and the ship winch-operated. Because of the river sandbanks, it was not possible to travel by night. We needed to sail as far as possible from each side of the tremendously wide river, owing to armed 'baddies' taking occasional pot-shots with rifles.

We were fortunate on the river. Reconnoitring Japanese spotter aircraft visited once or twice each day, yet, for some reason, they never chose to direct an attack on the paddle steamer. Aware of the possibility that Japanese assault columns might be moving across country from east to west, as well as from south to north, we were ever aware that the spotter planes might be directing a land based attack, particularly at the various landing stages, where passenger halts were reduced to an absolute minimum. Fortunately, the Japanese were attending to their own wounds and sores, while spending many days resting, regrouping, and rejoicing, in Rangoon.

Benny Mee must have had some kind of intuition when, at Tharrawaddy, he suggested that I approach Ted Hewitt from Doncaster, to take on the job of my batman.

"I don't want to be a bloody servant", said Hewitt.

"I don't want you to be a bloody servant. I want you to be my batman".

"It's the same bloody thing, isn't it?"

"No, it's a very different bloody thing. I can't manage without a bloody batman".

Having explained my philosophy, that no man would ever be my servant, and that my job as an officer could not be done without a batman functioning in his own responsibilities, Hewitt agreed to 'give it a run'. It was the start of over three years of teamwork. Hewitt never hesitated in speaking his mind, never once carried a word of 'tittle-tattle' about his colleagues or N.C.O's, He would anticipate my needs, and he did not hesitate to give me a bollocking for getting 'too regimental', or for roughing-up the bed sheets. It was a fantastic relationship. Hewitt never changed his views on his sole concern; – "to get this bloody war finished and get me home".

Having been trapped in the roadblock, and seeing the possibility of future glory slipping from his grasp, Alexander wasted no time in getting out; roadblocks in south Burma are no place for a future Governor of Canada. He was off, over 400 miles up-country, to Maymyo. Here he joined Lady Dorman-Smith, General Hutton, Sir Rupert Clarke, General Stilwell, and General Dennys (the Chief British Liaison Officer with the Chinese, who was killed in an air crash in the next few days). Stilwell despised 'British Raj' types as having a 'superior race complex', and asserted, 'they will pay dearly for having been colonisers and occupiers of Asia for so long'. The archtypical British aristocrat, Alexander, with his immaculate guards officer uniform, and the punctilious speech of a Harrow and Sandhurst man, overawed Stilwell. Alexander, considering himself to have overall responsibility, requested – almost demanded – Chinese Army support in Burma. Stilwell, who thought that he had absolute command of the Chinese Armies, was not keen on supporting anything British. The Chinese general, Tu Yu-ming, the man on the ground, also considered that he commanded all Chinese forces. Alexander was snubbed.

The truth of the matter was that Chiang Kai-shek, and he alone, ran the Chinese Army. Nothing happened without Chiang's approval and authority. At all times, Chiang insisted that any Chinese involvement should be conducted 'within a self-contained sector'. Having such a sector prevented misunderstandings; in due course, we were to see the sense of this autonomy, owing to the completely different organisation of the British and Chinese forces. Chiang was obtaining Lend-Lease from America in return for his reluctantly accepting Stilwell; Stilwell, however, would not accept that he was no more than a puppet.

The speed of action undertaken by Chinese Divisions was determined by the four or five days required for a message to travel to and from Chiang, at his Chungking H.Q. Nothing happened in haste, and quite often, nothing happened at all, except that Britain continued to feed the Chinese Army in North Burma. The cost of this was to be amply repaid in a few short hours, some days later.

There was little to celebrate on St Patrick's Day 1942, as about 100 remnants of the KOYLI Battalion disembarked from S.S *Japan,* having enjoyed five relaxed days, sailing the Irrawaddy. Knowing that Japan targeted the precious oilfields, we were cautious in approach, lest infiltrating columns had advanced across country, and occupied during the course of our river trip.

We were relieved to meet the destruction team of engineers of the Burma Oil Company. They remained, resident in bungalows and were delighted to see British troops. This dedicated team had the job of destroying several million pounds' worth of oil equipment. They knew that the minute they commenced sabotage, the township would erupt, with hostility directed against them from Burmese Nationalist groups, in addition to the impending treachery anticipated from the workforce, led and incited by former clerical assistants. A second oilfield to be destroyed was the smaller one at Chauk, a few miles to the north of Yenangyaung. Both oilfields lie close by the Irrawaddy River.

Burma's oilfields, the country's greatest assets, were the targets for rival political parties and factions; as they vied in villages and bazaars, all were competing for Japanese favour, and distributing anti-British propaganda. Considerable hostility had been generated and promoted within Burmese Nationalists' movements before the war, when the British had refused to hand over independence. Aloof and indifferent to politics in the pre-war period, the Burmese Army was now thought to be ready to join with the Nationalists, to preserve the oil, if given the opportunity. Tension among the dedicated oilmen was relieved with the arrival of armed British soldiers; no matter how badly equipped, we would assist them.

Smithy was a small man, one who left no room for error in his plan for destruction; drawings and diagrams were consulted in order to ensure maximum impact, and to make further oil production impossible. Day by day, the controlled destruction continued; pumping engines were vandalised, drills, some weighing up to three hundredweight, connecting rods and cams from engine houses were dropped down wells. A similar operation of destrution followed at Chauk. Several million pounds of deliberate damage were done with but one isolated attempt by the Burmese at intervention.

With a small force, I was given the job of security at Chauk, the second field to be destroyed. Smaller than Yenangyaung, it was somewhat isolated. In the early evening, as we were about to enjoy the daily meal, the small school building situated at the northern edge of the deserted village was burning, and flames and dark smoke were rising perpendicularly into a clear sky. The smoke was a perfect marker for any advancing ground troops or spotter aircraft. There was no obvious reason for a fire. Grabbing the jeep and taking Ray Elsworth, Steve's batman, and a Brengun, I circled around the buildings and fencing, coming up on the outside of the village, to see a group of 18 or 19 Burmese men assembled on a small rise, a short distance behind the blazing building.

The men were dressed in trousers and shirt, of a uniform clerical type, rather than the conventional *longyi,* the dress generally worn by both men and women throughout Burma. They were all of an age, about twenty to thirty. They were laughing as they pointed and joked about the fire in broken English, and it was obvious they had ignited it.

Benny Mee had warned me about evening fires appearing as troops neared a village, which for some reason, were ignored by senior officers. As Benny had said, 'The silly buggers think they are playing with kids. They can't see that these fires are signals for the Japanese to march on.'

In less than two seconds, I assessed and acted. A gathering of five or more persons was illegal, and regarded as an unruly mob; a closely-packed mob of this nature might well have several firearms among them. We were in an isolated situation, one in which many men had already fallen to the *dahs* of Burman dacoits. I grabbed the Bren gun and blasted a short burst into the legs of the mob.

The group had not expected a British officer to fire at a group of Burmese. Reaction was dramatic and instantaneous. Men scattered in all directions at speeds to defy Olympic records. The few with bullets in their legs hopped. Having dispersed the mob and got them on the run, I grabbed the rifle, set the sights at 800 yards, and fired, speeding them along the riverside track, and across country. With heat shimmering from the baking earth, and sweat running into my eyes, it was not easy to take good aim. Leaving those limping to manage alone, I picked off three others following the contours of the river, and one or two of those crossing the baked earth. When I reported the incident to the oilmen, they expressed surprise that so large a party should be so close by, and assured me that such a mob were indeed hostile.

Enjoying a dip in Chauk club swimming pool, I panicked as a huge snake appeared through the fencing, and settled on the edge of the pool. I thought that it must be coming into the pool, but it merely dropped its head into the water for a brief drink before leaving the premises. 25 to 30 feet of six-inch snake can be disconcerting in a swimming pool. The oilmen laughed at my discomfort.

Rations remained constant, one reasonable meal of soya sausage and hard biscuits in the day. It pleased me when Smithy invited me one evening to a cold beer from the fridge, and a chicken curry. Never before or since has a meal tasted so good. The huge meal of white rice, sultanas and spices, to accompany the chicken, was superbly cooked.

The destruction at the oilfield completed, I ensured that these dedicated British civilians were adequately armed. I wished them well, and, at their request, detailed a small escort party to accompany them a few miles along the road on the start of their long trek into India, well beyond reach of the mutinous Burmese.

Second in Command of the battalion, Major Geoffrey Chadwick, arrived at Yenangyaung to assume command. He had previously been 'B' echelon commander, responsible for provisioning from the Maymyo base. Chadwick was accompanied by a number of N.C.O.s and men; some recovered from illness, others having 'missed' the battalion in one or other skirmish. The battalion strength was increased to a little over 200. Apart from our draft of new officers, the remainder of the battalion had suffered greatly from the start of the Japanese onslaught; it was unrecognisable as the smart and efficient unit at the commencement of hostilities.

Restructured, the change was considerable, and there was no A.B.C. or D. company. It was now under Captains Maurice Green, Geoffrey Baxter and 'Dusty' Miller, the first two recently promoted from subaltern, and Miller from Company Sergeant Major. Few regular officers remained, and both Green and Baxter had received accelerated promotion. N.C.O.s and men were shared randomly, about 70 to each company. As a specialist

3-inch mortar officer, I was retained by Chadwick at H.Q. My platoon consisted of Sergeant Mee and eight men. We had three mortars, and twenty-four mortar bombs; the pitiable arsenal could be loaded onto a mule cart. With no central mess or gathering of officers, those of us new to the unit were unsure who was who. Having had no briefing or introduction, we felt as though we were resented, or at best tolerated. We were not consulted on any matter, and kept our opinions to ourselves.

Brigadier Bruce Scott, an 'old friend' of the battalion, appeared in order to show his face shortly after our arrival at Yenangyaung. He assured everybody that as he could not help in re-equipping or reinforcing the unit, and following destruction of the oilfield, he was withdrawing the battalion. 'Scottish troops and Fuzzy Wuzzies from Africa would be taking over'. No attempt at provisioning or re-equipping was made, and rumours of troop movements, including Chinese, circulated each day. All was quiet as we occupied bungalows vacated by the oilmen; but gradually, and with stirrings among the few remaining Burmese, we realised that the lull in activity was about to come to an end.

Apart from local defence guard and patrols, other duties evolved, and it became my day for courier service, carrying messages and mail 100 or so miles south to the 17th Division H.Q. at Prome. My transport was a small open truck with an Indian driver. From here on, as well as my revolver I also carried a rifle; men without rifles become prime targets, easily identified as officers. All officers had removed the shiny pips from the epaulettes of their shirts. One's own men knew one's rank.

The journey to Prome was uneventful, except for the gruesome happenings, on and beside the road, which was no bigger than a country track and much dilapidated. A few tanks and troops with mules and carts represented the military. Stragglers moved some distance off the road, in order to avoid strafing by aircraft. Refugees – mostly Indian – streamed along the dusty, tree-shaded verges, with a fortunate few riding on bullock carts. Women in saris and men in dhotis were coated in sweat and dust, carrying their few possessions in tiny parcels. They appeared as a stream of dusty earth, moving on thin legs, with occasionally, a pair of sandals. Some women carried children, already dead for days. Pushed or pulled off the road at intervals, were dead bullocks, mules and refugees.

All shot by Japanese aircraft as they strafed and machine-gunned the escaping columns. The stench of death permeated everything, with a numbing effect on smell, taste and touch. Hovering vultures, appearing as specks spaced out in the sky, would await absolute evidence of death before spiralling down. Once one vulture left its sky station, it became a signal for the remainder, as they centred on the corpse to clean the body down to bones.

Approaching the town of Prome, the guns of a Punjab Regiment Mountain Battery opened up, firing from our left, the eastern side of the road, seeking out an enemy target. Startling though the noise was, it was comforting to recognise friendly guns. My driver panicked, halted the truck, and starting turning round.

"Wappas, Sahib?" – (Go back?)

"No you bloody don't!" And we continued down the road. The driver realised that his brains would make one hell of a mess spilled out on his knees. I held my revolver in my hand for the remainder of the journey, and on arrival at Prome, I made sure the vehicle's distributor arm was in my possession.

Unable to find Divisional Headquarters, I saw Bill Riddell walking across the *miadan* (village green), along with Tim Watson. The two were attached to Division, as Pip Moran had put it, 'in the hope of shielding younger members of the draft in the comparative safety of rear situations'. Pip Moran of the Dukes had sense enough to be selective. Now they were with another, a far less sensitive major.

"We're the divisional sweepers", said Tim.

"How do you mean, divisional sweepers?"

"Oh! We're pulling out of here; we've been given the job of ensuring the area is cleared".

"You mean to tell me that you don't leave until after everyone has gone?"

"That's right; Brigade have moved back to Allanmyo, about fifty miles up the road".

These were two good friends of mine, and here was some stupid, brigade major condemning them to the task of covering his mistakes.

I delivered them back to Allanmyo; it was well that I had no sight of the brigade major. Both of these two beloved friends were to die, some time later, when I was not near.

The arrival of a photographer at Yenangyaung was something of a surprise. He wanted a few shots of British troops in action, for use in a new newspaper that was about to be launched in India, specially produced for the forces in India and Burma. He had taken shots of a few individuals prancing around with fixed bayonets, posing in 'pretend' observation situations, which purported to be authentic action shots. Several professional writers later used the bogus shots as authentic war photographs, obtaining them from the War Museum.

Geoffrey Chadwick asked me to use my platoon and perform for this man. This I did, reluctantly, by advancing across open land with fixed bayonets and jumping over a small *nullah* (dried stream). The cameraman then said, "That was fine, chaps", and requested a re-run: – "this time with a film in the camera". He was told exactly where he would find as much action as he wanted, fifty miles down the road. He got himself out of Yenangyaung, and on a plane out of Burma with all speed. Those 50 or 60 miles away from the action was the nearest a war correspondent got.

The period at Yenangyaung was one of mixed activity, in which there was no immediate threat of attack, although we were ever alert for possible infiltration. Numbers of refugees passed through and there remained a steady flow, trekking along the roadsides. Many had suffered atrocities at the hands of Burmese, particularly those wealthy Indians who had made a late decision to flee their businesses.

A few elderly Burmese women ran food stalls, smoking their huge cigars and trading at what had been a small roadside bazaar, selling tea, curry, betel nut, and the odd chicken and eggs at exorbitant prices, or barter in exchange for jewellery from the starving refugees. There were indeed few civilians to be seen: pro-British Burmese had long since fled in fear of the Nationalists' vengeance, and the remainder, it appeared, had gone 'to bush', far from the obvious target area of the oilfields. What is certain is that there was not the slightest sign of communications between the KOYLI and the indigenous community. This struck me as being singular, considering the unit had been stationed in Burma for nine years, long before the outbreak of hostilities. The situation, however, suited the occasion; the present scorched-earth exercise of destroying oilfields in order to ruin the economy of the country was better done without sentiment. Having completed the task of destruction, and bade farewell to the Burma Oil staff, we awaited Brigadier Bruce Scott's orders for travel north, and the promised march, or flight, out of Burma and into India.

Except for minimum rations, we remained unprovisioned. No ammunition or equipment, no clothing, and seemingly, no interest.

12

'WISEST STROKE FOR JAPAN,' SAYS CHURCHILL

On 1 April 1942 Churchill dispatched this message to Roosevelt:

*"Speaking as one amateur to another, my feeling is that the wisest stroke for Japan would be to press on through Burma northwards into China and try to make a job of that. They may disturb India but I doubt its serious invasion".** *

In the light of this 'top secret' message, we of the British Army in Burma were officially discarded. This decree was never disclosed while Churchill lived. We were subsequently dubbed 'The Forgotten Army'; in reality, the army in Burma was not forgotten – we were 'abandoned' by the British Prime Minister and the War Council.

The next Churchill message was on 15 May. Churchill suggested 'offensive schemes' against the Japanese, to give Chiang Kai-shek some encouragement 'to hold out' against the Japanese in China.

Churchill's message to Roosevelt carried no solace for the British, Indian, and Gurkha troops, or the Chinese army supporting the British in Burma; all of them struggling in conditions brought about by Churchill and his government in their blindness. One wonders what Stalin would have made of Churchill's signal, had he seen it. At the time he was already counting more than two million servicemen and civilians killed. Roosevelt was to lose no more than 250,000 men in the whole of the war; Stalin lost that number every two weeks. What a pity that

---

* Winston S Churchill VII (1941–45) Martin Gilbert (page 82) Wm Heinemann Ltd.

Chiang Kai-shek, with his army force committed in Burma, did not have a copy of Churchill's message, or John Curtin, in Australia: particularly the change of tone in the two messages. Churchill was demonstrating here the same indifference to the British Army in Burma that he, and the British Government, had previously shown the Irish. He ignored the recent loss at sea of the cruisers *Dorsetshire* and *Cornwall,* operating against impossible odds; they were bombed and sunk in fifteen minutes by Japanese aircraft, costing the lives of 29 officers and 396 men.

The Far East conflict remained one great embarrassment, in which he could do nothing to influence events. He couldn't withdraw his forces, he couldn't reinforce them, he couldn't arm or equip them, he could neither feed them, nor could he ease their thirst. Survivors would receive a medal, 'The Burma Star'; we would forever remember chums left behind, and wonder what we were doing there in the first place.

Unaware of Churchill's betrayal, Wavell, Alexander, Dorman-Smith and the recently arrived brigadier, Bill Slim, met together for a meal at Maymyo, planning and puzzling on the impossible. They considered the withdrawal of the army, or the alternative, surrender; but all such plans would be greatly affected by the very hostile Japanese army command. Rangoon had been closed for the last month; this left Myitkyina airfield in northern Burma as the only point of possible departure, providing we had the aircraft. The airfield survived solely because the Japanese wanted the use of it when they captured North Burma, as surely they must.

Japanese aircraft carried out frequent machine-gun attacks; wives of soldiers were shot attempting to leave from the airfield. One officer's wife was killed when about to board a plane. The alternative way out was on foot, subject to roads being opened and passable before the start of the May monsoon. But, of course, they were not. The pre-war Government Survey was 'referred, not-implemented'. It meant foot-slogging through hundreds of miles of jungle, crossing mountains and massive rivers. A daunting task to undertake, terrifying for women and children with no alternative other than capture or death. It was an impossible situation.

After the meeting, the Dorman-Smiths, disregarding the perilous situation around them, set off on a five-day tour of the Shan States, the pleasantest part of Burma. Lady Dorman-Smith noted in her diary,

"Delighted at the prospect of going on this trip, as a distraction from the daily round of duty and service". Dorman-Smith found the Burmese he visited 'not totally indifferent to the British', and greatly concerned about the killing and looting by the dacoits. He himself missed, by only one hour, being kidnapped by dacoits.

The Burmese attempted to warn the Dorman-Smiths of the danger they were in as they travelled around areas known to be thick with dacoits, members of U-Saw's private Galon Army and Aung San's 'Thirty'. The village of Thazis, where a kidnap point was set, was also a direct target for the impending Japanese infiltration. The Japanese were already attacking the Chinese at the town of Toungoo, only a short distance away.

However, the Dorman-Smiths were lucky; they returned to Maymyo in time for them to entertain Chiang Kai-shek and his wife to dinner. The meeting was arranged in order to discuss the general situation, about which the Dorman-Smiths knew nothing. The following day, however, accompanied by the Chiangs, they visited the burning town of Mandalay and witnessed the devastation, obviously caused by very recent Japanese bombing. The Dorman-Smiths had known nothing of the carnage. "A most convenient misunderstanding!" commented Madame Chiang.

Imagining that he commanded Chinese Forces, Stilwell had reluctantly offered Chinese support to the British. Chiang furiously countermanded the support; whereupon Madame Chiang seized the opportunity to turn both this and the Dorman-Smith 'misunderstanding' into Chinese advantage, becoming conveniently affronted by the gaffes of the ill-informed British Governor, and the presumptuous Stilwell. She used the situation to get herself and Chiang onto centre stage, putting pressure on Churchill and the other world leaders.

Alexander, having ordered withdrawal of all troops northwards, from Prome to Allanmyo, a town 50 miles south of Yenangyaung, was at the same time concerned to close the gap between the two British columns, travelling on two almost parallel main roads, both leading north from Rangoon. One road defended by the 17th Division followed the Sittang River to Thazi, in the east. The one to the west, with 1st BurDiv defending, followed the Irrawaddy River.

Unaware that the oilfields were already damaged beyond repair, Alexander expressed a hope of saving them and also the airfield at Magwe, 20 miles south. Magwe had, however, ceased operation some weeks beforehand.

Bill Slim sought, 'a little time', after his arrival to reorganise his new command. As with all the Burma Army hierarchy, he had not assimilated the changed situation, and time was a luxury denied by the Japanese. In consequence, Slim's first operational instruction as Corps Commander was on 6 April, for the withdrawal of 1st BurCorps to Migyaungye, a small village in the Allanmyo area. Alexander's decision to move back was now being implemented. The new official word was 'withdrawal'; it had been the unofficial action since the closure of Rangoon on 6 March, one month beforehand.

13

DESERTED OR DISCARDED

From the time of his arrival, Bill Slim had no opportunity to inspect the condition of troops under his command, although he knew them to be greatly weakened. He accepted that reorganisation was impracticable, and with little transport available, operations had of necessity to be piecemeal; utilising whatever troops might be available, particularly as the reinforced and well-equipped Japanese assault force was known to be moving rapidly northwards from Rangoon. They were focused on one objective, capturing the Yenangyaung and Chauk oilfields, which they sought to capture intact.

On 6 April, 1st BurCorps was struggling to make its way north to Migyaungye. It meant travelling the final 25 miles through scrub country and over rough jungle tracks, and it was difficult terrain for the few motor transports available. Short of fuel, and with damaged axles, most of the vehicles were eventually abandoned. Becoming dependent upon the few commandeered bullock carts and pack mules, troops arrived at the town hungry and thirsty from the cruel heat, and dust raised from cartwheels and tired feet.

Japanese advance units followed closely upon the heels of BurCorps, causing them to turn and fight, almost immediately upon arrival at Migyaungye. No more than a shadow of its previous fighting force, BurCorps adopted a position astride the main road, and contained what must have been a small enemy advance force for six days. Other Japanese forces were building in strength on the flanks, and attempting the familiar encircling tactics.

Deducing that the Japanese might be using river craft to encroach up the Irrawaddy, Slim decided that his troops must withdraw, or be overrun, in the very near future. He was particularly concerned not to yield the main road to the north, the direct approach to the airfield at Magwe, as well as the two oilfields. The defended road junction was the vital cross-country escape route for 17th Division, who were scheduled to join with BurDiv.

Unaware of the drastic developments taking place 50 miles south, we of 2nd Bn. KOYLI rested. There was a movement of personnel as a few of the sick returned to rejoin the unit. It was surprising how news of Bruce Scott's proposed evacuation of the battalion brought a number of officers and men, miraculously recovered from wounds and illness, returning to duty. The battalion strength on the morning of 11 April 1942 was about 220. Numbers varied by the hour. It was eleven o'clock in the morning as we listened to Saigon Radio on wireless sets bequeathed by the departed oilmen; we heard Tokio Rose's taunting news bulletin, issued by the Japanese. It contained the threat announced in perfect English,

"The British Forces at present stationed at the central oilfield of Yenangyaung will be annihilated. The Imperial Japanese Army will attack and leave no way of escape".

News of the threatening broadcast from Saigon shocked the unit, insofar as it specifically targeted us, the sole unit on the oilfield. It was fortunate that our men were unaware of Churchill's discardment message to Roosevelt; even so, the Japanese broadcast was traumatic for troops in the present circumstances, knowing the Japanese to have total air superiority, plus field guns, and equipped troops, augmented by the Nationalist Burmese (some of whom, ex-members of the Burma Rifles, were, ironically, trained by the British).

Nevertheless, our reaction to the Japanese message was unexpected: we were spurred into action, and in an atmosphere of tension and expectancy, everything tightened up. Men moved with purpose, weapons and equipment were double-checked, the three small company identities became more marked. It now seemed only a matter of time before we won or lost all, including our lives.

With no apparent route out of Burma, our landlocked, semi-relaxed unit had to become, once again, a fighting force. The atmosphere became electric: – Let Japan attack!

The impact of the Saigon broadcast had hardly penetrated before we received a second devastating message. It was noon, an hour after the broadcast; Brigadier Bruce Scott made another one of his rare appearances.

"Sorry KOYLI, I have bad news for you. We cannot get the reinforcements promised. I have to send you down the road again, to Migyaungye, to cover the withdrawal of BurCorps. I am arranging for transport to be here at 16.00 hours, it will be insufficient to move all in one journey; it will have to be 'ride and march', with transport 'leap-frogging' to and fro. I hope it will be for only this once, and then I want you out of Burma, as fast as possible".

To undertake a 'do or die' defensive operation on the oilfield was one thing. The sick and injured were prepared to shoot it out to the death, but to be ordered onto the offensive with a 50 miles forced march, ill-equipped and debilitated, was suicide. This insensitive order brought the unit within an ace of mutiny. What we newly-joined officers did not know was how little confidence N.C.O.s and other ranks had in the regular officers of the battalion. Fifty years after the event, men still talk of one officer going into a 'bashah' (straw house), from which they then heard a single shot, after which he came out with a minor upper arm wound. There was no identified enemy in the area.

No sooner had Bruce Scott departed than a steady stream of men made off, deserting, across the hard, undulating surface of the oilfield. These men were at the end of their tether, exhausted and malnourished. Those fit enough to do so were nursing their sick 'muckers'. They realised that going 50 miles down the road meant returning 50 miles, should they survive. In view of all that had gone before, they could not trust those in command to arrange supplies of food, ammunition and return transport.

'We'd better check these bloody things.' Benny Mee was an exacting man when it came to supplies. We had, by some miracle of war, four three-inch mortars. Cannibalising the four, we salvaged three, which meant that with the 24 ten-pound bombs, we could maintain a rate of rapid fire for a period of considerably less than one minute. It was useless.

Having checked the tools, we checked the staff, only to find that two long service sergeants, Moorhammer, and my namesake, Fitzpatrick, returning the previous day from being sick with malaria, had now decided to 'go walkies' along with the others attempting to make their way out of Burma. They had deserted. 59 N.C.O.s and men vanished in the short period of four hours. Most of those deserting were recently returned from hospital, and it is possible that they had better information about the chaotic state of affairs up-country. Mostly though, they were disillusioned with their commanders, particularly with their incompetence at the Salween and Sittang Rivers, and were well justified in their action.

It would have been easy to shoot those deserting, but a futile waste of precious ammunition. It required bravery on their part to take matters into their own hands, and face isolation in the hostile environment, reliant upon themselves for food, water, and survival against the debilitating illnesses many of them were already suffering. Many of those remaining with the unit wished them well.

Few deserters escaped to survive the long lonely journey into India, where they were sentenced in due course to long terms of imprisonment when the battalion was eventually settled in the beautiful hill station of Shillong, in Assam. Moorhammer and Fitzpatrick vanished, and were not heard of again. (Moorhammer, being of German descent, was suspected within the battalion of having Nazi sympathies, and this may well have influenced his decision to desert.)

Churchill's perfidious betrayal of the Burma Army was not revealed at the courts martial trying the so-called deserters. Churchill's endless prevarication ensured the state of chaos at present existing in Burma. Totally unaware of Churchill's washing of hands ten days beforehand, troops ensconced on the oilfield were in the centre of the turmoil. The surreptitious 'Top Secret' message of 1 April to Roosevelt was possibly confirmation of our expected early demise. In the eyes of the British Prime Minister, we were doomed.

Long departed were the dithering, doddering, and moribund Major Generals, roused from sinecures of comfortable appointments in cosy eastern outposts of the Empire. Men brought back from the seeming dead to direct and command. They had failed miserably.

The mayhem brought about by Churchill was likened to the boy with his finger in the dyke attempting to stop the flood. Churchill did not try hard enough, and he did not try soon enough.

Churchill had retracted.

These intelligent soldiers were not morons; many being conscripts, serving reluctantly and not in this morass of their own choice. Unaware of Churchill's treachery and his reneging on them, they were now beyond the bounds of tolerance; decimated, virtually unarmed, and hungered for weeks.

There are no adequate words to describe such a predicament, particularly for men serving a supposedly proud nation. In these circumstances, no man owed allegiance to Britain, its King, or its generals.

It would have been fitting at this point to have Churchill and his generals indicted for their failings and their treachery, rather than those unfortunate absconders. Many of whom perished in their taxing and hopeless quest for freedom.

Preparing for the move south to Migyaungye, nine batmen were sitting in a circle in one of the bungalows cleaning weapons, when a short staccato burst from a Bren gun caused a stir. The walls were splattered with blood and brains as Harris, batman to Company Commander Geoffrey Baxter, placed the Bren gun muzzle in his mouth and squeezed the trigger. Without a word, this tall, handsome young man had seen this as his way out. He was laid to rest in the garden of the bungalow. With 59 men deserted, and one now shot, the unit was left with a strength of about 160.

The move south began immediately; several pack mules accompanied our marching company, plus three mules and carts acquired during the stay at the oilfield. We were to be 'leap-frogged' in due course, when? and if? the unreliable 'promised' transport arrived.

The first sight of transport was as it sped south, past the roadside checkpoints, with no indication of its destination, until the four three-tonners returned about two hours later. Now speeding north, this time filled with Royal Air Force personnel vacating the base at Magwe. It was a big surprise to see them, or to know they were about. In the five weeks I had been in Burma, there had not been one Allied plane in the sky, other than the one flown by the Australian airmen crashing in the jungle area, near Pegu.

The chaotic priorities of command and planning were amply illustrated in the transport arrangements. We were 'urgently' wanted 50 miles south, well beyond Magwe. Our task was to defend a vital road junction and provide cover for BurCorps and the Gurkhas to pass through before the rapidly advancing Japanese cut them off. Transport would have got us into position three or four hours earlier, had we been given priority. 'Command', however, wanted the airmen out, and we were downgraded, to a secondary priority.

We now had to make a more desperate dash to undertake the vital covering action. Nothing would have been lost in giving the airmen second priority, but Brigadier Bruce Scott and his planners had their own peculiar priorities. The 'urgent' need for infantry action, in support of infantry, was superseded by the need to get the Royal Air Force personnel out of danger. With priorities determined in this manner, could a man be blamed for deserting? The deal in supplying transport, could have had the same effect as the Sittang Bridge, when Smyth cut off the means of withdrawal, losing hundreds of men. Bruce Scott almost cut off the transport, which would have lost all forces in Burma, including the airmen.

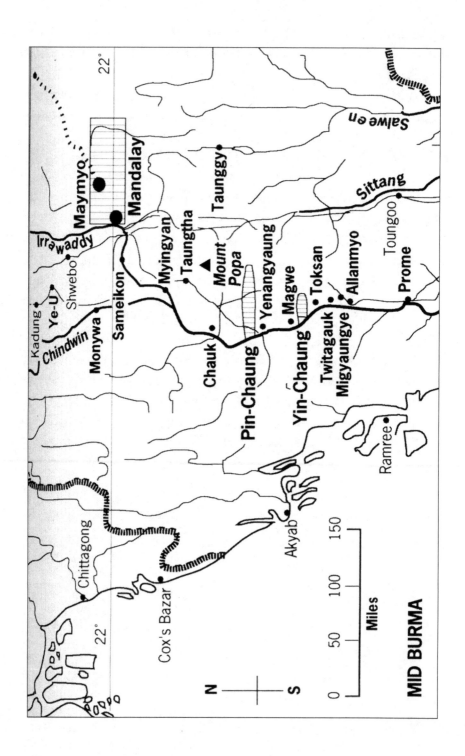

MID BURMA

14

A VERY GREASY HOLE

I had shared the company of established officers of the battalion for a brief period, and it was plain to me there was little comradeship amongst them. They were mostly former juniors, now promoted to captain, with many competitive jealousies. Former seniors had, one way or another, managed to be eliminated; others of senior category were absent and employed in, 'vital extra-regimental employment', on staff appointments, or commanding camps of all kinds, anywhere except Burma.

The newly-elevated officers considered themselves an elite and had no time for us, the newly arrived draft of E.C.O.s. Those with Burma experience distanced themselves, when a little guidance and a few advisory words would have helped settle us newcomers. The cool indifference possibly stemmed from the belief that Bruce Scott was about to evacuate the battalion out of Burma. It appeared that the newly promoted were competing, one with another, all with a view to future promotion.

Regardless of the friction, the move south was on. Four three-ton trucks arrived and loaded the main party, consisting of two companies. 24 or 25 men crammed into each vehicle. This was no great problem, as all that each man carried was his possessions; basic webbing, with two front pouches, a full water bottle, a rifle, and if lucky, a side haversack. No man had more than fifteen rounds of .303 ammunition, and many had less. Two reserve ammunition boxes were placed on one of the trucks, each box containing 1,000 rounds (10 rounds per man), making an average arsenal of about 25 rounds per man. However the transport was organised, it meant for every man at least 20 hot speedy miles on foot, in boots already well worn. All knew that the possibility of transport for the return journey was remote, particularly in the event of contact with the enemy. In such event, the likelihood of any return was extremely small.

There was silence and a lack of humour as transport moved off. No man was in doubt; we were inadequately equipped for offensive action. The feeling was one of going to inevitable doom, as though sliding down a huge tube with greasy sides.

Off to war, with ammunition sufficient for less than one minute of firing, enough for a suicidal defensive action, but hopeless for even a modest offensive. The prospects were grim indeed.

Passing by Magwe airfield, recently vacated by the Royal Air Force personnel, there was a rare sight. Twenty-three black plumes of smoke, spiralling perpendicularly into a windless sky, were ascending from aircraft destroyed at dispersal points around the airfield perimeter. There must have been some reason why these aircraft were not seen flying in recent weeks.

There is little evening or dusk in the tropics; the sun falls rapidly from the sky. It was after nightfall, and moonless, when we arrived at what we thought to be the correct junction of the road. There was great heat, silence, and an air of expectancy, as we moved into position in total darkness, forming a rough defensive perimeter. Using materials scavenged from houses and damaged bullock carts, we established a rapidly prepared block on the road, and waited into the night.

Morning came after the quiet yet alert night, only for us to realise that we were in a most open situation, and vulnerable to Japanese observer aircraft. Moving rapidly into cover, we found we were defending the wrong road junction. We could hear shooting, and as a few wounded men arrived, we were advised that Japanese motorised units were beginning to infiltrate forward defences. There was no transport for a speedy move to the correct location. In the heat, we ran the 15 or 16 miles south, in order to commandeer the road junction at Thitagauk, a little behind the forward troops who continued to be engaged in heavy combat.

This was an unusual situation, made all the more weird by the total lack of movement: (Gurkhas don't move easily). There was no troop movement on the road, other than of a few wounded, and no more than a trickle of refugees. The heat intensified, and men were warned to conserve water, as it was now almost impossible to obtain.

We established that the fighting troops to our front were the remains of a brigade of Gurkhas, who, themselves short of ammunition, had fought a tremendous battle before having to withdraw from the desperate situation. The Gurkhas had taken a great toll of the Japanese, before withdrawing through our cover position. The warmth of feeling for these men was expressed by the Yorkshire troops sharing their most precious commodity, a swig from the water bottle. A man really had to love another to offer his water bottle.

Bruce Scott had the knack of creating situations requiring initiative and dedication. It certainly required both for us to take on the Japanese advance as the Gurkhas moved through, leaving us to hold the road junction. Defences tightened as four or five Japanese fighter aircraft patrolled and strafed at random; eight or nine bombers followed, seeking out targets on the road, the only axis for movement north or south. Fortunately, we suffered no casualties from this action, although a number of refugees, always reluctant to move off the road, suffered greatly.

I targeted the three-inch mortars, and Johnny Welboume sited the anti-tank gun to cover two or three prime areas to our front, making ready for the Japanese advance. Geoffrey Chadwick, our battalion commander, instructed that the weapons should stay on the mule carts. We reloaded, and the mortar platoon operated as infantry within the perimeter. Chadwick was for some reason reluctant to use specialist weapons. Benny Mee was not enamoured with Chadwick, whom he knew of old; he was angry and disillusioned to find him in command. Here we were, once again, detached, isolated, and almost unarmed, with a commanding officer afraid to have support weapons unloaded from the transport.

We remained in the isolated situation throughout the day and night of 12 April. The anticipated assault did not materialise, as the Japanese had suffered greatly in attacking the Gurkhas. Injuries had given them cause to withdraw, rest and regroup. Apart from air action, there was no sign of offensive, yet we knew that we needed to remain alert. Our situation became ever more vulnerable, as an attack by the enemy was inevitable, and we knew that we could be eliminated in the event of attack by a strong and well-armed force.

Aircraft bombing and strafing had become more intensive on the morning of 13 April, when, as though from nowhere, five or six trucks loaded with Gukhas passed across the track behind us. All were singing, as though on a working men's trip: 'Lucky! Lucky! Lucky!'

They were part of the 17th Division, evacuating from the eastern sector. Within minutes of the Gurkhas passing, there was ground movement, a party of about 100 Japanese, possibly more, well-deployed and advancing cautiously. They were crossing open ground to our front as we stayed heads down in the cover of rough scrub. When they were halfway across the open, and at a range of less than 80 yards, we opened fire, knocking over many of the advancing enemy. Survivors retreated at speed, appearing to be in disarray, and it was tempting to follow and attack, but discretion was the better part of valour, and we stayed put, in solid defence, keeping strict control on our ammunition. Perhaps the advancing Japanese were survivors of the combat with the Gurkhas. Our solitary casualty was Private Harold Wilson, of Leeds, shot through the thigh; he was fortunate in obtaining a lift to hospital on a tank.

Before the outbreak of war, Geoffrey Chadwick had occupied a passive role as second in command of the batallion, his responsibilities being administrative, organising 'B' echelon services and provisioning field operations. Assuming command at Yenangyaung was an unexpected role for him, and he was greatly perplexed at Thitagauk, finding himself out on a limb, lacking directions and instructions. In that situation, Chadwick ought to have got out once the Gurkha transports passed; but reluctant to move, he was seeking to make contact as a messenger arrived, saying that 2nd Royal Tank Regiment would be arriving to assist in conveying the battalion back almost 30 miles, to a position near the Yin Chaung. This was our first operational meeting with the tank regiment, and what a blessing they were to be in the days ahead.

Tanks arrived in mid-aftemoon. Only then were we informed that we were situated in enemy-occupied territory, 40 miles behind advanced Japanese lines. There had been no enemy attack as we awaited the passing of the Gurkhas, so we had assumed that the Japanese patrol we ambushed were themselves in isolation and disarray. Other enemy advance formations had been outflanking and infiltrating towards the oilfields, and Magwe airfield to the north.

The tanks and our two unit vehicles moved off, carrying headquarters staff and two rifle companies, leaving Captain Frank (Dusty) Miller, Vic Stevens, and myself, with two small platoons, totalling about 35 men. We were escort to three mule carts carrying the weapons. The march was 28 miles, and movement was restricted to the main road, which was vulnerable and debris-littered.

I had by now developed a rather painful boil on my right buttock, which hurt as I moved, and in the intense heat, it was not easy to sit on the ground. With no means of treatment, I began to worry that the boil would turn septic. It was a risk, but not worse than for the malaria, dysentery, cholera, and beri-beri sufferers in the unit.

'Dusty' Miller was a regular soldier; he had been a Company Sergeant Major, squat, with ginger hair and a short waxy moustache. Following the departure of the tanks and transport, he waited a while before giving the order to move out of the defence perimeter, 'just in case' the Japanese might be waiting to follow-up.

As we vacated Thitagauk, it was late afternoon, and the sun was scorching the ground, causing reflective heat and a blinding glare from the sandy dust at the roadside. Salty sweat from the forehead ran and smarted into screwed-up eyes. Water bottles were already less than half-full, with no prospect of a refill throughout the long march. Fortunately, there was a small quantity of hard rations on the mule carts. The extra bonus, if it could be called so, was that we were moving rapidly into the welcome shelter and coolness of a jet-black night.

The march was strength-sapping; escort duty to the transport was necessary, as were flanking guards during daylight hours, and they travelled in the more open agricultural ground, well clear of the road. This was to prevent Burmans taking pot-shots or raiding from the cover of distant trees or vacated villages. Numbers of refugees were attracted, and travelled with the column; they were pleased to have protection against Dacoits.

We were thankful to enter the blackness of night cover, knowing that we were unlikely to be attacked in this situation; it was relatively safe on the main road. Outstanding among the accompanying refugees was an Indian woman of most unusual height; she was like a beanstalk, easily six foot six inches. Her only garment was a totally inadequate sari; it looked incongruous, covering a lump in her belly that indicated a well-advanced pregnancy. She travelled alone. This unfortunate woman vanished in the dark into a small copse at the roadside; yet, within two hours, she was back in her place among the moving column. She was carrying a newborn child. The life expectancy of the child must have been zero. Many wondered if it was ever alive.

That not one British soldier could offer assistance to the woman emphasises the parlous situation of our party. The condition of the refugees was no better and no worse than our own, except that we carried weapons for protection in the event of attack. Fortunately, there was no attack.

Well past midnight and with the moon not yet up, we had marched 20 miles along the road, unsure where we might find either the remainder of the batallion, or a Japanese roadblock. We came upon Johnny Welbourne; it was a surprise as he emerged from roadside scrub. He had been detailed to remain with one or two men to meet Miller at the road junction. Avoiding possible roadblocks on the main road, he was to lead us a further 8 miles, along a track going off to the left, to where the main part of the battalion were transported on the tanks. Marching 20 miles on the road, and in roadside fields had been strenuous, but the next 8 miles, off the road, were to be hell.

The night was black; too dark to see a man at more than arm's length. The narrow track had no surface, other than several inches of fine sandy dust, churned up by bullock carts and tanks. The two-wheeled mule carts became bogged down and had to be pushed, with as many men as possible around the wheels and rear of each cart, in order to make any progress. Pushing the carts brought sweat on top of sweat, with dust rising in clouds and sticking on clothing and body. The depth of dust and narrowness of the track brought the column to frequent halts. It was easy to hear sounds from great distances in the stillness of the night.

During listening periods, we could hear the squeak of turning axles some distance to our left, in the direction of the river. We wondered whether a second track ran parallel to the one upon which we were travelling, with Burmese travelling on an illicit journey; or it might be Japanese. We could not reconcile this with having such free movement along the main road for more than seven hours.

What we did not know, because Chadwick failed to tell us, was that when receiving instructions to withdraw, he was also warned that the Japanese were moving in considerable force around the west flank, and that they were advancing between our group and the river. They were attempting to reach the Yin Chaung, and possibly capture the airfield at Magwe.

The movement we could hear to our left was in fact a Burmese-guided Japanese column, moving with equal difficulty to our own, along a similar track parallel to our own. Flames some distance ahead of our column illuminated the skyline; obviously a fire lit for the benefit of the Japanese on the parallel track. There were occasional animal noises in the night, noises often given as recognition signals between Japanese troops; we realised that these could be from troops, already infiltrated and ahead of our party. We guessed that, in the night, and with restricted communications, the Japanese might possibly assume us to be a second Japanese column, also moving forward. In darkness one has no means of identifying troops, and it is difficult to attack; therefore we were free to progress. Speech distance is bayonet distance. A change was coming about as the moon began to rise, and there was a measure of visibility.

Chadwick had made no mention of Bruce Scott's 'pie in the sky' plan for 'two brigades to move into position south of the Yin Chaung, in order to repel the Japanese', thought to be advancing to our west, close by the Irrawaddy. He had also maintained silence about the unit being ordered to the village of Myingun, a short distance south of the Yin Chaung, to act as 'a stop'. Bruce Scott's message was:

1. Hold the enemy at all costs during the night of 13 April until 1st Brigade arrive.

2. 1st Brigade will come and get the battalion out of any fix on the following morning.

3. In the meantime, the Cameronians will be put out south of the Chaung, as a screen.

4. Chadwick must move and act on the assumption that he would meet the enemy at some time.

Chadwick failed to inform us of these instructions. Miller and our party were left in ignorance of possible events before starting out on the long march. As a final blunder, Chadwick managed to get his party lost. They finished up at the small village of Toksan, a good mile from his Myingun objective, and about two miles to the east of the Irrawaddy.

The Cameronians did not appear, as a screen.

1st Brigade did not arrive on the South bank of Yin Chaung.

Chadwick did not meet the enemy; Miller did.

Information, command, and control were chaotic. Wherever he was, Bruce Scott had clearly lost control. In view of Chadwick's finding himself in the wrong village, it came as no surprise to find that John Welbourne, acting as guide, did not know where to find him, or the battalion. The moon was beginning to rise, and it was between 2 a.m. and 3 a.m. when we came upon two trucks that had managed, by some quirk, to become parted from Chadwick. The moonlit ground, upon which the trucks were standing, was heavily ploughed, as a crossing point for bullock carts. An area of deep dust in the base of what, as we were to see later, was a huge shallow saucer-shaped area of land, not easily defined in the dark.

Here we encountered a man I had seen only briefly at the oil-fields; he had travelled from start to finish on the transports, hardly a foot touching the ground.

None of us had seen a bedding roll, blankets, or sheets, for weeks; yet here was this man settled in a bedding roll with white sheets, brought with him when he joined Chadwick at Yenangyaung; Nicholas Throckmorton, with a crown on his shoulder to indicate field officer rank, a major in the British Army. As such, he should have commanded respect; he did not. In earlier days, he had illustrated his infantry skill by placing a compass behind his back, and looking over his shoulder, to take a back bearing. Emerging from the jungle, he placed a compass on a railway line, to find to his surprise, the needle swung north-south.

Detailed as our guide to the battalion location, he had, 'absolutely no idea where they were'. His explanation was that things look different at night. Throckmorton's reaction to the arrival of our party, after ten hours of thirsty, dust-choked marching, pushing mule carts for a large part of the way, was a curt, "Settle down, over there!"

Lieutenant Quartermaster Taffy Phillips was soon on his feet; when told of the arduous journey, he requested a water issue for the men. "There'll be no water issue tonight, you must wait until morning", said Throckmorton, from within his sheets.

"They need a drink now", said Taffy, as he unloaded the container, and started a water issue. "I'll shoot the bastard if he has any more to say".

"You'll be after me in the shooting, if there's any more from him", Miller rejoined, and Throckmorton went quiet. There was no doubting the mood of the men by this time; any further delay in issuing water, and they would have taken matters into their own hands. One or two men had collapsed and fallen behind, and possibly died, in the march along the hot dusty track. The desperation and determination in the remainder was quite unmistakable; they would kill for water.

15

TOKSAN VILLAGE

With the men settled and supplied with water, Steve and I slumped down on the track some yards from the transport. Less fatigued than most of the troops, we realised that we must continue to stay alert in view of the noises heard in the night, and determined to make an early start at daybreak, in order to get everybody under cover as rapidly as possible. Suspicious of movements on the track to our left throughout the long march, and with the pain of the boil on my bum, I got no sleep. At first light, I stirred, finding Steve alert and ready to move.

"Come on; let's have a look up here". We started up the track in the silent, colourless world of first light; that period of about twenty minutes before the sun begins to rise over the horizon. There was no birdsong or movement at this hour and the shapes of trees, houses, and men showed themselves in silhouette, just a misty outline haze of bluey grey. We knew this to be the most vital time of day, and we must use it to carry out rapid reconnaissance.

There was no question of dressing; no man had removed a single item of clothing for days now. At night, boots and puttees remained fastened, the bush hat was simply moved to the back of the head as a pillow, and the belt buckle loosened, but not removed. Rifles were secured to the body by the sling.

The position in which we found ourselves was at the junction of several tracks, a huge saucer shape of agricultural land and bare open scrubland, with fields rising gently away on all sides. Overlooked from surrounding ridges, this was no place to be, particularly as spotter planes might become active overhead, and we were easy prey for ground attack. Finding cover rapidly was essential if we were to stay alive.

We inspected the only feature of note, a *pongyi kyaung* (church or village school), which stood on higher ground about 100 yards away, surrounded by a few trees and a little cover, and with a view across an expanse of land. Assured that this place would suit our immediate needs, we walked back to where the exhausted and tired men lay, as a few of them were beginning to look around.

Bending down to pick up the small haversack from where I had lain in the night, all hell broke loose. Machine-gun bullets thumped into the trackside under my nose, causing me to look up very sharply indeed. There, almost unbelievably, no more than 25 yards away, was a Japanese, squatting behind a machine-gun; his face looked enormous, with lips parted showing tombstone-like teeth. The next thing I felt was puffs and eddies of warm air on my temple and right ear, as bullets whistled at head height between Steve and me. I shouted "Down!" to Steve; not that it was necessary, as the bullets had gone between the two of us. Yet, in this smallest fraction of a second, I had time to think, "You ugly bastard! What a bloody awful shot. You wouldn't do for me if you can't aim better than that". Dropping flat into the powdered dust of the track, using the trackside *bund* for cover, we crawled like two overgrown geckoes up the track towards the *pongyi kyaung*. There was no time for niceties like giving orders; it was a matter of; – get out of here at speed! The Japanese had used the black of the night, and first light, to good effect. There was pandemonium as men and mules scattered away back up the northern slope.

Apart from our weakened force being caught in isolation, there was a detachment of Indian Army Mountain Battery over to our left. This accounted for some of the squeaking noises heard in the night. 'The Gunners', it appears, were themselves being followed by the main Japanese assault force, now joining in the attack.

Within seconds, what had been a huge and quiet expanse of open hillside became alive with movement, as men, horses, and mules stampeded in front of a hail of bullets. The big *Pathani-wallah* sepoys of the Mountain Battery hurdled small fences and scrub at Olympic speed, some mounted on chargers, some with part-shackled gun carriages, all running like stags as firing now concentrated from many sides.

Getting over the first element of surprise, and having crawled, stomach-deep, in the sandy soil for thirty or so yards up the track, then ran halfway up the slope, I stopped for a second, and I decided that if Japanese were such bloody awful marksmen, there was little choice if I was to survive. Move I must! There was only one way to go; – at all speed towards the northern slope, at the same time shouting, "Keep together! This way!"

Halfway up the rise, I joined about a dozen men, including Benny Mee, Danny Lobben, and Jacko. Serious as it was, some were laughing at the show as we dropped down into firing positions to take on the Japanese. My 'big faced, slant-eyed Japanese', remained squatting in the open behind his gun, another coming forward, carrying an ammunition box. A beautiful target. Setting my rifle sights at 200 yards, I took aim and fired. The first shot hit the machine-gun; it splattered, and the big face split up the middle, before the man slumped forward. His friend dropped to one knee before being hit in the middle, and as he grabbed his stomach, I thought 'Abe would have liked that'. It was satisfying to have killed the first Japanese I had fired on. There was a thrill, a feeling I had previously experienced in a boxing ring, or playing rugby; only this was like captaining Ireland, or England, in the biggest game of all.

Shortly after the start of the firing, came the whistling sound of big Japanese mortars, and shells began to fall all around. With a five-inch barrel, against the British three-inch, and a range of over 3,000 yards, – British 1,600. More devastating in blast and shrapnel than British; they could blanket an area requiring twice the number of British weapons. Lying on a long, exposed slope was no place to be, once the shells began to fall.

Calling, "Danny! Jacko! Let's get out of this", back we went up the rise. The two chums were feeling better, having managed a few hits in the firing. I was annoyed, because we had lost my three-inch mortars, as well as bombs, transport, mules, and carts, along with the 2,000 rounds of reserve ammunition, the rations, cooking utensils, and the water. It was a tragedy, after sapping our strength pushing the carts throughout the previous night.

We were fortunate, at the crest of the rise, to find Chadwick with the main party, occupying a small village in which they had spent the night.

They were alerted on hearing the firing, and 'standing to,' at the village of Toksan. We had halted for the night, less than half a mile from the battalion group, but how would Throckmorton know this?

Joined again with the main body, it was difficult to assess the losses in the morning fracas. Some men had dropped out from fatigue on the strenuous march under cover of darkness, and we had no way of knowing whether they had caught up. Others were killed or wounded in the morning attack, and some may well have completely passed by the battalion in the frantic escape dash and gone north, or possibly west to the Irrawaddy River.

Captain Allan Bootland had travelled with the main party, and was in a hell of a state. He was lying on the ground, a bullet having passed through his throat and out through the jaw; blood was pumping out at a rapid rate. Before being recently commissioned, he had been a most unpopular Regimental Sergeant Major, particularly vitriolic towards a recent draft of 'Belisha Boys' (twenty-year olds, conscripted for training in pre-war months, and mobilised on the declaration of war). Bootland's wound was far too big to have been inflicted by a small zippy quarter-inch Japanese bullet, particularly at fairly long range. It had the nasty look of a British .303 inch bullet, and many speculated on this being 'a debt repaid', by one of Bootland's pre-war victims.

Without a doctor, or medical aid of any kind, we could do nothing for him. I placed him on a bullock cart. Being semiconscious and unsecured; – he fell off. Stripping a length of rough rope from a bamboo house, I secured him to the cart as he passed out, unconscious. Giving the bullock a slap on the arse, I set him on his lonely way, along a track, towards the north-east, in the hope that he might reach the main road we had used earlier. He would have a soldier's chance of living or dying, according to his luck. His life depended on the bullock keeping going along the track for several miles, and eventually reaching assistance. In the mid-day heat, he had no real hope of survival, so he must have had a charmed life. In stages, he managed to progress several hundred miles to the airfield at Myitkyina in North Burma. He was flown out for treatment and rejoined the battalion in India some time later.

14 April was a long day of subterfuge, with transport already lost, along with arms and essentials. Geoffrey Chadwick sent two companies forward in abortive attempts to recover the lost equipment. Toksan is a small, remote village of few houses, self-contained within an ill-defined rectangular perimeter, a fair growth of trees for cover, and some cool shade, isolated away from the main flow of refugees, well clear of the main road.

In such a place we expected to find some form of life, chicken, goat, bullock, or maybe an elderly person, but there was none, and the place was dry with no available well for water. Apart from two or three containing a little water, a number of large earthenware *chatees* (water pots) were shattered on the ground outside bamboo houses. This was clearly the outcome of a 'scorched earth policy', decreed by one or other of the Nationalist groups. It did not help us accomplish Wavell's order to 'live more off the land'.

Our few rations were held centrally, and as a result of the morning's loss of containers, the water situation was desperate; everyone was into their second or third day on one full water bottle; and there was no let-up in the heat.

Japanese movement was seen on all sides around the village, and we were deployed in the sparse cover around the perimeter, several miles forward of British lines, and completely surrounded by enemy. They were infiltrating towards the Yin Chaung, a short distance north of our position. A white Japanese plane with large red circles on its wings patrolled to and fro above the village, maintaining close observation.

The promised, 1st Brigade and Cameronians, had failed to materialise. Bruce Scott had a vivid imagination, great enthusiasm, and many flops. So much of what was promised never materialised, that the troops believed the battalion to be entirely alone.

Chadwick became concerned at having no news from Bruce Scott, and decided to send his intelligence officer, Arthur Watts, on foot to ascertain the position of 1st Brigade (whose commander had, unknown to Chadwick, requested a move to north of the Yin Chaung). With no wireless for communication, as Bruce Scott explained later, he had in fact attempted contact by sending a boat down the Irrawaddy at night, and signalling by lamp: 'Chadwick come back'. Yet he had ordered us to the village of Myingun, two miles away from the river. Where did he think we were? We were in fact one mile further adrift, at Toksan.

It was no surprise to find that liaison officers, using trucks, had been unsuccessful in attempting to get messages to the battalion. There was some luck, however, when mounted officers of an Indian Mountain Battery, carrying Bruce Scott's message of withdrawal, met Watts. The Indians gave Watts a horse, and he set about returning to our lost unit, only to fall, break his arm and lose the mount. Understandably, Watts did not get back with the message; hence we remained in our familiar state of isolation.

The enemy were seen to be building up a considerable force all around the village, and although they continued observation, aircraft made no attempt to attack, possibly because they too were capable of shooting their own ground troops, or were short of ammunition.

In an attempt to deceive the enemy on the strength of the unit, Chadwick created heavy movement within the village, by ordering frequent changes of observers between guard posts. Although the enemy were seen moving around, well within rifle range, ammunition was far too precious to waste; it was reserved for emergency in the event of enemy attack. We chose not to commence hostilities and thus attract enemy fire. In view of the reluctance of the Japanese to attack, it was thought, they might be equally short of ammunition.

Only as the excitement dimmed a little did I begin to feel the pain of the huge boil on my bum; it was now almost impossible to sit on the ground for rest, even for brief periods. Doctors were out of the question, and I became a bit scared, convincing myself that the boil might become gangrenous. This really worried me, but, being behind Japanese lines, and seeing the enemy's strength, I also had a feeling that I might not be using legs for much longer. Toksan village had the look of another good spot for annihilation, and we could well be the victims. Now a battalion of less than 80 in strength, we were isolated from troops of Burma Division.

Clearly, the Japanese were becoming impatient with our unit; we had shot up the party on the previous day, and further checked their advance for twenty-four hours. Excessive patrolling within the village was clearly deceiving the Japanese into believing the battalion to be much stronger than it was.

Calling a brief meeting of officers, Chadwick's indecision showed, and he sought our guidance. He was clearly in some degree of panic at having unwittingly delayed the enemy for so long, and he accepted a unanimous decision to act. We agreed on withdrawal; – to be carried out by companies independently moving out under cover of darkness.

16

YIN CHAUNG

The plan was to move out northwards, towards the Yin Chaung, and find a village track in the hope of it leading to a crossing point. We were to use the North Star for guidance; cross the *chaung,* and continue across country in the same direction for one hour, a distance of about three miles. Then turn eastwards to meet the main road, which at this point traverses for a short distance east to west; follow the road north, to the first 'ten-mile stone': – (These stones are particularly prominent). Here, take defensive cover, and await the remainder of the battalion.

No sooner had I made the rough sketch than each of the three companies requested a copy. These I made on any old rough piece of paper or card, and also a diagram showing how to locate the North Star in the night sky. Using the sandy soil as a blackboard, I spent a happy hour conducting a course on astronomy for senior N.C.O.s.

At nightfall, the Japanese were seen to be active on three sides of the defence perimeter; observation posts reported movement at very close range. I, along with the mortarless mortar platoon, was detailed to join Captain Geoffrey Baxter and his company on the withdrawal. As 'cartographer in chief', and having planned the operation, we were first to lead out of the perimeter into the pitch black night. Unsure of enemy dispositions, I carried a primed grenade in my right hand, for accurate throwing, and a 0.45 inch revolver in my left. A rifle was slung across my shoulder.

So dark and precarious was the night that, for guidance and silence, each man held the bayonet scabbard of the man in front.

Darkness made the indistinct tract hard to follow; the terrain alongside was hard scrub-country with many deep crevasses, causing stumbling and falls. A good curse seemed to ease the tension somewhat before someone said, 'Shut up, you noisy stupid sod!' and on we would go once again, unhurried and in silence.

Yin Chaung is one of the large dried up river beds running across country, east to west, towards the river Irrawaddy, and almost bone dry at this time of year, before the monsoon rains of late May. Three or four hundred yards across, with sharp sheer sides some 18 feet deep and a fine sandy bottom, it was impossible for wheeled transport, except at prepared crossing points, somewhat like a ford on an English river, only gargantuan by comparison.

As on the previous night, it was moonless and intensely dark. We reached a more defined track leading northwards, and started along this to a point where the track began to slope down through a cutting, into the bed of the *chaung*.

Descending the slope into the cutting, we heard the sounds of men moving around above us, and to the left side of the track. There was an unmistakable rattle of equipment and weapons; men were obviously lining the near side of the perimeter of what was possibly a *pongyi kyaung* compound. There was no time for second thoughts or turning back. The sheer desperation of our men in this perilous situation favoured us Yorkshiremen, and we continued forward, down towards the *chaung*. Movement and noise of the men above was repeated, with the same rattling as they moved through 90 degrees to occupy a new position, to face the black chasm of the *chaung*. There was no other reaction; whoever they were, they knew not to waste ammunition blazing off into darkness at an unidentified target.

It was a case of mutual respect, and we moved forward to cross the sandy bed. The Japanese above could not be certain whether we were British, or Japanese, and they made no attempt to challenge, or drop a 'friendly' grenade. Had they made any offensive movement, there would have been a bloody event: – Yorkshiremen hacking in with sharp steel. The surprising ability of the Japanese to leave a way free out of a desperate situation was illustrated once again. They knew that we must retaliate, and inflict merciless casualties, if cornered and attacked from the front.

The close encounter with the enemy caused Baxter to have cold feet, at the idea of our crossing the *chaung* as an independent company. He considered the idea of halting and waiting on the south bank, 'in order to meet up with the remainder of the battalion'. With some persuasion, he eventually opted for an immediate crossing, using the cover of darkness, and to await the remainder as previously arranged. Baxter was not a happy man to be operating independently.

Starting out across the *chaung* was easier and more relaxing than it had been on the hard undulating ground. There was a feeling of freedom as we moved away from the south bank. The situation changed drastically, however, as we arrived a little over halfway across, our troubles really started. Fortunately, visibility remained zero; nothing could be seen as we began to stumble, and fall over *bunds* of sandy soil, built up around water tanks (ponds) in the bed of the *chaung;* possibly it was a series of paddy fields. We floundered in water up to chest height in places.

Suddenly, this was, as Scott said of the Antarctic, "an awful place". Men and mules floundered in the morass, first on the *bunds,* then splashed into the water. Subduing noise in these circumstances was quite impossible; the silence of the night was shattered. Shouts and screams reverberated through the vast expanse.

Unable to stand, unable to speak, and unable to see, we were totally incapacitated. Machine-gun fire opened up from the north bank of the *chaung,* about 200 yards to our front. It was all hell let loose. Here we were, totally out of control, floundering from *bund* to *bund,* through water at chest height, while at the same time being fired on by weapons easily recognisable, Bren guns.

Desperate, and uncomfortable though it was, there was room for a little ribald humour. Diminutive, in height, Regimental Quartermaster Sergeant 'Dogger' Riley was struggling, a non-swimmer, with water coming up to his chin.

"Help me! Don't leave an old man!"

Danny Lobben dragged him out by the neck of his shirt. "Come on, you silly old bugger. You'll forget this when we get out of here".

It was possible to distinguish the steady Da-Da-Da-Da-Da of the Bren gun from the accelerating, staccato Di-Di-Di-Di-Di, of the Japanese machine-gun. The one-in-three tracer bullets revealed gun positions and line of fire. It did not take long to deduce that these were half-trained Indian troops. No British or Gurkha soldier would be so stupid as to open fire with tracer bullets, on fixed line firing, without knowing for certain that they were engaging an objective target. Furthermore, British troops did not have ammunition to squander in such a prolific manner. With tracer bullets passing less than 15 feet overhead, it was easy to identify the two gun positions. They were predictably located at the base of two tall palm trees, the only identifiable features, 300 or 400 yards apart, silhouetted and, as the moon began to rise, easily discernible, on the skyline of the north bank of the *chaung*.

Stuck as we were, literally in the mud, in the middle of nowhere, there was the option of turning around to the south and re-crossing the *chaung,* or continuing the few hundred yards, moving in under the challenging fire of two Bren guns. We decided against returning as it would be doubly hazardous; it meant retracing our tracks into where the bullets were falling, and to the Japanese-occupied crossing point.

Under Bren gun fire, we continued forward, walking, floundering, and almost swimming, towards the north bank, aiming to arrive at a central point between the position of the two machine-guns. We were pleased the Indians had ammunition to burn. Had they stopped firing and listened for a while, they must surely have heard our movements and turned the Brens on us.

Moving cautiously, the line of fire never faltered. Aware that random firing into darkness is ineffective, we gambled on this and doggedly stuck to our task of moving foward, in the hope of meeting no further opposition. Being the first company to cross the *chaung* in defiance of the thick mud and two Bren guns, we proved to be the fortunate ones. With relief, we reached the north bank, precisely at the bullock track leading out of the *chaung,* and between the two Brens. From this situation, we knew the Indians would not fire at us, as it would have meant firing at each other.

Company losses were minimal; one or two were known to have collapsed, and fallen by the wayside approaching the *chaung,* and an unknown number were shot, exhausted, or drowned, in the swamp.

The following two companies met with absolute hell, as, with the rising moon, the Indians realised their faults, and began to think for once. The Japanese also became alert and active, firing rifles and mortars from the south bank. Caught in the swamp, and being fired upon from front and rear, the following companies suffered casualties.

Reaching the north bank, and appreciating the worsening predicament of the remainder of the battalion, there was no time to waste as we set forward to locate the main road. Knowing we were behind British lines, it was a matter of getting the Indian firing stopped with all speed. The darkness of the night, and now with the rising moon, was no help as we set forth across the rugged countryside.

Hardly had we moved before Baxter turned to me and said, "Fitz, you'd better take command of the company".

I had my revolver in my left hand and a primed grenade in my right as I said, "But you're the Company Commander, you have the three pips on your shoulder".

"You take over the company. It's an order".

I had been made aware of his shortcomings, as he had won few friends in the short time he had been with the unit; like me, he had no knowledge of the country. He was a stranger to the men of 'C' Company, the nucleus of the present one, with problems in communication. I realised that Baxter was 'sold out', and, for whatever reason, was incapable of command.

"Supposing I don't?" I said.

"You'll be shot".

I thought these to be brave words from a man who looked more like a frightened mouse, particularly as it would have been the easiest thing in the world for me to have shot him as he spoke. And I very nearly did.

"In those circumstances, I'll take over. But I want no interference from here on".

Douglas Haigh, having listened in silence to this little altercation, turned to me and said, "Here, Fitz, take a swig of this."

"That's two rapid promotions you've had". He offered me a drink from the spare water bottle he was carrying.

"Thanks", I said, as I took a good mouthful, thinking it to be water, only to explode as the neat rum scorched the back of my throat. My empty stomach wanted to retch and throw up, but there was nothing to throw, and my head spun. I felt far worse than before.

"I'll back you", said Douglas, as we moved off.

I had not gone five yards, however, before falling and sliding eight or ten feet down a small *nullah,* (crevasse) in the ground. The boil on my arse burst to form a big, sticky, congealed mass. It was by far the most scaring part of the night; I feared the boil turning septic and the loss of my leg, or worse. But there was no time for self-pity.

Having been delegated to command, I was now leading the company, and there was no time to be lost if we were to help Chadwick and the reminder of the battalion struggling in the *chaung.* Holding bayonet scabbards once again, we continued northwards with added caution, seeking the main road. After about one hour, we halted and listened. Arriving near the road, we could hear, once again, the gentle rattle of harness, and deduced that mules were standing close by. We had no idea whether they belonged to friend or foe, and required to find out.

There was no particular reason why it should be so, but when I asked for two men, it was Danny Lobben and Jacko, who had seen fit to stay with me, who now came forward. "Fix your bayonets! Quiet!"

The three of us moved forward to examine the road. There were a number of mules, with carts, all pulled well into a small copse of trees on the side nearest to our position. Two men were stretched out, asleep on the ground, with legs going in under the cart from the back.

"There are two blokes under the cart. Put your bayonets to their throats, and if they don't speak English, bayonet them!" I said, quietly as possible. We crawled forward, the heavenly twins each taking a throat as I gently shook one of the men by the shoulder. We did not want undue noise.

"Phwat the –? Who the –? Holy Mother of God! What the f------ hell's up?" said the man. With such eloquence, I realised this was no Japanese.

"Put your bayonets away!"

"What's your unit?"

"We're 1st Inniskillings, attached to Brigade Headquarters".

"Good. Where's your Brigadier?"'

"In the field on the far side, a few yards down the road".

"Thanks! Come on!'

By this time, it was about 2.30 a.m. and there was slight visibility as the moon began to show. The noise back in the *chaung* was unmistakable; heavy machine-gun fire, accompanied by exploding mortar bombs. It was clear, the remainder of the battalion was getting pounded from both sides, Indian machine-guns, and Japanese mortars.

Security at this Headquarters was nil. Finding the Brigadier was no problem; the nice, well-pressed white sheets on his camp bed standing out clearly in the middle of an open field. He was cosily bedded down, quite oblivious to the heavy firing a short distance away. I shook my first 'brass hat' by the shoulder, in the same manner as I had shaken the Inniskilling, but sparing him the bayonets, although I still had revolver and grenade to hand.

"Are you the Brigadier?" I didn't know his name.

"Yes, what's the matter?"

"Your troops are firing on the KOYLI Battalion, crossing the Yin Chaung. That's the firing going on now."

"I can't do anything about that at this time."

"Can't you get a message for them to stop?"

"No. There's nothing I can do at this hour."

"Useless twat!"

It was later, when I realised who he was, I regret not leaving him snuggled up in bed with my grenade for company. He would most certainly have been left nursing the hand grenade had I been aware at the time that he was Commander of 1st Brigade, whose troops were, "weakened and weary", as he said. No one would have known, and he wouldn't be missed.

Caught in the *chaung,* the remainder of the battalion became a target from both sides. Suffering casualties, they decided to avoid the swamp and return across the easier ground to the south bank. They took cover under the bank for the remainder of the night, and were locked between

British and Japanese guns. They were lucky as, once again, at first light on the following morning, there was the incredible escape route. Battalion H.Q. and one company crossed the *chaung* without a shot being fired. Chadwick was unaware that the third company, under Green, had gone missing in the night. Maybe the North Star had moved for them, as they finished up going west, to the bank of the Irrawaddy River.

Amongst the tragic losses at Yin Chaung was Lieutenant Quartermaster Taffy Phillips. He had chased every possible avenue for food, ammunition, and clothing, winning the esteem of all. Halfway across the expanse, Taffy collapsed and died of a massive heart attack. There was no possibility of help, and he remained in the sandy vastness. All regretted the tremendous loss of a man lacking nothing in courage, particularly when it came to dealing with dithering superiors.

Three companies from the 1st Indian Brigade crossed the *chaung,* to the position they should rightfully have been on the previous day. Fortunately, Green's company was located and escorted across the *chaung,* to join with us at the set milepost, and for us to re-form once again, as a more depleted battalion.

It seemed a long time between the morning of 11 April and the morning of 15 April. It was incredible to think of the miles covered by day and by night, marching, running and pushing. And for one whole day we had been virtual captives, locked in a village behind Japanese lines. We knew that every man had done all that had been asked of him, in what now seemed to be the only place in the world for a man to be.

Throughout the four days of activity, I felt the change. From being a very insecure junior, I knew that I had come of age, and that I was 'all man'. I had been fired on by machine-guns, and felt no fear, just the soft warm wind on my cheek. I had shot saboteurs at Chauk. I had shot, and killed, the first two Japanese I had seen in my sights, and loved it. My endurance and leadership had been tested and not found lacking. Apart from taking over from one senior whose nerve had gone, I had 'bollocked' two senior officers for their indifference and incompetence. In the short period of my involvement in the war, I had realised that my survival rested in my own hands, and it was to be 'survival of the fittest'. I now had no regard for seniority of rank; for a man to order me, he must justify the action.

17

MAGWE

For a man to command others, particularly in war, he needs to win their esteem. Without that, he may 'have command' and pronounce orders, but will not command with belief, or be followed by the heart. As it says on the Crown and Colonial Territories Memorial, in Westminster Abbey, 'Whosoever will be chief among you, let him be your servant'.

In our predicament, each man knew that he was on his own. If wounded or sick, he could expect no help. There was no doctor, and no man could expect to be carried or assisted by men already at their limit. Every man had one interest; that of self-preservation, and woe betide any aggressor. To shoot and kill a man in these circumstances was not difficult. Each new day was the one a, 'slant-eyed bastard from the East', might put a bullet through one's head.

Crossing Yin Chaung in daylight, with minimum harassment; the main part of the battalion, and Green's 'lost company', joined us at the ten-mile post. All assembled, we set forth across country, deployed as a wide, irregular formation, in order to present as difficult as possible a target for attacking aircraft. The nine or ten miles across dusty fields were exhausting, but had rewards. Arriving at the small town of Magwe in the early afternoon was like having a surprise Christmas. Although local Burmese had already raided the food dump, vacated by the Royal Air Force, sufficient food remained to provide a meal, and there was fresh water in the wells to replenish water bottles, and have a good drink. My boil had, amazingly, healed up cleanly, as though nothing had happened, although the sticky underpants were to stay on for weeks to come, with never a time to wash them. It was good to have a brief period of 'alert rest' after the strenuous nights and days of activity.

The afternoon peace of Magwe was shattered by a single shot. C.Q.M.S. Gledhill was busy sorting rations in the back of a three-ton lorry, he had acquired by some means. As he bent down, he was shot and killed. After a quick search, revealing no other person about, it was accepted that a hidden Burmese must have taken a random shot. Another view was that this was the settlement of yet another old score by one of the unit. The remainder of the day, and night, was quiet.

Peace did not reign for long. Bruce Scott appeared, like the proverbial bad penny, and at 5.30 a.m. on the following morning, 16 April, 'Christmas' was suddenly over. Within minutes we were on our way, carrying in hand whatever food we could grab, eating as we made the dash back, once again, 'down the road'. Passing Indian and Burmese troops of 1st Brigade, who were streaming north like men demented. Japanese forces had crossed Yin Chaung in the night, as we had done twenty-four hours earlier. They had penetrated Burmese and Indian positions.

With men returned at Magwe, and a rapid battalion reorganisation, forming two companies of between 60 and 70 men each, from the previous three companies, appeared to give a new zest and confidence to all. The few hours of rest, a meal and, most of all, water, revitalised the battalion. 'Buggered about' by Bruce Scott as we were, and constantly short of ammunition, this was a battalion seeking to get at the Japanese.

It transpired that Gurkhas of 1st Brigade were withdrawing to Magwe; once again on transport, they were to travel along the road we had followed, the part that traverses east to west. The Japanese were known to be moving north on foot, which meant they would be astride the road, some time before the Gurkhas arrived. Uncertain of the exact point at which the Japanese would cross, following our 7 mile dash, we deployed widely, taking positions facing south. Speculative as it was, it proved absolutely accurate. Within minutes, the Japanese advance was seen approaching with some haste. No Japanese was going to pass this territory, now full of Yorkshire grit and determination. Our resolve was to get a Japanese with every shot, and make every precious bullet earn its keep.

The selection of position was perfect, similar to the one adopted earlier near Migyaungye; open ground to the front and light scrub and bushes for cover. It was obvious that the Japanese expected no opposition as they advanced on a wide front with the usual two Burmese guides, easily identified in their native *longyis*. They were walking alongside a tall Japanese commanding officer. With no time for digging in, experience had trained our men to adopt good firing positions, behind any clump of stubble or bush.

The Japanese were chattering amongst themselves as they neared us, 60/40 yards away. Corporal, 'Geordie' Bareham had not been battalion marksman for nothing; he dropped the Japanese Commander and the two guides before they blinked. From that range, no man could miss, and what Japanese remained withdrew at speed, a number of dead left on the ground. It was estimated, that about 100 Japanese were killed or wounded, from a force of less than 200; the remainder scuttled back for cover, and possibly to reorganise, as we had done at Magwe.

Within minutes, Japanese mortar bombs began their whistling descent from on high, with no ill effect. Their aim was well off the mark, and we realised they must be short of ammunition as only a few intermittent bombs were fired. A Japanese spotter plane patrolling in advance of their troops, indicated that there must be ground markers, showing their forward positions. The plane had little effect on our actions, other than to ensure alertness all round.

It was a little time before the first transports, full of Gurkhas, began tearing past, exactly as they had done near Migyaungye, with the driver's foot hard down on the accelerator. The Gurkhas were once again delighted to be having a fast ride on a 'motorcar', oblivious of the perilous reception the Japanese were arranging. Our two depleted companies had gone in, almost unarmed, and thrown down the challenge to an advancing Japanese column; but it was the Japanese, with their dislike of direct attack, that suffered, withdrew, and held off. This was one occasion when the Burmese guides did not know their way around the defences, and paid the price.

'The yellow-bellied bastards won't come when we're ready for 'em!' the men often complained; but here, they did come, and they got hurt. The feeling of exhilaration was terrific, and the adrenalin flowed. I knew I was among real men, the ones who had not walked off at the oilfield.

We had insufficient ammunition to follow-up the attack. It was like winning the war, to arrive in a defence position before the enemy, and then knock hell out of him. We had the satisfaction of seeing truckloads of Gurkhas pass safely, once again, smiling and waving, totally unaware of the vital action only a few minutes beforehand.

The last of the Gurkha transports had departed some time ago, but we remained *in situ,* awaiting orders. Once again, Bruce Scott failed to appear with orders for withdrawal; he could find us when needed, but not when we were in trouble. Geoffrey Chadwick demonstrated his usual reluctance to show initiative and make a move. It required one of the officers at Brigade Headquarters to suggest that it was time for withdrawal, and it was late morning before we started the move out of the defence position, marching north in the heat with some urgency. It was known that the main Japanese push was being made by encirclement, with assault concentrated on both the airfield at Magwe, which they were now approaching, and the oilfield further north, at Yenangyaung.

This was open country with loose sandy soil, and the temperature was over 120° F. Tremendous heat reflected from the hot soil. Boots were burning feet, sweat carried salt down the face and eyes, and moisture darkened the yoke of shirts as we trekked through the lifting dust. Beards were flourishing on the darker men, as dust settled on the sweated strands.

Passing close by the fringe of Magwe airfield, my feet were caught in small wiry roots in the soft sandy soil, and pulling at the roots, I found them to be cultivated groundnuts. Quick fingers soon filled pockets in the ensuing scramble before we moved on; as Wavell had said, 'They must live off the land'. This one pocket of nuts was all the sustenance I received, 'off the land'; still, I was in compliance with the order. Nearby, on the very edge of the airfield, were a number of bamboo houses occupied by a few villagers; probably former employees of the R.A.F.

In passing, I noticed the exceptional depth of two protective slit trenches, at about eight or nine feet. Looking into them, I was surprised to see, buried in the bottom, the tops of rifle cases. They looked new, and might possibly still hold rifles. We were tempted to shoot the villagers, but with women and children among them, they were given the benefit of the doubt. They may have been loyal workers for the R.A.F. and may eventually have used the arms on the Japanese. With little opportunity to use them on the British.

Halting a little further on, at Kantha village, our divided companies joined up, after conducting a tactical encircling movement. Resting awhile before moving off to cross the next objective, yet another *chaung,* the Kadaung Chaung, seven more rough miles to the north. With Japanese aircraft patrolling incessantly, and little cover from trees in this central plain, traversing hot sandy fields parallel to the road for about two hours, crossing the Kadaung Chaung between Magwe and Yenangyaung at nightfall. After a further half-hour of marching into the sheltering dark of night, we halted to form a defence perimeter: – Having had almost 25 miles of running and marching in intense heat, through burning sand, and a heavy skirmish with the Japanese, all in the cause of extricating some fine Gurkha soldiers.

18

THE QUEEN

Magwe was vacated on 17 April, and left to the Japanese column, which halted at this point to consolidate. Having taken the airfield, they needed to nurse their wounded and bury their dead; by tradition, as rapidly as possible after each action. Having delayed the advancing enemy column for a while, we managed to take a most uncomfortable rest late in the day. In the torturing heat with the sun sapping the body, water became the need above all others, and we never forgot the value we placed on it at this time. (Sixty years later, my former colleagues and I find this the worst, or best remembered, period of our lives; values were set that were to shape everything to follow. Money had no value; it could buy nothing, a totally useless commodity; cool clear water was what we coveted).

Strict wartime security prohibited mention of even the humblest of troop movements, and certainly not a unit location. It was criminal to discuss deployment of any kind; posters, press and wireless repeated the slogan; – 'Careless talk costs lives'. It was, therefore: – (In view of Churchill's 1st April 'abandonment signal' to Roosevelt), a considerable departure, on 17 April 1942, when *The Times* newspaper headline proclaimed, "New positions held on Irrawaddy". "Magnificent Action by the KOYLI", "Days of fierce fighting", and "KOYLI's rearguard action", and continued:

> *"The following report on the situation in Burma was issued by the War Office yesterday. Our forces, who withdrew from Migyaungye, have established positions near Yin Chaung north of Minhia, covered by the The Kings Own Yorkshire Light Infantry, who for days have fought a magnificent action at Myingun".*

Comment of this nature was sufficiently rare to bring congratulations from our beloved Colonel-in-Chief; Her Majesty the Queen, no less, (now the Queen Mother). Her wireless message was despatched from London on 24 April:

"As your Colonel-in-Chief, I have learned with pride of your splendid fight in recent days. You are all much in my thoughts and I send my best wishes to all ranks!"

The message did not reach the battalion until five months after dispatch. We were safely back, re-mustering in Assam, at beautiful Shillong, when receipt of the delayed royal message was announced. Such a delay to this unusually high-powered communication, seems to emphasise our isolated, abandoned situation. In calling us, 'a Battalion', the War Office speculators, in concocting their own version of events, obviously considered us to be at full strength of over 500, whereas we were in fact little more than 100 Yorkshiremen; 'The Best of British!'

No man was in doubt; the army in Burma was forgotten and written off. Desperation and expediency ruled all action; there was no such thing as overall strategy, it was simply a matter of living from day to day, hour to hour. Water and food, – in that order, – overruled all else, and any man standing in the way of them would be shot without question.

Miserable hours spent near the Kadaung Chaung came to an end in the late afternoon. We were detailed as Divisional rearguard, and moved off, towards Yenangyaung oilfield; once again, off the road, trudging through dry, dusty fields for four or five hours. It is easy to expend energy at the rate extracted by those temperatures, when there is no input of food or water. Men lost weight, day by day, growing gaunt and desperate.

After the excitement of recent days, this action became a long, boring slog to nowhere. Morale sagged. Any man with a cigarette to smoke was instantly surrounded by six or seven smokers, all seeking 'a puff'; anything to feel something entering the stomach.

There were additional problems for those of us new to the battalion. There was time to think, and for each of us new officers to wonder, 'How am I getting along with my men? Do they have confidence in me? Do they respect me? Am I a good officer?' Thinking in this way gives one the wrong priorities; an officer must assess matters from the other side. 'How do the men get along with me? Do I have confidence in them? Do I respect them?' It was a relief to me to find that I loved and respected these men.

I knew that I would do anything for them, and in turn, they had noted my conduct in recent action. I had a feeling of great confidence. Bareham was a cynical but fine soldier, and his cynicism was aimed a long way above me, the new boy. The greatest vote of acceptance by Bareham, Benny Mee, and the squad, was my overhearing their conversation at one halt, when doubts were being expressed, and reassurance sought. A question was raised, and it was good to hear the response 'Fitz will see to it'. Not 'Mr Fitzpatrick', or 'that pillock'; 'Fitz' was good enough for me, although whenever one of them addressed me personally, it was politely, as 'Sir'.

The ties of my birth, my name, my schooling, coupled with the bigotry of my Catholic religion and the history of my youth, had made me more proud to be Irish, rather than English. The hostility of the times, Protestants against Catholics, only strengthened my feelings towards the Irish cause, to the extent that, had I been approached in the pre-war years; – I would willingly have become a most ardent and active I.R.A. member. A Yorkshireman, born of an Irish mother, and a Mayo-man at heart, I had not waited to be called up on the declaration of war; I enlisted freely to serve the King and a country I loved. There was never a doubt about where my place was in this war, and now, benefiting from my Irishness, I was putting the lot together, busy proving myself a proud Yorkshireman.

From Maymyo, Governor Dorman-Smith continued to demonstrate his remoteness, and his ignorance of the true situation. In his 17 April 'message of the day', to Foreign Secretary Amery, in London, reporting, 'Military situation is far from cheerful', is one of the understatements of the century. He also stated that he was moving north from Maymyo to Myitkyina, the last operative airfield. One can only imagine that Churchill received the news from Amery, 'with no great comfort'. Dorman-Smith could know little of forward military activity, treated as he was, with indifference, in Maymyo, by senior Army Command, who themselves knew little of the happenings in which we, and they, were involved. It was difficult to know what was happening even within one's own unit. Events would overtake plans by the hour, and action was mostly dictated on the spur of the moment.

General Alexander, meanwhile, continued badgering General Stilwell and the Chinese, seeking to extricate the British Army from the Yenangyaung area, and across the huge Pin Chaung, immediately to the north of the oilfield. This area was clearly the objective, and next point of major attack by the Japanese. Stilwell was no help; – ever ready to denigrate and deny the British, he regarded Alexander as having got 'the wind up', and stated that there was, 'no fight left in the British'. The Americans at the time, were continuing to let Russia do their share of the fighting.

Eventually, Stilwell, having received the O.K. from Chiang Kai-shek, his puppet-master, promised a division of Chinese troops. A signal of recognition was agreed, whereby each force would identify itself on meeting, by holding rifles 'above the head and in the horizontal position'.

The Chinese were to move south, and at the Pin Chaung, cross to the west side of the road. From this position, they were to attack, and dislodge the occupying Japanese from Yenangyaung town. With the objective achieved, they were to withdraw back to eastern Burma. The attack was agreed to commence at 4.00 a.m. on the morning of 19 April, timed to coincide with 'first light'. Or so we thought.

19

YENANGYAUNG BURNS

Nightfall, following the long march from Kadaung Chaung to the oilfield, was memorable. Diminutive miracle-worker, Quartermaster Dogger Riley, proved himself a worthy successor to Taffy Phillips, lost so drastically in the Yin Chaung. Waiting by the roadside, he welcomed the battalion.

'Come on, get this inside you. The bastards have got round us once again. You're going to need this.'

Dogger had uncovered a few sacks of beer, hidden on a mule cart; fifteen to eighteen bottles to a sack, sufficient for one bottle per man; plus some bully beef and vegetables. Also setting up a stew in a couple of dixies. Best of all, he had obtained water from a 2/R.T.R. tank squadron. Two 40-gallon petrol drums had been filled with water, the fact that the drums had not been burned out in order to clear the petrol was of no consequence. In taste, it was like drinking neat petrol, but what mattered that? It was water, wet, as much as one wanted, and we could fill water bottles. In pulling Dogger from the swamp, Danny had done a fine thing.

At Magwe, Dogger had managed 'Christmas in April', it appeared that this meal might be the 'Last Supper'. The mess tin of food was like a banquet. However, the joy of the feast was unfortunately tinged with bad news. The Japanese now occupied the oilfield; – by an outflanking movement into Yenangyaung. This news meant that we were positioned, once again, behind the Japanese front line assault force. Dogger was right; – we were going to need the food.

Acting as rearguard, we were covering the possibility of enemy attack from the south, and, at the same time, allowing BurDiv to establish forward defensive positions. All now changed, it was 'Action', superseding 'Plan'. Our role was changed, as BurDiv had now to consider the daunting prospect of launching an attack on the Japanese, they were ensconced in numbers on the oilfield, and occupying Yenangyaung town.

As ever, Japanese commanders had avoided direct assault. What remained of the Burma Army was now firmly enveloped in a Japanese sandwich, the encircling assault force having secured the valuable oilfield. At the same time, approaching from the south, and now re-formed, was the attack column we had shot up the previous morning. BurDiv was ensconced between two Japanese columns, and truly in the killing fields, a prime position for 'annihilation', as promised in the Saigon radio broadcast one week earlier.

The terrain around the oilfield is hard rock, and brown earth, baking hot, like bricks new from a kiln; burning feet through the soles of one's boots. There was no shelter or shade as we slowly inched our way around the rough track to the east of the town, and oilfield. The Burma Oil Company euphemistically chose to call the track, a 'by-pass road'. We were, to say the least, most uncomfortable. It was impossible to sit or squat on the hot ground, and drinking from water bottles filled from petrol drums only increased the thirst; there were no white chlorinating, or blue taste tablets, with which to treat the water.

Unaware of our assisting oilfield officials in rendering the oilfield useless, some senior army officer had ordered destruction by arson, and it was ablaze. Temperatures, well in excess of 125°F were added to by acrid smoke and noxious fumes; spreading in all directions from burning oil tanks, derricks, and pumphouses. Crude oil, spilling over and flowing down crevasses, was burning along the Irrawaddy River, and in the ditches and drains of Yenangyaung Town. Oily soot and dust falling from the sky clung to sweaty shirts. Breathing foul air scorched the throat. The combination of smoke and heat haze made one feel the earth was dancing a rhumba; everything appeared to wobble. Each man felt himself already halfway to hell, the hell painted so vividly by missionaries.

It was ludicrous to be British troops in this situation, in the forefront of action, eager and hungry for battle, in what might be the last throes of a fatal combat, and almost eager to die. Depleted to less than one quarter of battalion strength, desperately short of ammunition and all material things, extermination seemed inevitable. For Churchill and the Army Council to hear of the Burma Army survival, following their discardment for the past three weeks, must have been a 'possible' source of great embarrassment? It would have been easy for Churchill to make a parliamentary announcement: – 'On the loss of the brave and gallant British Army in Burma', than to attempt helping in any way. At this stage, as for months past, he could do absolutely nothing to alleviate the situation.

Continuing edging our way around the ill-formed, rugged and rutted 'by-pass', Regimental Sergeant Major Gerry Delaney appeared. He was standing quietly, over to the left. Detecting a slight silly little grin, I spoke to him, and noticed there was a tiny stagger, and a slur in his speech. I was green with envy: – "You rotten bugger! Where the hell did you get the booze?"

"Didn't you get some, Sir? There was some in a bungalow back there". The lucky sod! I could not believe a man could look so smug and contented in the present circumstances, but I was never to forget the timing of his stroke of luck. It would have been wonderful to be, 'stoned-drunk in hell'.

Throughout the day, sporadic action and firing could be heard from ahead. The Japanese had established a roadblock, at the crossing point for the massive Pin Chaung, two or three miles to the north of Yenangyaung Town, near the village of Twingon. One could only deduce the route of the main Japanese force approach; – possibly using the river coming up west of the oilfield, and into the town. Held passive on the 'by-pass' throughout the heat of the day, we could only guess at developments. Moving forward at dusk, it was soon dark, and we formed a rough perimeter to the north-east side of the oilfield, around the single hill feature, Point 512.

The night temperature contrasted greatly with the baking heat of the day, and with the cold penetrating the body, sleep was no more than a catnap of a few minutes. Flames from the burning oilfield illuminated the skies with orange, red, purple, and green. Spasmodic bursts of gunfire ensured that one was alert throughout. Nothing of the shooting, fires, or the cold worried me anything near so seriously as the penetrating, variable-pitched and constant buzz of mosquitoes, the dreaded carriers of malaria. It was odd to think that a nice clean, small bullet hole would be preferable to a nasty little sting from the malaria-carrying gnat.

Dawn of April 19, (was it Easter Sunday?), started with increased activity, as enemy artillery and small arms fire fell around Hill 512. Firing was intermittent, and at a steady rate, indicating a shortage of ammunition supplies to the Japanese. Shooting of this kind did little damage; it was the occasional hiss and crack of mortar fire, with the burst of shrapnel, which caused bodies to drop defensively to the ground. Fortunately, Japanese mortar shells must have been in even shorter supply than small arms ammunition, and were well spaced between shots.

Throughout the night, there had been a measure of panic amongst the few Indians, and the rapidly diminishing number of Burmese troops, all taking cover inside Point 512 perimeter. Many had broken from the Japanese-occupied western side, to establish themselves within our battalion area. By chance, we found 512 to be close to the Japanese-held roadblock. With one British battalion, and a mix from Indian and Burmese units, along with refugees, the total strength in the vicinity of Hill 512 was considerably less than 500 men, three quarters of them, totally unreliable, and many unarmed, merely seeking protection within the KOYLI position. Most settled in a small hollow below the hill.

Frantic for water, some 'itinerants' attempted to crack the six-inch cast-iron pipe that crossed the hollow. They were encouraged by seeing odd drops of water falling from a small leak in a joint. Some attempted cracking the pipe with rifle butts, others attempted firing bullets; the pipe was unyielding and the polished glaze remained intact. One of the Indian troops got the scare of his life, when opening a handkerchief containing sugar he had stashed away. He must have fastened the package in the dark, as out popped a three-inch long white scorpion; the man screamed and ran as the scorpion scurried away.

Previous attempts, by the Inniskillings, to dislodge the Japanese, by attacking the Twingon roadblock from the north had failed. One company of 'Skinns', mistakenly thinking a Japanese column to be the long-expected Chinese, were taken prisoner, to a man, and all were herded into Yenangyaung town. Totally unaware, and regardless of the unfortunate Inniskilling action, and hearing nothing of any orders, I felt that some early move must be made to clear the blockage; otherwise, with the Japanese in absolute control, our unit must surely perish.

Alexander, having earlier escaped the roadblock to the south, was no doubt remaining in Maymyo; we received no order from him or his subordinates. Without orders, Chadwick would dither, and eventually seek a collective opinion; – but there was no time for that. My concern was self-preservation, to get myself out of a hole, and I must do it my way. We were cut off, and denied, the crossing point of the massive Pin Chaung. It had 20 foot perpendicular walls, and several hundred yards wide. The enemy-held crossing point was several hundred yards to our west, along the Chaung. Recent experiences had taught me, there would be no 'Command' orders, or senior control, in such a situation. The fat was well and truly in the fire, and there was no possibility of help. All were now equally desperate, and contained within a zone of death.

This was the moment of truth, and I considered the options. Do I die here doing nothing, or do I die doing something? The answer was simple: – You do something! I put the idea to Steve, who was close by with his platoon, and, along with our two depleted platoons, of nine and ten men respectively, we began reconnoitering along the rim of the *chaung,* simply to find out what was happening. Advancing along the southern lip of the *chaung,* and deployed across a 50 yard frontage, we moved towards where the roadblock was reportedly sited. Anticipating heavy resistance, we were convinced that the Japanese had moved in strength, in order to take this strategic objective.

Advancing steadily across the rough undulating ground, I looked down the 20 foot sheer drop into the base of the Pin Chuang. What I saw there was a sight of chilling horror. There below, in perfect training manual formation, as an inverted 'V', was a section of Inniskilling Fusiliers. The numbers one and two on the Bren gun were in position at the apex of the V, with five men fanned out on either side, in the flat sandy soil. There was no response to calls; they were all dead, and there was no sign of a mark on them. It was impossible to know what had killed them, except to speculate that a mortar shell, or grenade, had landed in their midst. What was surprising was that they should be in such a vulnerable situation in the open flat expanse of the Chaung, at the foot of a sheer cliff, and caught in this manner.

To have been detailed to patrol in such an open expanse of ground, only emphasised the inexperience of the 'Skinns' officer during the action. To have time to deploy and adopt such perfect formation, with all weapons directed towards the north, indicated that they had identified a target. The killer was certainly not a random missile, a shell or aircraft bomb. Our two platoons could do nothing for them, lest the enemy had the position covered from the northern bank, and were now cynically using the dead as bait. As with our own men killed in action, we left them and moved on.

This was a desperate situation; all were in no doubt that we would die in a similar manner, should the Japanese continue to block and cover the crossing point. Knowing the Japanese to be responsible for the Inniskillings' deaths, Steve and I became more determined to continue with all speed, attack the blockage and clear the Japanese, rather than give them the opportunity of destroying ourselves and BurDiv.

I had learned a lot in the few short weeks, and much of the seniority, rank, title, or appointment was of no significance, if it did not meet immediate life-saving requirements. There were too many instances of failure; three generals, Smyth, Hutton, and McLeod, had been sacked for incompetence and kicked out of Burma. Alexander had become captive and cost beloved Abe his life. Bruce Scott had lost, and failed our battalion time and again. Commanding Officer Keegan had got himself wounded unnecessarily, and Tynte lasted less than two hours. Bill Riddell and Tim Watson had been left to rot by a brigade major. Throckmorton had got himself lost, and failed to locate the battalion. Chadwick dithered over everything, particularly in the departure from Toksan village, whilst surrounded by Japanese. Baxter had threatened to shoot me if I refused to assume command of the company. Brigadier, 1st Brigade, had been indifferent as KOYLI were being, 'hammered'.

This tricky situation allowed for no hanging about; minutes of delay could prove fatal, and there were no orders for an advance. All knew that this was looking death in the face, but act we must. More determined than ever after seeing the dead Inniskillings, Steve and I continued advancing forwards towards the roadblock. At first, moveing in an irregular manner, fanning out, away from the edge of the Chaung, I took the left flank, on the slightly higher ground, Steve the right nearer the rim. I allocated the centre ground to marksman, Corporal 'Geordy' Bareham, ordering him to operate independently. Short as we were of ammunition, Bareham was given extra. No man had more than ten rounds; many had no more than two or three.

Things were indeed desperate. Adrenaline ran high in every man; the game was on, with the stakes as high as any man can make them. These self-selected men, the very best; each was present of his own free will, otherwise, he would have walked off with the vanished fifty-nine, several days beforehand. Our band were far beyond caring whether they lived or died; the sheer desperation of the situation allowed for no fear. With Sergeant Benny Mee driving like a tornado, whipping up movement, no man questioned the absurdity of going into battle with less than a full magazine; that's all he'd got!

Visibility was poor, with the combination of heat haze, smoke rising from the burning oil, and salty sweat running into the eyes as we moved forward. Advancing leapfrog fashion, from hillock to crevasse, moving from east to west, over undulating ground towards the road. The stench was horrible but who cared? Advancing for possibly three-quarters of a mile, we began to wonder about the strength of Japanese holding the position, when suddenly the situation was confirmed, and shooting started. This was the first response from the enemy, and we were about 400 yards short of the crossing; it was then that the Japanese opened up, firing their zippy small-bore bullets, very surprisingly, in single shot!

Steve and I glanced across at one another with great relief, and nodded. It was immediately clear to us that the Japanese did not have machine-guns, otherwise, they would have tried mowing us down, as they had done with the Inniskillings in the Chaung. Moveing relentlessly forward, in turn, first one, then the other. Me to the left, Steve to the right, each move was a dash at speed, and for no more than ten or twenty yards.

Equally affected by sweat and heat shimmer, the Japanese shooting was miserably erratic, compared to Bareham's marksmanship. We had to take full advantage of the weak Japanese shooting, although in no position to waste ammunition. Minimum covering fire was given from one platoon as the other moved forward, amounting to no more than three or four shots. Leap-frogging from hollow to hollow, each platoon edged closer to the enemy.

No situation can be more exhilarating than to know that one has the chance to live or die, according to one's own skill and guts. Bareham contained the Japanese firing, with a minimum of support from the rest of us, until it became clear, with another 50 yards to go, the Japanese were routed. Resistance at the roadblock ceased, and a force of about 20 Japanese dashed to the west side of the road, dragging off a few wounded, leaving several dead lying around by the road near the small circular police, or customs post. The final move, to occupy the road, and the small circular stone building, was the ultimate test. Had we cleared the Japanese? Was it a trap? Were we about to perish?

The whole action had taken less than one hour. It was midday and very, very hot: – Exhilarating beyond measure; KOYLI had won! There was no thought of the fact that two junior officers had acted independently and, with depleted platoons, conducted our own little war. We were now, in that most vulnerable of situations; – 'complete isolation'. We didn't care. This was teamwork at the highest level. Steve and I thanked one another, briefly, and immediately, set about preparing a rapid all-round defence, before longer-term action could be planned. Surprised to have survived, we could not delude ourselves: – We were sitting targets for artillery, aircraft, mortars, or machine-guns, and we knew it.

Fortunately, thanks to deplorable shooting by the Japanese, we suffered no casualties in the action, and morale was high. Any attempt at pursuing the enemy, we considered suicidal; territory to the west of the road was obviously, strongly held. We could see considerable movement as the retreating Japanese joined others, in what were clearly prepared defensive positions. We had neither numbers nor ammunition for pursuit; it was sufficient for us to contemplate defence arrangements, in anticipation of a counter-attack.

Having settled temporary defences, covering the road to north and south, Steve and I approached the small building. It was prominently sited on a small hillock, and overlooked both the road and the Pin Chaung; little larger than a sentry box, about ten foot in diameter, it was either a police, or customs post. Approaching, with extra caution and suspicion, to within five or six yards, when four Japanese emerged, attempting to make a dash for freedom, to join their fleeing colleagues. They had no chance. Three of them were shot within yards, and as the fourth hesitated momentarily, he was pounced upon by Ray Elsworth, Steve's batman. One savage lunge with the bayonet as he yelled, "That's for Steady! You yellow-faced bastard!" (Elsworth's mate, Private Stead, had been hacked to pieces by Burmese *dahs* after the crossing of the Sittang River, in the early part of the campaign).

As the Japanese lay dying on the ground, Elsworth grabbed his haversack and pulled out a small marker flag; the white cloth with red circle containing names of the Japanese squad radiating from the centre, like rays of the sun. "I'm keeping this", said Elsworth, as he held it high. It was the first flag captured in battle from the Japanese, and we were proud of that. Elsworth used the small flag to cover his head and shoulders each night, against cold, and mosquitoes.

Our two, much depleted platoons, had dispatched a force of Japanese, killing several; ourselves suffering no casualties. We were in no doubt that supplied, and reinforced, the British could defeat the Japanese, but where were these essentials? This was the first occasion in the campaign that British troops had actually moved forward, in attack, on a prepared and held Japanese position. Other battles had been defensive, or essential counter-attacks.

This desperate offensive was an almost private affair, so private that it was never recognised, or brought to Churchill's notice, or recorded by the War Office. Not of their planning, Bruce Scott, Alexander and Wavell, remained unaware of it. So much was it out of Chadwick's, and others' hands, that it is not recorded in the official KOYLI regimental history. So little is the action known within the regiment, that when Ray Elsworth's widow handed over the flag, for display in the Doncaster-based KOYLI Regimental Museum, one of only two items captured from the Japanese; – it was relegated to a stock room, and remains so.

In the small stone building we found a large cooking pot, full of hot rice; there were also items of Japanese equipment, with sheets and blankets, which were obviously British loot. We were able to dole out as much rice as anybody wanted. A thermometer, hanging inside the building, recorded a temperature of 126° F. Steve and I remained isolated, in a state of quiet unease, and pondering on what action to take. We needed to alert Chadwick, and the battalion, to the open Chaung situation, and rapidly.

Suggestions of support, or assistance, at this time were treated with the greatest cynicism; we'd heard it all before. Bruce Scott's many promises of withdrawal, Australians? Cameronians? Assistance from 1st Brigade? A promised artillery concentration? All had come to nothing. As recently as that morning, the promised Chinese Army had failed to appear, and this had resulted, inadvertently, in the capture of an unwary company of Inniskillings, and the death of those stranded in the Chaung. The latest rumour was that; – 'the Chinese are due to appear at four o'clock'. Nobody knew whether that meant morning or afternoon, English time or Chinese time. The plan, as reported, was that 'BurDiv are to remain on the east side of the road, as any Chinese advance will be down the west side, as previously arranged'. After all that had gone before, who was going to believe it?

Nothing was happening, certainly no Chinese appearance. The quiet unease continued; the air was full of expectancy, the tedious waiting made minutes seem like hours. Anticipating a rapid Japanese counter-attack, Steve thought to break the tedium by conducting a personal check on the Japanese. It seemed suicidal.

'Cover me, Fitz! I'll take seven men down this *nullah* opposite, to see how far I can go. Any shots, or sightings, and we come back.'

There was no time to call Steve a 'stupid prat', as the small party moved off, on the trail of departing Japanese. I was busy setting the remaining men in position to provide covering fire, in order to get Steve back, should the Japanese attack. Tension built as time passed into mid-afternoon. There was eventually, movement, over to the east, and back along the Chaung, far beyond the custom post. At a distance of about three quarters of a mile, a column of troops were crossing the Pin Chaung, moving to the north, and with two guides wearing the familiar *longyi* at their head. With the shimmering heat haze over the sandy Chaung, it was not possible to identify the nationality. It was however, a party of Japanese, being guided by two Burmans. We were delighted to see the column given one hell of a pounding by a flight of Japanese bombers, obviously thinking them to be our British force, attacking the roadblock. This deviation was watched with some pleasure, and it briefly eased tension in the defence position.

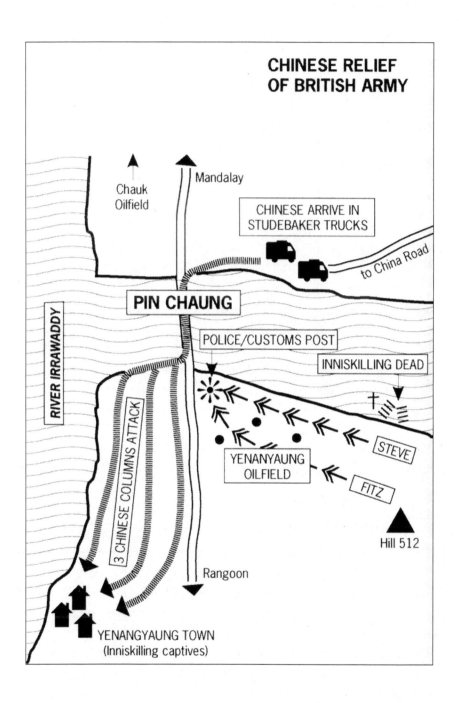

CHINESE RELIEF
OF BRITISH ARMY

Chauk
Oilfield

Mandalay

CHINESE ARRIVE IN
STUDEBAKER TRUCKS

to China Road

PIN CHAUNG

POLICE/CUSTOMS POST

INNISKILLING DEAD

RIVER IRRAWADDY

3 CHINESE COLUMNS ATTACK

YENANYAUNG
OILFIELD

STEVE

FITZ

Hill 512

Rangoon

YENANGYAUNG TOWN
(Inniskilling captives)

20

CHINESE SURPRISE

No handshake or ceremony was necessary on the north side of the Pin Chaung, as the big six-wheeled American Studebaker trucks, spewed out Chinese troops, seemingly, 'by the million'. The most spectacular show of the war was about to begin, one comparable with any medieval pageant, except this one was for real.

Assistance promised at four o'clock on the morning of 19 April, had arrived at four in the afternoon, and thankfully, the date was right. In view of the language barrier, there may have been problems, and uncertainties, in the communication of times and other messages. There was however, no problem with language in this unfolding spectacular. Witnessing the show was sheer magic, hardly one word was spoken, and troops moved rapidly into position, deploying into practised formations. As the magic unfolded, we were to witness an operation which fully justified Chiang Kai-shek's requirements, for 'a self-contained sector', for his forces' operation.

Each of the Studebaker trucks carried 50 or 60 equipped troops. Systematically, as men dismounted, they streamed across the huge flat expanse of the Chaung, to the west side of the road, and without further survey or reconnaissance, deployed rapidly over a wide front. Each man knew the job at hand, and the long-awaited Chinese support and attack on Yenangyaung had begun. The timing could not have been more apt. With a few men, Steve and I had cleared the pivotal Japanese outpost overlooking the Chaung, in which the Chinese would most certainly have been ambushed, and all British to the south, annihilated. This was the identical spot at which, two days earlier, the Japanese had captured a company of Inniskillings; they had crossed in the same manner as the Chinese.

From the vantage point of the stone building on the hillock, it was a rare treat to witness the assault. It was spectacular and efficient beyond belief, absolutely suited for the rough terrain around the oilfield. Most observation of action in war is restricted to only a few yards to right and left, whereas in this situation, I had a panoramic view of the whole disposition and action, as the Chinese set to the task. To Western eyes, the disciplined automation was astonishing; each of the three commanders in their colourful uniforms adopted pre-planned positions. Each, accompanied by a standard bearer carrying distinctive marker flags. Alongside the commander, was a young bugler relaying calls and messages, as troops moved speedily into their respective unit and formed behind the flag. There was no delay, and the whole contingent moved forward in unison. It was a three-prong attack; one column going westward, towards the Irrawaddy, one centrally, and the other by the road to our front.

The astonishing, and most amazing scene, was the follow-up 'B' echelon support contingent. Following immediately upon the heels of the troops; came camp followers, some older men, but mostly women, all with duties, carrying ammunition, cooking pots, medical aid, and rations, all loaded on the familiar bamboo poles, and balanced across the shoulders. Immediately the fighting units dismounted from the transports; they became totally self-sufficient, and independent; with no reliance on animal or mechanical assistance. This Chinese force had the ability of total self-containment. I was the sole British officer, along with my men, privileged to observe this rare spectacle; it was basic, primitive, and functional; – the perfect fighting machine for the conditions of Central Burma. Indeed, I was a most privileged officer.

The intensity of rifle and machine-gun firing increased immediately, as the Chinese started the advance, indicating the strength of build-up by the Japanese: – Obviously, in preparation for a counter-attack on our position. All hell broke loose as the Chinese swarmed forward, and further support troops arrived.

They, in turn, adopted similar formation, and advanced rapidly. Each independent contingent was equipped with flag, bugler and camp followers. The movement was like poetry, or a dance, with these highly disciplined troops.

As the Chinese advanced, I noticed a movement on the platform of an oil derrick to my front, and above the heads of the advancing Chinese, 40 or 50 yards away. This was immediately above the spot where Steve and his small party had gone down the crevasse; and now, embarrassingly extricating themselves from underneath the Chinese attack. Steve and his boys were directly in the line of assault, and almost walked over by the attacking Chinese. They were fortunate in suffering no casualties.

It took me only one shot to dislodge the Japanese observer from the oil derrick platform. Bareham took another Japanese off the next derrick, a little further along. The two signallers had obviously been reporting developments to the Japanese command.

No other person was so privileged as to see the two most spectacular shows of the war; – 'and both from seats of privilege'. When training as an officer cadet in August and September 1940, at 163 O.C.T.U. (The Artists Rifles), we were moved four miles from Shorncliff Camp to Folkstone, and with a most favoured position, accommodated in a goods wagons along Folkstone harbour pier. I watched, as pilots of the Royal Air Force, in Spitfires and Hurricanes, scattered the German Luftwaffe, in their Junkers, Heinkells, Stukas and other German aircraft. The action was known subsequently as the Battle of Britain. I was now witnessing, in Burma, this equally spectacular show of a superbly trained and drilled Chinese Army, moving like clockwork, to the bugling and signalling of the boys, and the calls of commanders.

As the noise of firing became more distant; – there was a realisation; the Japanese might be the ones in danger of; – 'being annihilated at the oilfield in Central Burma', contrary to the threat from Radio Saigon, eight days earlier.

The Chinese began to suffer casualties, and a steady flow of wounded individuals made their lonely way back along the road. We set up a reception point in the stone building, and did what we could to treat and dress the wounds of casualties, as they followed, one after another, with holes in arms, legs, and bodies.

Although, only twenty-two years of age myself, I thought the Chinese soldiers to be very young; they had the ethereal look of good porcelain. Wounded as they were, through the leg, chest, shoulder or arm, they could smile their acknowledgement, as British troops ripped the recovered sheets and blankets to make bandaging. Each of the wounded Chinese was delighted to see a friendly face, and to receive a helping of warm Japanese rice. They were soon on their way to rejoin the transports. Appreciative though they were of the medical assistance and food, no Chinese soldier would part with his short, lightweight rifle, not for the briefest of moments; one could look at the spotless weapons, but they never left the hands of those disciplined and heaven-sent soldiers.

Receiving a second, more noisy, rush along the road, we were surprised to find it to be a number of Irishmen, men of the Inniskilling Fusiliers. They followed the Chinese wounded. These men were visibly shaken and frantic, thirsty and hungry; they could barely speak, and showed signs of complete exhaustion. They devoured the rice handed to them, as bit-by-bit, their story unfolded. At this time, apart from having seen the unfortunates dead in the Chaung, we were completely unaware of the Inniskillings being in the vicinity. Two days earlier, a Company of Inniskillings had occupied the Pin Chaung customs post, and observed movement on the north bank. Advised of possible Chinese support, and the agreed signal of recognition, the company commander had displayed the rifle, held horizontal above the head.

On receiving acknowledgement by a reciprocal signal, he moved across the Chaung, in order to establish contact. It was only when the 'Skinns' were stretched out across the open flat sand, the oriental officer announced, in perfect English, – "I am a genuine Japanese officer. You are my prisoners". The Japanese either knew of the signal and the expected Chinese assistance, or they were quick-thinking enough to deceive Captain Murray, the company commander. The main body of the Inniskilling Company was stretched back across the open sand, and covered by hostile Japanese rifles and machine-guns. This left the company commander with no option but to surrender, or to be mown down as they stood. The company was disarmed, and escorted at bayonet point into the town of Yenangyaung. Denied food and water, they had been forced to carry water to Japanese troops occupying the oilfield, in temperatures of over 125°F.

The Japanese Commander, must have received instant information of Chinese developments from the two oil derrick observers. He immediately ordered the Inniskillings, along with Indian and Burmese prisoners, to be herded into the upper floor of the only two-storey building in the town. As the Chinese attack closed in on them, the Japanese ignited the building, and endeavoured to 'barbecue' the Irishmen, before the Japanese themselves were pushed back into defence positions. Many Inniskillings failed to escape the burning building. Survivors were badly shaken, and sought to escape up the road as rapidly as possible.

The Chinese withdrew shortly before nightfall, the movement being almost the exact reverse of the advance; quietly, they crossed to the north, and re-joined the transports. The spectacular operation had taken less than four hours, yet the consequences must have been devastating to the Japanese, and their prospect of annihilating the British Army were severely set back, with they themselves suffering many casualties. The Chinese losses, in an open frontal attack of this nature, must have been considerable, although we did hear of them suffering extra casualties in travelling to join the battle at Yenangyaung. Apparently, several of the fully-laden Studebakers, travelling at great speed, crashed, lemming-like, over a precipitous hairpin bend, in a mountainous section of the Burma-China road.

Both, General Wavell, and General Alexander, attempted to belittle Chiang Kai-shek; they expressed misgivings regarding the efficiency of Chinese forces. Wavell had obviously forgotten what soldiering was all about, whilst Alexander knew something about Guardsmen, but nothing about line or county regiments, which is what this kind of soldiering was all about. It takes a soldier to recognise a soldier, and when seen in action there was no doubt about the performance of this Chinese Army; it was excellent in its efficiency, and effectiveness, particularly in the exacting combat met with on that Burma oilfield

Unaware of the gallant 38th Chinese Division offensive, the remainder of the KOYLI battalion arrived at the customs post. They were also unaware of the independent attack conducted by Steve and me, with our two small platoons, which had made safe the ground for withdrawal. The Chinese would have suffered horribly had I not had the co-operation of Steve, and taken unilateral action to clear the Japanese from the roadblock. What is more surprising, is the fact that Wavell, Alexander, Slim and Bruce Scott, appear to have been in complete ignorance of the few short, and vital hours of superb Chinese action. It is an action that has never been recognised in British historical record, certainly not in the history of the two regiments involved, and is long overdue for acknowledgement by the British Government.

Moving off, crossing the Pin Chaung as though nothing had happened, into the cover of trees in a plantation that was not difficult to locate; one simply followed the scent of cooking soya sausages and vegetables. It was a collecting point with a treat; a field kitchen, erected by the wonder men of 2/R.T.R. The smell of cooking stew was like a magnet, instantly improving the bearing and morale of every man.

Aware of the effects of malaria and dysentery, seeing men delirious, shivering, vomiting and tearing their guts out, it was a relief to me at the customs post to have acquired a Japanese shoulder-slung haversack of light green material. I stuffed into this, one half of a grey army blanket, and half a white sheet. I covered myself with these each night, with the sheet over my head and blanket down below; the mosquitoes could buzz their heads off outside.

Sleeping that night with the blanket and sheet was no problem. At first light, however, I was awake, and accompanied by Benny Mee, and four men, we went back through the plantation. We were seeking stragglers, lost in the night, and also trying to ascertain whether the Japanese were crossing the Chaung in pursuit.

At the approach to the Chaung, Bill Kibbler, the leading man, signalled 'Halt!' On moving forward, a few yards out in the sandy bed, a short distance from the road cutting, I was surprised to see three stranded ambulances. The vehicles had obviously been freed during the Chinese assault. With all caution, and two men covering the approach, we advanced to the leading ambulance, to find once again, horror. Five men inside the ambulance were mutilated and hacked, as though with Burman *dahs,* and there was the familiar stench of death. It was the same story with each of the ambulances, all were full; it was hard to distinguish Indian, British, Gurkha, or Burmese; and all appeared dead,

Drivers and keys had vanished, and there was no time for delay in this exposed situation, as nothing could be done to help those casualties. We needed to be out, and away, in the minimum amount of time, and the three ambulances were too good to leave for the Japanese. Bayonets penetrated petrol tanks, and out of charity, the dead were spared the bone-scraping of the vultures; flowing petrol was ignited and the vehicles sent up in flames. It was only as we reached the top of the Chaung, that a piercing scream rang out from one of the ambulances. I made the sign of the cross as we silently walked on, back to rejoin the unit.

This had been one hell of an Easter weekend. How ironic that a Chinese Army, considered so ineffective by the Guardsman General, had so convincingly come to the aid of 'His' British Army, saving it from annihilation. It was becoming increasingly obvious that Bruce Scott considered us moribund, having failed to honour his promised evacuation, and there was no hope of further supplies of any kind. We were to depend on good fortune, to fall back on supply dumps, or to receive whatever rations the tank squadrons could scrounge, providing of course they themselves could be maintained with fuel.

21

MOUNT POPA

The eight days between Bruce Scott sending us south from Yenangyaung oilfield on 11 April to our return on 19 April seemed like a lifetime. And for some, it was the time of death. Casualties from Japanese action were few; it was the many debilitating sicknesses, now taking an increasingly heavy toll. Sickness indeed was becoming the greater enemy; with the constant tightening of belts the truth was evident. All men were weakening, and none could expect to be favoured. Sickness was no respecter of rank.

The battalion 'friend?' Brigadier Bruce Scott, had said, when sending us, "Down the road, once again!" – "KOYLI You've had enough. I'm getting you out of Burma", only for him to return four hours later, with neither food nor ammunition, to retract, saying, "I'm sorry KOYLI, I'll have to send you down the road, for the last time!" – That was some promise!

We had certainly 'been down the road'. We had returned, once again, after the gruelling eight days and nights of non-stop action, to the starting point at Yenangyaung. Maybe there was some significant undertone in Bruce Scott's phrase, 'for the last time.' It proved to be fatally so for Taffy Phillips, and an unknown number of others. It had been a bloody long road, and Bruce Scott did not bother coming back to say that we still had to travel, as best we could, probably the longest, and most arduous road of any British Army.

No senior commander could take credit for the actions of 2/KOYLI in the last eight hectic days. In truth, the 'top brass' in command, did not know where we were, or what was happening for most of the time, with companies, or parts of companies moving as best they could. Our situation was well illustrated when tanks, rather than wheeled transport, were 'sent down the road' with instructions 'to proceed south, as far as the Pin Chaung, and attempt to make contact with the KOYLI'. Fortunately, the attempt was very timely.

In order to make whatever ground they could, weak and sick members of the battalion were first to make early moves out of the night area. It was anticipated that the Japanese would follow up in force, once they realised the Chinese Army had withdrawn.

We had no idea of the strength of Japanese forces; they were thought to be considerable. It seemed however, in view of the lull in their activities, they had suffered heavy casualties, and possibly over-estimating our strength. They had problems of re-mustering, and awaiting replacements and reinforcements, thus allowing a little breathing space before we were to meet with them once again.

Tanks in Burma had a completely different role to that in Europe, or in the Western Desert. Operational manoeuvre space was mainly limited to roads and agricultural areas. They could not operate on the fissured ground of the oilfield, but how well the 2nd Royal Tank Regiment and 7th Hussars used that limited space to best effect, and how welcome they were. The 7th Hussars operated with 17th Division in eastern Burma, while 2/R.T.R. earned eternal gratitude, co-operating with 1st Burma Division, particularly when operating as transports, carrying nine or ten men, clinging on the outsides. They brought food, drums of water, and packs of 'Polo' and 'Victory-V' cigarettes, for the unfortunate smokers, while most of all, they boosted morale, and never hesitated to seek out and hustle the enemy, in suitable situations.

Tanks made a timely arrival to taxi strugglers as they began making their move to the north; it was essential to ensure that those in greatest need were given priority. About 40 men were loaded onto the tanks and despatched on their way. We of the remainder followed with care, marching defensively, and spread around on the road, and in the fields, travelling in anticipation and hope of further tanks arriving.

After the first hour, a second squadron of tanks arrived and lifted all but about 24 of us. This period of marching was one of alert suspense, and no rifle was slung over a shoulder; all were held at the port position, across the chest, with a round in the breach. This was known to be an area of intense Burma Nationalist hostility; also, having recently shot up Burmese at nearby Chauk, we fully anticipated some resistance from dissidents, most of them being former staff at Yenangyaung and Chauk oilfields.

Terrain in this agricultural part of central Burma is a little more flat and open, with cultivated land on either side of the road, and trees in the distance. We were making ground as rapidly as possible by remaining near the road, moving along both sides, well-dispersed in order to present a less vulnerable target. As usual, apart from the stream of ever-weakening refugees hustling along at the roadside, there was not a soul to be seen on the land. There were, however, sudden signs of movement across fields away to the right, and there were noises which indicated some unusual activity.

My operational plan for the move was simple and direct.

'In the event of any attempt to ambush, fix bayonets, charge, and assault the position, with every man in attack'.

Being desperately short of men and ammunition, hopes of survival depended upon total commitment, and a ruthless assault on any enemy or point of hostility.

Other than the 'own-goal' raid, in the air attack on the column of Japanese being guided in crossing the Pin Chaung on the previous day, Japanese air attacks had ceased throughout the last few days of inter-mixed conflict. Pilots could not differentiate between interlocking rival forces. We could now be easily identified, having broken away and travelling north on the road. Therefore, it came as no surprise when a flight of eight or nine planes did appear, after little more than one hour of marching. The aircraft came in low, dropped a few indiscriminate bombs, and strafed with machine-guns, to no effect. We continued, until once again, hearing the happy rumble of tanks.

The main party boarded the tanks, and I travelled with two bullock carts, recently accquired. We had travelled no more than four or five hundred yards when a hail of shots rang out from a belt of trees to the right of the road, much too far away to be effective. This was possibly the action of oilmen, turned Dacoits, or the column that had been strafed by their own Japanese aircraft, on the previous day. Relieved for the sick to be mounted on the tanks. The attempted ambush was certainly set just a little too late to have the desired effect.

We had no idea of the destination of the tanks, and it was a treat as they climbed the cooling heights of Mount Popa, about twenty miles north east of Yenangyaung. The large extinct conical volcano is, possibly, the geographical centre of Burma. Renowned as a home of hamadryad, the king cobra. This oasis of lush green grass, and cool clear water, was like being close to heaven, after the roasting, energy-sapping days on the oilfield. To partake of yet another soya-link meal, and enjoy a wash, to escape the torrid heat of the lower plain for a brief period, restored vigour and vitality.

Satisfied that the Japanese were delayed 50 miles distant, as a result of damage sustained in the Chinese attack, we had a welcome rest in this, the heaven of the snakes. Although to see two king cobras move across a green expanse, with heads held high, and at the speed of racehorses, was a bit off-putting; fortunately, moving away from our position.

Day temperature at this height (about 5,000ft) was much cooler than the plain. Smoke at that altitude was not easily visible in the dark, and a fire, started among some ruins in the dead crater, became the focus for a ritual. With our small companies suffering frequent changes of personnel, and being constantly widely deployed, it allowed no time for communication between individuals. We of the new officer intake were strangers to most of the older, pre-hostilities officers. They were the former juniors; all recently promoted, and considered themselves, – 'Very select!'

It was something of a surprise when two further tanks arrived later in the day, bringing with them, among others, two officers, recently promoted from being senior N.C.O.s within the battalion, and commissioned at the same time as Bootland, the man shot in the jaw some days beforehand. The newcomers had been convalescing, back at the peacetime barracks in Maymyo. In the cool of the evening, as the tanks returned to base, and with no general announcement, there had been a discreet evacuation of a few of the sick. Chadwick had personally selected the men for evacuation, arbitrarily and surreptitiously. Among those chosen were two company commanders, Captains Green and Baxter. The two newly-arrived, former senior N.C.O.s, now full two-pip lieutenants, were given command of Green and Baxter's Companies. Once the clear-out had taken place, and replacements were settled in, it was amusing to observe 'the hierarchy' revert to type, and the 'very select' officers became settled around the dying embers of the fire.

There was a new, immediate and vociferous 'pecking order', established among the 'new breed' senior officers, no matter how recently jumped-up, each one jockeying for prime position, close by the fire. In this semi-relaxed situation, we of the *Strathallan* draft of juniors were relegated, unnoticed, to the rear, and our opinions were not sought. The discussion round the fire was in no way concerned with, 'How the hell are we going to get out of Burma?' Confidently expecting Bruce Scott to honour this commitment, to evacuate the battalion from our present predicament, all was thought to be in good hands.

The subjects of discussion were future command, and promotion prospects, for those present, coupled with anticipated military decorations. Major Geoffrey Chadwick returned from convalescence, and assumed command at Yenangyaung, for the last two hectic weeks. With universal fireside acclaim, Chadwick was to receive the Distinguished Service Order. Military Crosses were considered the 'order of the day' for all regular, and supplementary reserve officers, remaining with the unit. The big problem was David Martin, who in a few short weeks was elevated from subaltern to the dizzy height of major, and for a brief period, he commanded the battalion. Active and inspiring, he had been to the fore, sparing himself nothing, and now he was self-appointed adjutant, and second-in-command to Chadwick. Not a shy man, he proposed himself for the Victoria Cross and there was considerable support. With no paper, pencil, or regular structure, it was difficult to define the adjutant duties. It did, however, preclude him having company command responsibility, for forty or fifty men.

What was not appreciated at the time; – In the British Army, particularly one already written off by Churchill, losers got nothing: – Certainly nothing was said of subalterns getting themselves killed, with unquestioned valour, as did Jimmy Ableson. Abe's valour merited the

Victoria Cross, not once was his name mentioned by those discussing merit around Mount Popa ashes. They never knew him.

Back in England, at about this time, a high-level subterfuge was concocted, a scheme designed to alleviate pressure on Churchill. His existence as Prime Minister, and head of the War Cabinet, was under threat. Successfully securing a parliamentary vote of confidence, this rang hollow as the press continued to decry constant losses, on land and at sea. Churchill sought to apply one of his principles; – 'Create a diversion!' With Malaya and Singapore gone, and now a discarded Burma Army, Churchill recruited Mountbatten as an aide, in seeking to deflect attention away from the lost Far East. Between them, they concocted a spectacular European show.

Seeking to get Burma off his back on 19 August, the Royal Navy and commandos, were launched on a 'mission impossible'. The two schemers dispatched excellent forces, attacking the German held, French dockyard, at Dieppe.

Several thousand good Canadians perished in the hopeless action. Churchill continued to insist that he remain behind the detailed planning. Dieppe was a suicide mission, doomed from the start for lack of simple intelligence. In undertaking the operation; – 'The Royal Navy was never going to fail Churchill'. Churchill got what he sought; a change of topic in the press and in parliament, – a diversion to get the opposition off his back. Survivors of the attack, few though they were, were rightly feted, and decorated for bravery. Dieppe was a show for Roosevelt's benefit, for him to use in conjunction with his reluctant promotion of American support for Britain. The extra bonus for Churchill, was that it also helped to put the problem of Burma, and the Far East, further to the back of British minds.

After two nights of rest on Popa, although ever alert in boots and equipment, the battalion was re-formed on the morning of 23 April. With a strength of less than 100 men, formed into three companies for the leapfrog march and ride. A move, authorised by wheeled transport, indicated that we might be in a safe area. Set to travel 30 or 40 miles north, to the nearby village of Taungtha. Assembling to move, the men realised that certain officers had departed, and made no secret of their objections to the favouring, arbitrary selection by Chadwick. Many men were in far worse physical condition than that of Green and Baxter the departed officers. Anger, inflamed by the constant inefficiency of command, was now at boiling point, with the increasingly hostile mood of the men, expressed in no uncertain manner. Favouritism amongst officers, was seen as, 'status inequality', totally unacceptable in our dire circumstances. No man could expect favours, and vehement voices were raised in objection, particularly by men with long-suffering 'muckers', men struggling, day by day, for survival.

Of necessity, incompetence of officers had been tolerated up to this point, so long as hope of survival existed. Now tolerance had cracked, hostility was further inflamed by the introduction of the two recently-commissioned, former N.C.O's, as replacements for Green and Baxter. The two men were regarded as scroungers, by those with whom they had been, in turn, private soldiers, corporals, and sergeants, and who knew them only too well as persistent bullies, particularly to recent conscripts. Both had a proclivity for young boys, from the villages and bazaars, and they were considered malingerers whilst at Maymyo. They were the least popular of men.

Much was now changed; – a disregard for discipline, and no man considered himself subordinate to another. In a desperate situation, anger was directed inwards, men with sick comrades confronted and harassed Chadwick over his actions. It was now, Chadwick realised that his life was in danger, and that he could be easily disposed of. Challenged and abused, fearing for his life, Chadwick made a decision no infantry commander should be required to make. He appointed Private, 'Geordie' Bill Tighe, to be his personal bodyguard.* He was instructed to remain, at all times, within ten yards of Chadwick.

Returning to the central plain from the cool of Mount Popa, the instant dry arid heat felt even more intense, with the choking dust of the road flavoured with the putrescent stench of death, sucked into the backs of the three-ton trucks. The slow journey seemed endless; dead bullocks and carts blocked the narrow road. Live bullocks with carts, and the

---

* 'Geordie' Bill Tighe corroborated this detail on 15 September 1996, at the parade of veterans at Eden Camp, Malton

ever-present stream of refugees, slowed down progress to walking pace. Every few yards, vultures and hawks cleaned up the bones of families, and animals, dead with disease or killed by Burmese Dacoits, men who robbed all they could before carving the unfortunates with *dahs,* as indicated by numerous cuts on bodies.

22

TAUNGTHA

Caught up in the melee like conditions, accompanied by six men, and two mules, pandemonium reigned; – as bullets came in, fired from a copse, over to our right. "My f—ing leg!" The cry was from Private,Gigger' Lee, who was walking alongside me, as a bullet passed through the flesh of his thigh. The big, handsome and powerful man was all set to, 'chase the bastards', wounded leg or not. He was slung onto a bullock cart, and the wound strapped with his, 'first field dressing'. Gigger was lifted back to Mandalay, and eventually flown out of Burma: – He was later reported killed in the 'D' Day landings in Europe. Taungtha was a completely different style of habitation to the random spread of villages passed earlier. Constructed like a medieval fortress, it was not the kind of place a European would enter easily at any time. The whole town was contained within stockade walls, of solid teak tree trunks, about 25 feet in height, and so close together as to deny entry for the smallest mouse. The one entrance was through a gateway, with width and height sufficient only to take a bullock cart. (with better news of Gigger later).

Alert to the hostility directed towards British in this part of Burma; oilfield officials had, for their own safety, ensured they were escorted, well beyond this most dangerous area. Reduced in numbers, and dishevelled, we heeded the oilmen's warning, and showed caution in choosing a night halt, about 400 yards from Taungtha, close by a small Chaung.

Companies were dispersed, and suitably settled, all was ready to prepare the daily meal. There would have been no cause for entry into the town, had not the tell-tale plume of smoke started its perpendicular ascent skywards. The familiar huge, dark pencil, writing out its silent message, informing the Japanese and others with anti-British interests of the presence of British troops.

There was no waiting; the drill was exactly the same as that ordered by me on the road march: 'Instant attack, as though being fired upon'. Grabbing six men, including Sergeant Mee, I ordered others to surround the village and allow no one in or out. I raced towards the place to find, almost inevitably, that it was a part of the *pongyi kyaung* (or school) that was going up in flames. On our approach, a gathering of very surprised, and unmistakably hostile, Burmese men began moving away from the burning building. It was as the men moved away, a stream of about fifteen to eighteen Indian girls came from behind the burning school, screaming in terror and desperation. They were all youngish women, escaping in ones or twos, following one after the other.

Dressed virtually in rags, they were being given the 'barbecue' treatment, as were those Inniskillings held prisoner by the Japanese at Yenangyaung. The young women, distressed, demented and screaming, wasted no time in accepting their freedom; they scurried away, joining with the fleeing refugee column moving to the north. Although further screams rang out from within the building, there was no time to seek out survivors damaged in the fire, or otherwise.

It was significant that, while Indian girls were held captive in the village, there were no Burmese women or men, other than the dissident group. Apart from being ill-used by the Burmese, the women would have been useful as barter or to seek favour from the Japanese. The unusually large, hostile-looking gathering of men, very few dressed in the humble *longyi* of a villager, was far in excess of the limited group of five permitted under government wartime regulations.

Without seeking further cause, 27 Burmese were rounded up and marched out of the village. All were of an age, none young, and none old. A gathering of this number, and type of individual, in a village, in this defiant manner, at this time, required some explanation. The Indian girls may, or may not, have served their purpose; the burning school, with the girls inside was no myth, and a rare illegal gathering of this nature spelled real trouble.

Fortunately, within the battalion were one or two soldiers, recruited locally, at Maymyo; – they spoke fluent Burmese, and readily identified some of the captives as former oilfield staff. On questioning the men, there were no satisfactory answers as to their presence in the village, or about the start of the *pongyi kyaung* fire, or why the Indian girls were held captive in the burning school. Bland uneasiness met questions on the shooting of Gigger Lee. Clearly, men organised in this manner, at this time and place, were enemies, despite the bland, innocent look. They were proven murderous in attempting to burn the girls; indeed fanatically seeking any opportunity to damage the British, and vulnerable refugees, of whatever race. (I learned many years later that this gathering was part of exiled Premier U-Saw's private 'Galon Army').

Weakened, and weakening almost by the hour, we were no more than nominally a battalion. Literally 'slushing' our many sick and wounded along, with an ever-increasing number of individuals losing hope, and falling back on the line of march. The desperate situation called for desperate action, in order to stay alive: Anyone considered to be even remotely hostile, and seeking to take advantage of our debilitated condition, must be eliminated. We were captured, in the sense that no man could envisage survival, and getting himself out of Burma. No prison could be more secure, or more environmentally hostile. Desperately, I must ensure that my fellow officers, along with Benny Mee and the platoon, were to have every opportunity of escape from this hellhole of a country: – (Every officer, indeed, every man in the British Army, has a prime responsibility, in the event of capture by the enemy, of attempting to escape, by whatever means).

Escape from this enclosed land, against sea, river, jungle, heat, sickness and menacing enemy, was virtually impossible. There were two mammoth rivers to cross, and hundreds of miles of torrid mountainous jungle to negotiate, in excessive pre-monsoon temperatures, with the added prospect of an imminent monsoon. Reinforcing the hostile elements, was an aggressive and well-equipped enemy, one threatening 'annihilation', supported by fervent Nationalists.

Burma was indeed a prison, with the luxury of walkabout facilities, although it did have some drawbacks. Normal prisoners have the luxury of regular water, and food; they get to wash, and to change their clothing. They have a bed to sleep on, and a nice man in a smart uniform to lock them in at night, protecting them from the horrors of the terrible outdoors. They have money, cigarettes, doctors, padres, visits from family and friends, and if they don't like what they get, they have reporters from newspapers nosing around. No Burma-based British troops had any of these joyful comforts. Considering all options, a decision needed to be made regarding disposal of the hostile Burmese, and made quickly.

As the man capturing the prisoners, and knowing the circumstances, I made the decision and put it to the titular commander, Chadwick. Reluctant to act, and skulking, Chadwick turned his back and walked away, chuntering, "I want no part in this". Chadwick washed his hands of the affair. He did not want to take the initiative in any decision regarding the dispatch of the hostile 27 Burmese. These were shrewd men, who had, no doubt, by this time, taken close stock of the appalling conditions, and state of affairs, of our men and equipment. Any one of the former oilfield employees was capable of giving detailed information on our condition, to the Japanese. Particularly when put under the pressure of Japanese torture. It was a question of, which one of them would betray us?

There was no time for prevarication. Chadwick was afraid to accept responsibility, becoming increasingly, and rightly, concerned at the growing personal hostility towards himself, following his favouring certain officers at Mount Popa. Chadwick was beginning to realise that in this situation, regardless of the crown on his shoulder, he was just another man on the ground. Interference with any decision, made by me, on the Burmese, might not be in his best interests.

British Army Training Manuals contain no, 'Code of Conduct,' for the desperate situation in which we found ourselves. Having assumed his shaky command, twelve days or so beforehand, Chadwick had no answer to the situation. It was easy to see why he was left behind at the depot on mobilisation of the unit. Cushioned by privilege and rank, Chadwick was unable to comprehend the present depth of our desperation. We had virtually no hope of survival beyond one or two days, and the officers and men of the unit had sunk to a point of mutuality, where all have equal voice, and responsibility. This was far beyond Chadwick's ken. As a result of his one rash act, the men were not now looking to officers for protection: – We were now a group beyond military comprehension, and normal authority was defunct.

As the officer impounding the prisoners, I was in no doubt about what action to take. The decision was mine, and I sought no further opinion. Only the few men entering Taungtha knew the facts, and this was no situation in which to be carrying out long discussions and explanations. As Chadwick had turned his back on the subject, there was no question of referring to higher authority. Where were they? Who were they? Although no more than, 'the senior junior officer', any decision on the culprits rested with me. At least one of the men was guilty. Not one of this group could be left alive, to inform others of the distressed condition of the battalion.

Whilst I could not promote myself, I knew that I must assert myself. Rank had no meaning. Long abandoned by Churchill and his government, and with no means of communication, I accepted the task of being their proxy: – In sentencing 27 men to death and seeing them dispatched within half an hour of capture. I was protecting, His Majesty, the King's soldiers.

Aware of the despondency, and distrust amongst the men, I felt that they must be treated with consideration, and not asked to perform a task for which they had no stomach. The necessity of which there was no time to explain. My decision was not taken lightly. I ordered: – "These men must be shot. They will be shot by the three company commanders".

Only in this way was it possible to maintain some integrity of command. The order had a salutary effect; it restored discipline, and a vital dignity amongst the troops.

Allocating nine Burmese to each company, I ordered how and where they would be shot: – "At the bank of the Chaung, and their bodies dropped into the bed". The birds would clean the remains. It was certainly no worse a fate than that of those girls, perished in the schoolroom fire. I joined Captain, 'Dusty' Miller, for the dispatch of his nine men. As they moved forward, the leading man drew a knife from his belt and made to strike towards me. The Burman's arm was broken by the barrel of my rifle, following a punch in the face with the end of the muzzle. I dispatched him with the same knife, and left Frank Miller free to conduct his own business with the remainder. I retained the horn handled knife, and the teak scabbard.

The Burmans were brought forward one-by-one to the Chaung edge; some with the traditional plea of hands joined together before the eyes, others arrogant and defiant. They were shot at close range by revolver or rifle, in order to use a minimum of ammunition; then, pushed over the edge, to drop into the hot dry sand below. Having seen the first man dispatched with such speed, there was no show of resistance from the remainder. Somebody was going to hold them in memory, maybe Premier U-Saw, as martyrs in their own land.

My involvment of officers in the dispatch of the recalcitrant group was a masterstroke. The common-sense appreciation of the necessity for officers to be seen carrying out a distasteful, yet essential duty, earned instant respect from my subordinates. The action had relieved private soldiers of a most unpalatable task. It upheld officer discipline and asserted authority that was in danger of slipping rapidly away. The ominous, almost mutinous, atmosphere among the troops, following the surreptitious disappearance of company commanders, from Mount Popa, was considerably dispelled.

Many years later, in my management days, I realised that this was possibly the most dynamic masterstroke of man-management and decision-making of the war; superbly balanced to effect equanimity within troops demoralised through indifference, incompetence, and inefficiency of senior commanders. It created a new confidence, in that men knew their officers really did mean to attempt to release them from capture in this vast hostile land. Having completed the business of Taungtha, and aware of the implications of the smoke plume, we moved on, one hour up the road, to take the delayed soya-link evening meal, and settle for night-time defence.

The episode of Taungtha was immediately 'forgotten', in the need to get on with the task in hand. The action was never mentioned, certainly not in the history of the regiment. Chadwick remained silent throughout, and subsequently, when the unit eventually returned to India. It was with some reluctance, and following a Serious Crime Squad inquiry from

Scotland Yard, that, as a much older man, Benny Mee was reminded of the incident. His comment was, "I brought them in, but I didn't kill any".*

---

* I offered the story of Taungtha to The Observer newspaper in 1984. Following visits by investigative journalists to my former army colleagues, in many parts of the country, the Observer editorial staff, in spite of assurances to the contrary, became selective in their use of the material. Much against my wishes, on 3 June 1984, they printed a distorted, sceptical, sensationalised version of the story. The circumstances at the time of the incident were ignored. This was, in my opinion, the British press at its typical worst. The Observer version went worldwide, and caused Mr Tam Dalyell M.P. to raise questions in the House of Commons. This resulted in an inquiry by Scotland Yard's Serious Crime Squad. The inquiry was conducted by Detective Chief Superintendent Hardy, and Detective Sergeant Tovey, on 24 October 1984. I considered it a "cover up". I gave the Scotland Yard men my full co-operation, which resulted in a very badly recorded interview, (the sergeant had difficulty in writing). They then followed the same line of inquiry as The Observer staff, except that they approached people in an accusative manner, as though about to prosecute, making these old soldiers feel uncomfortable and defensive. However, my story was corroborated, and to the surprise of nobody, I heard nothing further from Scotland Yard. I was told by my Observer contact, 'Bob Low', that Brigadier John (Everest) Hunt, a director of the newspaper, had repeatedly lambasted the editor for carrying the story in the first place. The same noble lord intervened with Scotland Yard, attempting to smother the story with the words 'The British Army can't be seen to be doing a thing like this.' It never occurred to him to ask, 'How the British Army got into a hole like this?' And, more to the point, 'Who was responsible?' All subsequent correspondence on the subject was proscribed by The Observer editors. Not one word of comment was printed.

Captain Maurice Green, and the timing of his departure from Mount Popa before the Taungtha incident, was particularly mentioned. It was at the instigation of Chadwick that Green was, some time later, given the responsibility of compiling the regimental history of the Burma campaign. Green's absence, from Mount Popa onwards, made easy the task of overlooking Chadwick's shortcomings. Having been evacuated sick, Green obviously had no personal knowledge of the happenings, or the repercussions, resulting from his contentious evacuation.

It is interesting to note that, in his investigations, Green completely ignored the contribution made by members of the squad of junior officers of the *Strathallan* draft, the men who became the battalion's driving force for ten long weeks.

Although I was assured of the report on the Scotland Yard inquiry finding, I heard nothing. *The Yorkshire Evening Post* 11 July 1985 reports;-

"A spokesman for The Director of Public Prosecutions said that no action would be taken over the allegations because of insufficient evidence."

The treacherous facts and perilous truth of the occasion would have been brought out in a prosecution.

23

COOKING OIL

Thoughts of conflict were fading fast as we set forth at dawn; no words were needed, signs of our debilitation said it all. Nobody wanted to know the date, or the day of the week, it was a simple matter of the sun comes up, and the sun goes down; do we have water and something to eat? Men were prone to fluctuating moods, and uplifted only for brief periods, at times of rest and food. Within minutes, the gloom descended. Moods, moans, and fading hope, rattled backwards and forwards throughout the column.

Not having been involved in the incident at Taungtha, Ted Hewitt, my batman, did not mince words as he approached.

"Who the bloody hell do you think you are, God?"

I simply asked him how he would like to be the one to fall behind sick, and to be captured by the Taungtha gang. In Hewitt's eyes, it must have looked a very glib decision; although with the degree of Burmese hostility, there was no alternative.

Many were refusing to surrender to illness, and those fit enough, and capable of doing so, stayed close by their 'muckers', encouraging them to keep going. Malaria was a constant companion, with its sweat, shakes and shivers; dysentery, with its diarrhoea, blood and weight loss, was rife, and contagious; 'dhobi-rash', for the want of clean clothing, was spreading scabs; 'jungle sores', 2-3 inches in diameter, open and festering, developed from scratches, or leech bites, and spread over legs and up the body, stinking to high heaven. Cholera had almost wiped out the remains of a nearby battalion, and it had left 80 Burmese troops dead. They had obviously found, and unfortunately used, an infected water point.

'Typhus tick', insect bites leaving unpleasant, itching coppery blue marks an inch diameter on shoulders and chest, were always evident as we arose from the sandy earth each morning, causing hallucinations in the last horrible pre-dawn hour of each night. Beri-beri, from lack of sustenance, was causing debilitation in many men, and constant perspiration running salt into the eyes, caused a steady, burning discomfort.

Rumours were rife; it was not surprising to hear of an episode occurring some days earlier on the track as we moved around Yenangyaung. Private Lacy was rough, tough, rugged, and ever ready for a scrap; known as 'a heap of walking trouble', permanently on jankers or in occupancy of the guardroom. The Rangoon Silver Grill Bar, of ill repute, was the main centre for illegal transactions, and a magnet for him. He knew all the naughty girls, and didn't mind the naughty boys, and was always flush with money, so easily and illegally earned, smuggling drugs and jewellery on the railway between, Maymyo, Mandalay, and Rangoon. Police and customs officers rigorously searched suspect Burmans, but not British troops.

Lacy recognised a 'fence' from his jewellery smuggling days, he was ill and struggling, among the column of refugees. The man must surely be well loaded with jewellery; Lacy escorted him to one side 'for protection', strangled him, and adjusted the man's body-belt to fit his own slimmer shape. There appeared to be no witness to the incident, yet Lacy was carefully watched, day and night, from the moment the story broke within the unit. Lacy's life was now in equal danger, and he knew it. Three days later, he himself vanished without trace. Did he desert? Or was he in turn, relieved of the booty? There was never an answer.

The 18 or so miles, in the heat of the day, from Taungtha to Myingyan proved a severe test. The hard task paled into insignificance when contemplating the territory ahead. Escaping Burma, with an untold number of miles to go, must be achieved before the onset of the monsoon, due in about one month, between 24 and 26 May. Otherwise, there could be no hope of escape.

Myingyan was a large, straggling town, deserted, and with highly-suspect water; cholera was rampant, with many deaths in the district. Orders were given not to drink or use the water, although in sheer desperation, as ever, a few ignored the order, taking their chances at a small slime-covered spring.

A little food was found in a large shed, a place previously used as a cinema, and now used as an emergency supply depot. This provided a meal, and in late afternoon, as we were about to leave the drab town, Major David Martin, accompanied by a four-man escort, set about destroying the store. Bayonets were plunged into tins of ghee cooking oil, until the floor ran with the oil, and the building filled with fumes. For some reason, Martin failed to appreciate the significance of the fumes, and, whilst still within the store, ignited the ghee.

A dull rumbling explosion shook the ground, and an inferno resulted, as the whole place went up in flames; three of the men were killed inside the building. Martin and the fourth man, Private 'Tommy' Mellia, were blasted out of the building with clothing in flames, and to have time only to relate what happened before they also died. This was a big loss, as David Martin was a popular officer, and with him were some of the most capable and likeable men of the unit. Martin, so full of energy and exuberance, had done a good job, particularly in the brief period when commanding the unit. Bodies were buried, with all due respect.

In view of the raging cholera epidemic, little time as possible was spent at Myingyan. It meant a further punishing 25 mile trek, to the small riverside village of Sameikkon, with hope that here, boats would be available to ferry across the great Irrawaddy river; otherwise, it meant either improvising on rafts, or swimming, as at the Sittang. The unthinkable alternative was to cross much further to the north-east, at the Ava Railway Bridge, near Mandalay. The prospect of this detour was dreaded; it would put between seven and ten extra days, travelling on foot, with not a hope of organised food supplies; being so far off the main axis of the divisional withdrawal.

Being rearguard unit meant precisely that; – we had no troops following on behind. Our weakening men were constantly falling back, and by the time they caught up, maybe two or three hours behind the main party, whatever food was available had been distributed. Our main communication appeared to be with stragglers from units ahead, and was always suspect.

The march to Sameikkon was agony; – Surreptitiously, the two officers, former N.C.O.s, vanished at this point, conveniently near to Mandalay. Relapse of malaria was given as the excuse. We were left to think whatever we would; I never heard of them again.

Commandeering three bullock carts, along with Burmese drivers, provided transport for a few of our sick. Animals were equally affected; we were all short of food and water. Mules are the most fastidious of drinkers, even when desperately denied water, they will not drink at polluted, or at muddied ponds, and at all times they were given priority in drinking. Mules were used by me, as my 'personal samplers', when coming upon a small pond with clear-looking water; if it was good enough for the mules, it was good enough for me.

24

GOVERNORSHIP AND GENERALS

Governor, Dorman-Smith, was hopelessly out of his depth in the situation in which he found himself. In a few short weeks, he had gone from Churchill's number one man in Burma, to a total nonentity. So much out of touch, and lacking in initiative, he said he was, "taken by surprise", when in late April he heard the Japanese were approaching his seat of government, moving freely up the eastern route of the country, towards Maymyo.

The situation deteriorating rapidly, Dorman-Smith should have been out of Burma, or at least moved across to the less vulnerable, more inaccessible, western side of the country, away from possible air attack. As an absolute last resort, he ought to have been in position to commence the long walk to the safety of India. Delighting in the high life of Government House, he showed great reluctance to leave his new-found luxury. Displaying an ignorant and myopic view of the situation in which he had placed himself, he assembled a staff fishing party, journeying 28 miles in a jeep, to the confluence of two rivers. Here they enjoyed a picnic before returning to Maymyo.

Hearing of the Japanese advance to Lashio, on his return from the fishing trip, within twenty miles of Maymyo, Dorman-Smith panicked. He realised how precarious and vulnerable his personal, and official, situation had become. Kidnappers of the British Governor, could demand a fortune in ransom from Churchill; – and he would pay it.

Japanese, occupying the eastern side of the country, were now moving in force towards the vital Burma Road town of Lashio: – As was normal practice with the Japanese, free-moving assault columns, accompanied by Dacoit guides, would be established ahead of the main force, closing rapidly towards Maymyo.

Dorman-Smith decided the time was right for him to leave, and made his panic move northwards, to the only available airfield, at Myitkyina. His life was now entirely dependent upon the Japanese tactical need to preserve the vital landing strip, for their own use. With the airfield destroyed, Dorman-Smith would have no alternative route out of Burma, other than three hundred miles of walking through rough jungle and hills to the west, which he would most certainly not survive. Isolated from the army, he felt, 'completely stranded'.

On 5 May, Air Vice Marshall Donald Stevenson, himself long ensconced in the safety of India, sent his personal Hudson plane to collect Dorman-Smith from Myitkyina. He flew to Dum-Dum airfield, near Calcutta, and on the following day, continued to Delhi. Meanwhile, G.O.C. Wavell was engaged in preparing his never-ending paperwork; appreciations, recommendations, pleas and excuses. This he did, in order to justify himself against Whitehall daggers, ever ready poised, to insert into his back; – Damning him as commander of yet another defeated army.

Wavell severed responsibility for the troops remaining inside Burma, and instructed staff at General Headquarters, India, to prepare preliminary plans for the return of the Army into Burma. Clearly there was no question of supplying the sad units remaining on the ground. His recommendations for the future may have been good, but they never benefited him. They came to fruition two years later, when Mountbatten was given Supreme Command of south-east Asia. Appreciating guidance, Mountbatten, in due course, adopted most of Wavell's paper work: – Wavell was removed, out of the army system.

Maybe Churchill was afraid of Wavell exposing the truth of his all-too-frequent interference, in the Middle East, and in Asia. Wavell, as Army Commander, was landed with the blame for each failed theatre of war, although throughout each campaign, Churchill imposed a tactical input, until the moment things went wrong. (See the Addenda, for copies of messages in which Churchill is fully exposed.)

Alexander, and Slim, did attempt to show some interest in the Burma Army, seeking to build upon the idea of a combined offensive, resulting from Chinese meetings, conducted with Stilwell, and with Chinese General Sun. These sessions brought varying degrees of encouragement and promise. With plans made, the two British withdrew, awaiting results.

Unfortunately, they were completely overlooking the one man of consequence, the controller of all Chinese Army Divisions, Premier, Chiang Kai-shek, and on this occasion he remained very, very, silent. Chinese Army Divisions varied enormously, in performance and efficiency, according to the general in charge, and his personal interest. Chiang, in turn, allocated tasks according to the degree of favour, and abilities, of each individual division, and its commander.

The eastern sector situation, with British 17th Division, was cause for the greatest anxiety; Japanese troop concentrations being guided at speed throughout this sector of the country, so much easier to negotiate. Plans were made between Alexander, Stilwell, and General Sun for an early offensive, and eventually, Chinese divisions were deployed. All was set, ready to launch an assault on the Japanese. This was fine, until Japanese forces attacked, over-running outpost units of the two central Chinese divisions.

Advised of Chiang's silence, Chinese Commanders considered discretion to be the better part of valour, and with not a word of apology, or farewell, Sun withdrew his troops and equipment from the action, scarpering off, back to China. On leaving the sector, the Chinese carried with them as much British-supplied rice, and goods, as the division could carry. Apart from the talking, the aborted action was the end of the Chinese connection for the time being, and the Chinese Army was withdrawn from Burma.

Pressure on the British Army, both in Burma, and the Middle East, prompted the Hindu Congress Party of India to take heart, and set about exploiting the situation. They knew that Churchill and Wavell, along with many others, believed a total British defeat in the East, imminent, and were confident they could profit, by increasing pressure in many ways: – Demonstrating, and demanding an early British evacuation of India. The initiative brought about further, and more intense, Indian civil disobedience. Acts of sabotage within the country became widespread.

Damage sustained made support for the remote Burma front, ever more problematic. Trains were derailed, and communications of all kinds interfered with; anything to hinder British progress.

Desperate, in the hope of countering unrest within India, Wavell sought to create a movement; – 'To reform the rapidly disintegrating Burma Army'. Planning proved useless, this Army was already discredited within its own country. Deserting individuals were known to be, rapidly, joining in the internecine chaos, existing between the various tribal, independent, and nationalist programmes.

25

IRRAWADDY STOCKTAKING

Romantic-sounding Mandalay, and Maymyo, remained distant as ever, passing me by, very slowly, a few miles to the east. Rangoon had been no more than a glimpse. There was no harassment on the hard march along the road, passing tended, flat arable land, now parched dry and dusty in the pre-monsoon heat. Arriving at the small riverside settlement of Sameikkon, a ferry crossing point close by the confluence of the Irrawaddy and Chindwin rivers, we faced the almost impossible task of crossing the seemingly, mile-wide river. With hearts in mouths, fully expecting all ferries to be bombed out of existence, and having to endure the ten day's foot-slogging detour, over the far off Ava Railway Bridge, situated near Mandalay.

Thankfully, a squad of Royal Marines had somehow found their way into Burma, and commandeered the one remaining small ferry. Developing lush curly beards, the marines had set up a thriving outpost; there was no waiting and hanging around here. A soya sausage sandwich was thrust into the hand of each man as he boarded the vessel. Where they procured bread was a mystery; we had seen none for weeks. Boarding in small groups, limited to the capacity of the boat, we crossed the huge river in stages, 30 or 40 men on each trip. With the sandwich, and an ample supply of precious clean drinking water, there was another quick boost of morale, and who cared if water was scooped from the river?

Time taken in crossing the Irrawaddy seemed an eternity, to those of us last away from the south bank, although once our feet settled on the safer north bank, the feeling of relief was enormous. It was like instant freedom, placing the massive river barrier between the Japanese and ourselves.

Fortuitously the Japanese spared this small ferryboat, as we heard of the destruction of the Ava Railway Bridge at midnight, the night that we crossed the river. Without the ferry, we would have undertaken the long detour to Mandalay, and almost certainly, into captivity or oblivion. The Royal Marines were well thanked, and their efforts appreciated. Sameikkon was the first river, or sandy crossing, undertaken without molestation by the enemy: – Salween, Bilin, Sittang, Yin Chaung, and Pin Chaung had each taken their toll of casualties. It could be that our execution of the Burmese Dacoits at Taungtha had remedied a further problem.

Mystery surrounded the three bullock cart drivers, they adamantly refused to cross the river, having a dread of crossing from the south to the north bank. They were clearly terrified, yet unable to explain their predicament. Promises of money and food were of no avail. There was no assuaging their fear, and they were relieved to be left on the south bank, although we retained the bullocks and carts. Reaction of this kind, however, was a warning that some form of danger lay ahead; as people from the south, they might be attacked by some other tribe on their crossing the river.

Resourceful Private Robson thrived, as he undertook the duties of number one bullock cart driver. Within minutes, he had the animals performing like racehorses by sticking a piece of wood in their rear orifice, where Burmese drivers use the big toe. Requiring no petrol and spare parts, as did army transport, the sturdy carts were tremendous assets in this type of action; no maintenance, other than dry grass, and ensuring harness functioned satisfactorily. Bullocks appeared capable of pulling whatever amount one loaded onto the massive carts, although we had little. Mules, however, remained the mainstay of the unit transport, long tested and well proven, and magnificent animals to work with; far less stupid or stubborn than people think. Aware when they are overloaded, they politely refuse to move until the load is adjusted. Loaded correctly, mules perform wonders, and make no complaints. It became unthinkable for any army unit to function without a contingent of mules. Tough as they come, Private Bill Kibbler handled Nelly, a misnomer if ever there was one. Nelly was in fact a 'mister mule', who occasionally grew a big nasty fifth leg between the back two. When it almost touched the floor, and then slapped back up to the belly, one knew, Nelly was no lady.

Leaving the huge river barrier to hinder the Japanese advance, was a relief and morale booster; it was also a time of appraisal and stocktaking. Of my 18 *Strathallan* colleagues, Jimmy Ableson was already dead, and Arthur Watts had broken his arm when falling from a horse. Seven had been selected, simply on the basis of junior commissioned service; Allan Ibbotson, Stuart Renton, Tim Watson, Bill McKillop, Bill Riddell, G.E. 'Chotta' Lawrence and Allan Whittaker; all had been posted back to various brigade and divisional appointments. Of those remaining with the unit, Victor Stevens had been brilliant in actions undertaken alongside me, first in the Tharrawaddy area, and later around the central oilfields. Andrew McLaren Young, Bob Rimmer, Leslie Wise, Jim Marsh, Johnny Welbourne, and Doug Oakley, all with small platoons, had constantly patrolled and manned outposts, particularly by night. Douglas Haig, a former trainee veterinary surgeon at Liverpool University, undertook all those duties, also ensured that animals were treated in the best possible manner. Designated Mortar Officer and answerable direct to Chadwick, was a farcical situation, Chadwick was allergic towards mortars, and I now had none. My platoon consisted of one sergeant, one corporal, and seven privates, with the blessing of three mules carrying mortar bombs, and no weapon with which to fire them. Protecting useless ammunition from the enemy, was my task.

The levelling down process meant equality for all. No man had more than the clothes on his back, the scant remains of military equipment, and the weapon carried on his person. There were no barracks, bed or food, to comfort him at the end of his duty. Night after night, the ground was our bed, and stars above the ceiling, yet no man wanted for anything more than to be with his mucker in this stinking hot country.

I regarded myself as particularly fortunate, to have worldly goods in excess of most, in that I had the only working watch in the battalion, the horn-handled knife taken from the Burman at Taungtha, and, most precious of all, I had the Japanese haversack with the half blanket, and half sheet, from the customs building at Yenangyaung. Here, semi-relaxed, I had the first opportunity to look at the photographs I carried in the breast pocket of my sweat-laden shirt. They were stuck together to halfway up the small photographs. This was my first indication of the depth of water in the Yin Chaung; halfway up the breast pocket of my shirt.

Sweat was ever increasing the width of the white salt-band across the chest of my shirt, which was now becoming greasy black on the yoke above the salt; yet it remained khaki down below. The discharge of blood and mucus from the boil on my arse remained in the underpants, to be tacky or hard, according to the time of day. Being fair skinned with a schoolboy complexion was an asset, as the bit of bum-fluff growing on my face made no show of a beard, whereas Steve and others were developing massive black growths. Geoff Chadwick had a splendid ginger display; no man now owned a razor, and beards of all shapes and sizes flourished.

Men previously referred to as 'Fatty', 'Tubby' or 'Busty', no longer lived up to these names; the weeks of hunger, thirst and marching had slimmed all into lean, gaunt figures. Awakening each morning feeling cold, and yearning for the warm sunrise, whilst at the same time knowing that within minutes, each day would become hotter than the previous one, as the monsoon season drew near. In my nightly hallucinations, I saw clearly a party of four men, all covered in mud, emerging from a swamp and carrying a fifth man. I considered the fifth to be me, carried by the arms and legs, although each time the vision appeared, the right leg was swinging loose, maybe from fear of losing that leg.

It was obvious that stamina was essential if one was to endure the three hundred and fifty miles to the Indian border, and freedom. Mileage on maps took no account of deviations, for jungles and rivers. The next major obstacle, many miles ahead, was another gargantuan river, the Chindwin. I had confidence in my swimming ability to carry me any distance, providing the excessive marching did not bring about stomach cramp, or one of the many illnesses affecting others, before reaching the river.

Incentive to keep going was easy to find. At Yenangyaung, I shot a vulture that perched on a tree in front of the bungalow, in order to have a close inspection of the brute. Its foul droppings had killed off all foliage and left only a stunted blackened perch; there was evil in its very presence, although the government imposed fines for the destruction of vultures, (they had sanitary value). I did not want the two foot long neck of this monster stuck up my arse, after having my genitals cut off and stuck in my mouth by some Japanese. This was the fate of those unfortunates I found in the ambulances, the ones left burning at Yenangyaung. With these thoughts in mind, it became easy to keep moving, whether it be for two hundred, or two thousand miles.

Each daily move was a further stage towards the limits of physical endurance. The ground occupied each night for rest and recuperation was chosen by the battalion commander, according to the onset of dark, and the prospect of food and effective defence. Fortunately, Bruce Scott had not needed KOYLI's services for some days; in consequence, we had not seen him around, although we knew that he would find us when required.

Resulting from numerous blunders tolerated beforehand, a new democratic control had evolved, and operated from here on. Responsibilities became a question of, 'How right are you in giving me that order?' and 'How fit am I to carry out the order?' Within the battalion, two men carried the crown of a Field Officer on their shoulders; one was the demeaned Chadwick, who found it necessary to appoint a personal bodyguard. The other was Throckmorton, a man with no concern other than for his own well-being, carrying a *chargul* (canvas water carrier) and a revolver, deplored by the men, as a farcical figure.

Major David Martin, now dead, had been a completely different kettle of fish. Martin had wanted to be in at everything, and he had clearly resented the fact that the dithering Chadwick was designated commander, simply on the basis of seniority. Martin had been a far more effective Officer Commanding. He had been disillusioned by the imposition of one he regarded, 'incompetent'.

The new pattern of discipline and communications percolated throughout the unit, unsolicited and unannounced. Men had matured as a result of the degrading conditions, suffered equally by all throughout the previous six months. If they wished to express an opinion, all men had a voice.

It was in another place, and at a later date, (1943), that the mutually adopted code of practice, became enthusiastically adopted, by General Bill

Slim. He was happy to discuss with our team of battle-experienced Officer Instructors at his Officers' Battle School, and Jungle Warfare Training Centre, based at Ranchi in India. Slim ordered essential attendance for officers, up to the rank of major. He placed great emphasis on the need for all eligible officers to attend the gruelling course. Speaking personally to as many officers as possible, when visiting, at the end of each three-week period. Slim insisted upon giving his 'update address', to those successfully completing the 16 punishing, live ammunition, days and nights of training.

Slim was something a bit different; a change from the pompous senior officers with whom one usually came into contact. Not only was he a man's man, he had the additional attribute of being a listening man, and he seized upon the idea of the modified disciplinary 'code of practice'. Fostering it throughout units of the 14th Army, with the resultant success achieved during the following three years.

26

IRRAWADDY TO MONYWA

The night of 29 April was spent observing the riverbank and guarding the precious river ferry. The whole of BurDiv was a considerable distance ahead of our position. We were rearguard, by many miles.

The one battalion charger was allocated to Douglas Haig, the only man with knowledge of riding. With mobility, he was also, ostensibly, liaison officer with Brigade H.Q. Having increasing difficulty walking, it was better that he ride, owing to the spread of large jungle sores on both legs. We had to lift him onto, and down from the horse.

Resting overnight on 30 April, in order to re-muster and invigorate the weak. It was too good to last; later in the day, a Gurkha soldier arrived with the message that, by some means, the Japanese had infiltrated ahead of BurDiv's position to the north, and closed the road, cutting off the line of our withdrawal. This scant information was all that was known of the situation.

Unsure of BurDiv's location, it was rapidly deduced, to be more than 20 miles ahead of our position. Easy to realise, a roadblock so far ahead meant, progressing northwards was virtually impossible. Bruce Scott, having secured himself among the 'big boys', Alexander and Slim, much further north. He, like them, was ensconced on the safe side of wherever the blockage was set. This, fortunately for him, precluded him from making his usual visit of doom. The Gurkha messenger was a good substitute.

It was vital, the battalion, now consisting of about 100 men, join as rapidly as possible with the remnants of 1st Brigade, about 20 miles further north; we could but guess them to be near the riverside town of Monywa.

At about 20.00 hours, we moved off, on the first leg of the Monywa march. Thankful of the brief rest, and a little food, before making the effort; as automatons, we moved under cover of darkness and travelled for more than 20 miles, before halting by a small village at about 3.00 a.m. for food and a brief rest.

Sergeant 'Busty' Taylor was another man unbearably troubled by dhobi-rash, and, as with Douglas Haig, the horrible soreness had spread over the lower part of his body, forming one huge festering scab from his crotch into his thighs, stomach and all around his bum and down his legs. This powerful, dedicated soldier could not accept his incapacitation, and was an inspiration to all, as he refused to be beaten. With nothing more to do, Busty ripped off his shorts, and, naked from the stomach down, making nothing of the pain or discomfort, he 'soldiered on'.

It was difficult getting tired and exhausted men to move on the following morning, 1st May, as the first warmth of dawn penetrated tired limbs, cooled in the chill of the night. Attempting to rouse fellow officer, R.E.O. (Bob) Rimmer, I met with resistance, a sign of exhaustion, as Bob had been fit and well throughout the previous day. He was not the man to scrimshank.

Giving Bob a nudge in the ribs with the toe of my boot, I stood back, and awaited the response one may expect from a dedicated and active platoon commander. Bob making no movement, I realised something must be radically wrong. I did not have the benefit of medical advice, or assistance, and could only deduce that he had been bitten or stung by a gnat, typhus-tick, or other insect. He had contracted some form of sleeping sickness, in addition to having a most awful 'jungle sore', covering the whole of his chin.

This was an unusual problem; no man could expect to be carried by men, themselves exhausted. Constant shaking and talking elicited no response. The consensus of opinion among the men of his platoon was that Bob should be left where he was, to take his chance with whoever might find him, Burmese or Japanese: – "Like Hell! We don't!" I said.

There was no way that I was going to leave Rimmer. I had not been there for Abe. Now Bob was here, in trouble, and with me by his side; although he might not be much alive, he was to be given the chance, and not left to die. I had no idea how to handle the situation, but I knew that I would.

As a boy, I acquired skills in animal management in the West of Ireland. I had loaded and led donkeys when carrying turf from the family bog, and when haymaking, pulling cocks of hay to the stack. I could mount and ride donkeys bareback with one short stick for steering. I had repaired creels, and as a trained engineer, was not going to be found wanting in improvisation. Although I had never seen anything done like it, I knew there must be some way to carry a man on the back of a mule. I ordered, – "Take the fuses out of the bombs on that mule, and throw the useless things away, bombs and all!" Chadwick had no say. He had been afraid to use mortars when in the Migyaungye area, where we faced the enemy. I was prepared to stick my neck out without seeking permission.

How to secure a man to a mule was a puzzle, but I knew the mule was going to carry Bob Rimmer, so long as he was alive. Setting men to stripping bamboo rope from village bungalows, I laid Bob face down along the soft haunch of the mule, legs to the fore, arms and head downwards, over the rump. Obtaining sufficient rope to pass some around Bob's body, arms and legs, and then around the four legs, tail, and neck of the mule. It was done in such a way that Bob was held at all corners, he could not fall off, and the mule was comfortable. Away we went, with two men responsible for the mule, and its precious cargo. Bob, showing no sign of recovery, travelled in this trussed-up manner for the next four days. Sick beyond measure, with no food and little water, he was eventually evacuated, and hospitalised. He recovered much later, back in India.

Joining with the Gurkhas, it was agreed that the amalgamated force should be called '1st Brigade', for one day only. Brigade, was another misnomer, as the total strength of the four constituent battalions was less than half of one normal battalion; a very weak battalion. There was no history of our units operating together, and, apart from the language barrier, none knew the capabilities, or inadequacies, of the other. The composite unit formed a defensive perimeter, and awaited information on the Japanese infiltration, only to find a variety of conflicting opinions. Unable to get a measured assessment, or report on the situation, it became a matter of conjecture as to what might be the true picture. It transpired that we were joined with no more than a detachment of 1st Brigade.

Considering the speed with which the Japanese set the trap, particularly following the devastating Chinese assault on them at Yenangyaung, it was reasonable to assume they were not holding the obstacle in great strength. Apart from the fact that the Japanese had to be dislodged from the stranglehold of the roadblock, for 1st Brigade to have any hope of survival, there was the essential need to find food. Arrangements were made to march out at first light the following morning, and with no more plans, than to seek out the Japanese at Monywa.

Only now did we realise that extra miles were to be covered, and at much more of a gallop, than a march, over the 14 miles; speed was essential in order to reduce the time available for the enemy to reinforce the blockage. It was an energy-sapping gallop, often across fields of fine sandy soil. The Japanese had apparently infiltrated by boat, coming up the Irrawaddy and the Chindwin Rivers, to set the blockage at the busy junction town of Monywa, tactically sited at a point where the road, railway, and river come close together, in a pass between hills. This, then, was the point at which the 'annihilation of British Forces', promised almost three weeks earlier, was to be carried out. Was it the end?

At Monywa, the Gurkhas were already in action. Being virtually unarmed, we were allocated a less committed reserve role, on the south-west flank, facing the river, in order to repel any attempted boat landings. 16th Gurkha Brigade was distinguishing itself, and with a measure of success, as firing became surprisingly heavy all around.

Desperately short of ammunition, in the late afternoon, we were called forward to join in what must be a futile attack. There remained many personal scores to settle, and this was, 'do or die'. Revitalised movement showed in every limb, and stretch of the leg. With fixed bayonets we moved up the slope, from the riverbank, advancing forward through the remnants of a Gurkha battalion, already pinned down under a hail of bullets. We had possibly 24 reasonably fit men. This being our most desperate situation to date.

Delight showed on Gurkha faces as we moved forward. This was the ideal; British showing pride when going into action alongside, 'Johnny Gurkha'. Bullets were flying in all directions as we approached the crest of the rise. One Gurkha, accompanied by his chum, was standing in the shade of a tree; he turned as I passed. A young boy, with a huge smile on his face, lifted his shirt to show seven small holes in a line across his chest; there was no blood, simply seven small, clean quarter inch holes, about one inch apart. They must have been inflicted only seconds earlier by Japanese machine-gun bullets. He must have died within minutes, as, ironically, by some quirk, firing ceased completely, the instant I passed this gallant young soldier.

The Japanese had broken and withdrawn, without further firing or obstruction. They were possibly only a small and well-armed raiding party, landed from a boat. Firing one or two shots throughout the engagement, we had insufficient ammunition, stamina or time, to go in pursuit. There was nothing I could do for the wounded Gurkha, other than ensure his water bottle was filled, and remember him.

Fortunately, the Japanese had once again, declined the offer to join in frontal battle with British troops, although on this occasion they certainly would have had total success. The Japanese withdrawal, as we approached, was obviously orchestrated by some observer, possibly in a tree, whereas on the oilfield they had observed from the derrick platforms. Could it be, they had seen the formidable sight of Sergeant Taylor approaching, naked from the waist down? One could only assume that the Japanese wrongly assessed, we must be a strong and well-armed unit, for us to be introduced at this stage. Halting, lest we run into an ambush; – This was no time for bravado.

Forming a defensive perimeter, we withdrew to the riverbank, awaiting the sheltering dark. Two hours after dark we moved out, taking the longer route, encircling Monywa to the east, as this was the side least likely to be ambushed. About three hours later, halted by a small village, adopted all-round defensive positions. The following morning was one of observation, patrol and rest, as an increasingly dense stream of refugees began flowing north, from Monywa. It was necessary to observe this unfortunate stream very carefully, lest there be Japanese infiltrators among them. It would be difficult for a well-fed and trained Japanese to impersonate one of these gaunt and dazed refugees, with the pencil-thin limbs.

Aware that the Japanese might attempt outflanking once again, at nightfall, we embarked on a race with both, the enemy, and sickness. Bob Rimmer remained totally incapacitated. Douglas Haig could not walk, and required help into, and out of the saddle each day. Busty Taylor was a pitiable mess without his trousers. So many others were struggling. A man got weaker and weaker, until eventually he collapsed off the road, to lie and die, or a parting shot would announce the end. Weakness was fighting the will to live in so many men.

Thwarting Japanese intentions, we moved on an hour after sundown. Tired men required aggressive command to get them onto their feet and marching again. Covering as much ground as possible meant pushing on non-stop; there was no thought of ten minute halts every hour, men would simply slump into deep sleep. After five hours of marching into the night, a halt was called, at 1.00 a.m. in order to give the men some rest. Starting once again was even more difficult, but it had to be done, knowing that we must get as much distance as possible between the Japanese and ourselves. By daylight, we could expect enemy fighter, and bomber aircraft, to harass at will.

Restarting the march at 3.00 a.m. in the rising moonlight, it was tragic to leave two or three of the sick behind. Our good friends, 2nd Royal Tank Regiment and 7th Hussars, were away, supporting Chinese up the eastern route, prior to their precipitous departure home to China. Stilwell had demanded Tank Brigade support, in return for the considerable, and very precious Chinese aid, given in the vital relief of Yenangyaung, and the blessed release of Inniskilling captives. It was timely that the tanks did eventually return, north of the Irrawaddy. They had crossed the Ava Bridge a few minutes before its destruction.

The moonlight march was agony, although it had the dubious compensation of our not sleeping in the increasingly bitter cold of the night. Halted at dawn for a brief rest, it was not the warm fingers of sunlight that stroked across the morning sky; rather a canopy of lead and a hail of Japanese bullets, shattered the dawn. Thwarted in their ambush at Monywa, the Japanese had pushed forward a small bicycle section, possibly on commandeered bicycles, and armed with machine-guns, in an attempt to fulfil their promise. In slightly different circumstances, they might have met with success, but on this occasion they failed.

Being rearguard battalion, we were halted astride the road, using the cover of a small wood, facing south over an area of open agricultural land, in a defence situation. Sudden shouts and the surge of a number of refugees gave warning of unusual activity. This slight alert was sufficient to arouse the men. The exchange of shots lasted no more than minutes, and the Japanese withdrew, after once again sustaining casualties. Had the Japanese waited and caught us on the move in the now more open country, it would have been the slaughter of the innocents. We were fortunately alert, and in a prepared defensive formation, and suffered no loss.

Departure from this encounter was instant, with the sick to the hindmost. There was no time for hanging around. Japanese machine-guns had sounded reveille, and the five mile dawn march was done at a rapid pace.: – Halted at 7.30 a.m. for two and a half hours, for essential food and rest, and in order to allow the increasing numbers of stragglers to catch up with the column. It meant, however, that men in most need of rest were getting the least, as some of them had just arrived, in time for the restart at 10.00 a.m. We had to start the next leg, of almost 50 miles, to the village of Ye-u. This was a gruelling prospect, marching through the heat of the day, after non-stop movement and defence in the previous 48 hours, and virtually no sleep.

Men had long adopted a fatalistic acceptance, – 'if your name was on the bomb, or bullet; — tough!' All realised that time was of the essence, and that casualties must occur in one form or other. There was no point in fearing the occasional Japanese air attack; bombs or bullets might hit some, but not all. Off-road travel in the sandy soil would have taken far too long, exhausting even the fittest. The strenuous Ye-u march was to be undertaken on the road.

Belts were now fitting several inches tighter than at the outset, and legs were like machines. Marching was the easy part for the fit, but it was the dread of sick men. Bob Rimmer, fastened on the mule, was oblivious to all movement; Dougie Haig grimaced at each stride of the charger, while Busty Taylor, bare in the arse and in agony with soreness, managed to keep up his ribald patter to raise a laugh. Taylor boosted morale, as he did later, after the war: – He became 'mine host' at his pub, the Malt Shovel, in Pontefract.

The 50 mile trek, in the heat of the day, was like the march to hell, and with no ending. No padre, parson, preacher, or priest appeared in this scene, and doctors far too precious to be shot at; they were retained at hospitals, or in aid posts. We had not seen any one of these at the battalion, from the outset.

Having progressed about 28 miles, we heard rumbling, from 2nd Royal Tank Regiment, and exhausted 2/R.T.R. task was, carrying the reduced battalion, in two halves, to the village of Ye-u. Clambering onto hot tanks, eight or nine men to each tank, the first half of the battalion got away, while the remainder adopted defensive positions to await stragglers, and to encourage them as they rejoined the group. It seemed a lifetime, waiting the three hours or so it took for the tanks to return, even then, a number of the stragglers had failed to arrive. Two tanks continued back down the road, in search of missing men.

Busty Taylor, Douglas Haig, and Bob Rimmer, along with others, were evacuated by the tanks from this point. Survive they did; Busty, to his pub; Douglas Haig, to qualify as a vet and serve in Africa, and the West Indies; Bob Rimmer, I believe, became chief executive, in a West Country, County Council; possibly Gloustershire?

A sound like a girl's scream, as we arrived at Ye-u, turned out, predictably, to be Nicholas Throckmorton. Having travelled back on the first tank, he committed the cardinal sin, getting into water to bathe before the animals had taken their fill. Rising from immersing himself into a natural spring of water, about ten feet in diameter, right by the roadside, he saw the two large black swollen leeches, forming a letter 'V' on his abdomen. The only man of the battalion who would consider bathing in the priceless, clean commodity, before the animals were given their drink. And all the men were yet to have a fill.

In little under three days – 2nd Bn, KOYLI, had marched night and day over 60 miles. In addition, had a lift of about 20 miles on tanks, distancing from the enemy, patrolled and attacked at Monywa, and repelled cycling Japanese machine-gunners; – Thirsted, and hungered, in the great heat. Losing men through disease and exhaustion, withstanding indiscriminate air attacks throughout this period.

As ever, we had not seen, or heard, of one senior British General officer. Far from finished, and still a considerable distance to go to get out of the land, improving in appearance each day as we moved north.

Strenuous though the last few days and weeks had been, it was no more than a practice for endeavours yet to come.

27

LIAISONS

With Douglas Haig departed, Chadwick appointed me, Brigade Liaison Officer. Fully aware that driving a bareback donkey, as a boy in Ireland, was no qualification for riding a horse, my mount had to be 'shanks's pony'. L.O. proved a futile exercise; it had no meaning, not one message was passed through me. The job necessitated being detached from the unit, and travelling with a very nominal Brigade H.Q., whilst at the same time, retaining responsibility for my small platoon. I was required to return to the battalion for food, as rations were issued there on my behalf; there was no chance of my feeding with brigade. This presented problems, as one never knew the time a meal might be prepared; there was never a chance of any *buckshee* (free). My batman, being uncertain of my movements, could hardly be expected to save my rations; he was more likely to eat the bloody lot.

Having been so active in the last three days, it was difficult starting on the following morning, 5 May. The lift on the tanks in the previous day had opened a generous gap between the battalion and the oncoming Japanese. This allowed for a slight relaxation, a less hectic pace; things became a little more leisurely as we entered pleasanter, and somewhat greener, countryside. A halt was called shortly after midday, close by the village of Taunbyinnge. Here, clear water was available, and men could take a brief respite. The new job required much walking about, tooing and froing, with nothing to show for the efforts.

Returning to the battalion late in the day, I asked Benny Mee, "Where's Hewitt?"

"I don't know, sir. I haven't seen him all afternoon. Anybody seen Hewitt?"

Nobody had seen Hewitt, and it was assumed he had cleared off, as no man vanished for such a length of time without somebody knowing where he was.

"Where the bloody hell have you been?" I asked, as a much relieved, ever so much relieved, Hewitt reappeared, as though from nowhere.

"Come on! Come with me! I'll show you," leading me round to a vacated, stilt-house of matting structure, and pointed to the underside; "I've been four hours parting with that!"

There, in the middle of the floor, was the biggest turd I have seen in my life; like a loaf of French bread, long and as thick as a man's forearm. It looked like a conglomeration of 'hard-tack' ration biscuits, and soya-link sausages, eaten in the last few weeks, but certainly not like anything human.

Hewitt's inspection completed, whoops of delight rang out, heralding the arrival of the two cooks, Danny Lobben and Jacko Jackson, accompanied by the battalion butcher, – Jim Major. Driving before them a pair of very young buffalo, found tethered inside a village house. This was unbelievable, fresh young meat on legs, walking in to provide an evening lash-up. It was too good to be true.

These most desirable animals were driven down a small slope, through the Rajputana Rifles' battalion area. The Rajputs, however, aware that the buffaloes were not coming to participate in a cattle show or a rodeo, became somewhat perturbed. The boys were putting Wavell's order, "They must live off the land", into practice.

It was, however, only minutes before Rajput's Commanding Officer, Lt. Colonel Rea arrived, slobbering off his fat chops. He was of the opinion that we were going to kill the animals, so much venerated by his soldiers. How right he was! Rea insisted, indeed demanded of Chadwick, that the animals be released, 'in order to avoid unpleasantness', as he put it. One of the tragedies of my life was to see that lovely grub walking away on eight legs.

'Unpleasantness' was a commodity not in short supply, with Rea. Hardly the word to describe what very nearly followed, in view of his untimely intervention. Rea's concern was understandable, and tolerated, until, unfortunately he made the mistake of going a step too far. His unpleasantness very nearly cost him his life. Returning to his unit, he passed by six KOYLI men sitting on a low, stone-built parapet, by a small culvert; a welcome rest on a low seat, and a pleasant change from squatting on the hard dry ground.

"Don't your regiment stand and salute when an officer passes?" With officers passing at all times, men would be up and down like yo-yos. However, they stood, and pleased Rea with a salute that belied the sentiments they felt. Not satisfied with the salute, Rea continued; – "If that happens again, I shall personally see to it that your officers are flogged!" This sort of stricture had gone by the board within the unit weeks ago, and for very good reason. No officer could afford to be pointed out to an enemy sniper, by being kow-towed to, particularly by so obvious a sign as a salute. Battalion Officers had won full respect without the nonsense of salutes; so much so, that the threat made by Rea brought a response and reaction he may not have expected.

Aware that I had overheard the exchanges, Bob Rimmer's batman, Johnny Raby, asked, "Have we to shoot the bastard, Sir?" Raby appreciated the care given to his officer, and he was not one to hesitate. The small band would willingly have shot him and not given it a second thought. This was a different matter to the shooting of Burmese at Taungtha, where officers, realising the delicacy of the situation, had saved the faces of the men, and possible arguments, by themselves carrying out the unpleasant task.

Rea was the British senior officer commanding troops who had fired blindly on the unit, as we crossed the Yin Chaung swamps three weeks beforehand.

"No, you don't shoot him! If there's anyone going to shoot him, it will be the officers; the first one he threatens, or makes any attempt to flog."

With no further mention of flogging, Rea needed eyes in the back of his head for the remainder of that day. Any one of the men on the parapet would willingly have dropped him dead, had the opportunity presented itself.

Not satisfied with the assurance that any attempt at intimidation by Rea, would be attended to by officers who were every bit as good as their word. Private Fletcher, without any more ado, upped with his rifle, and was about to put Rea out of his misery, for denying the unit a meal. It was only rapid intervention by Jim Marsh that saved Rea getting on the list of those; – 'slightly damaged'.

Renowned as a hothead, Fletcher rounded on poor old 'Cloggy'. He was unaware that Marsh was a fine athlete, as well as achieving a degree at Oxford, through sheer hard work. It was the fact that Marsh came from a village near Barnsley, and in Fletcher's eyes, no man from Barnsley should be of commissioned rank. Fletcher referred to Marsh as, 'a jumped up pit rat!' Marsh was livid, he could have set to and half slain Fletcher. Considering all options, Marsh was at a loss to know what he could do, to punish a man, any more than he was being punished, in the present circumstances.

The next surprise intervention pulled me up sharp. "You silly bastards, haven't you had enough?" It was Private Michael Mycock, the silent man of my platoon. Benny Mee, Bareham, Hewitt, Bill Kibbler and others, all had had their say in the weeks together. I realised suddenly, these were the first words I had heard spoken by Mycock. This short, silent man, with a chiselled face, sharp eyes, and red hair, pushed straight back from a high forehead, had been in every action, from day one. An outstanding soldier, his boots worn down at the heels until they looked like rockers, a man totally committed, accepting the rigours of his existence without one word of complaint. Maybe in his silence, Mycock was master of Fletcher; however it was he, brought the altercation to a rapid close, with no more than one word to Fletcher.

The following day was another, 'march and ride', to a junction in the track, at Pyingaing, a small insignificant village. Tanks shuttled to and fro, giving lifts of about ten miles, before going back for more. I remained on foot, accompanying Brigade, until late in the day, when transports failed to return. In the circumstances, and having covered almost thirty miles on foot, I expected to be fed by Brigade. It was not to be, I was refused. Setting off to cover the eight or so miles to find the battalion, it was night and very dark before I found them, and what food there was had been devoured long beforehand.

The previous day, 5 May, I had had one small meal. Throughout 6 May, without a bite of food, or a fill of water, I was on the move all day, and was dehydrated, dizzy and aching, for want of sustenance of some kind. In sheer desperation, I sounded out men of the platoon, seeking the puff of a cigarette, a tab end, anything to feel the comfort of something entering my stomach, even though I was a committed non-smoker. A cigarette would have made me sick, as Douglas Haig's rum had done at the Yin Chaung. I realised my mistake; I should have shot the insensitive, and arrogant, Brigade Major, who so adamantly refused me food at H.Q.

It was a bad day that got even worse. The gestation period was over; malaria, and dysentery, had overtaken Steve during the day, and this dependable colleague, in all action to date, was now shivering and shaking like a leaf. He made no issue of his problem, simply said, "There are many worse off than me". He showed great stoicism at all times.

I had a rough night, unsure of surviving the dark hours in my weakened condition, cried a little, and said a prayer or two, as I thought of the family far away, and of what they might feel at my failing to return. It was a horrible feeling. Awakening on the following morning, I was a little surprised to find myself still alive. Without conscience, I was first in the queue for the deliciously cooked sausage, and I spared no blushes as I told Chadwick he could go to hell, and 'Stuff it!', for a liaison officer. There was no requirement for one, to be buggered about by Brigade idiots. It served no purpose.

28

THE WORLD OUTSIDE

Isolated, cocooned for weeks on end in a remote hot land, we lived from day to day, unsure whether we were to live, or to die. Nothing was known of the outside world; it was as though it did not exist, and was not given a thought. Our world was contained within the group we were with, each waking day, many thousands of miles and a million light years away from our background, training, and culture, and what we rightly considered to be British Army conditions. The real life existence of this Army in Burma was like being in another world, a world of fantasy, a world where words were the sole private possession one could part with. There was no currency, or goods, to bestow or to barter; nor anything to barter for. There was no news of the outside world, and we wondered, did it exist? It was many years later, long after the timid post-war period, one was reluctant to relate wartime experiences lest one be considered a braggart, news releases from a variety of sources told the story. It was from reluctantly divulged reports, and documents, we heard retrospectively, of activities taking place throughout the rest of the world, whilst we stewed in Burma.

These were delicate times, for both Churchill and Roosevelt, each seeking to impress and outdo the other. They were aware at all times of the effects on their personal, jealously-guarded status, within their home governments. Ever wary of Stalin, observing from behind his Russian armies, in constant and deadly combat with Hitler's Nazis. Churchill was sickened by his series of losses. Roosevelt, newly committed into war, was forever looking for a minimum of military commitment, seeking the soft option, to look impressive in the press. Roosevelt eventually demonstrated his commitment in a gentle manner. Entering America into the western war, starting with a spectacular armoured dash, across the wide open spaces of North Africa, against no enemy. But it looked good, and the cameras attended.

Whatever action Churchill undertook had to look good, and feeling that Roosevelt held him in awe, as an experienced war leader, he exploited the situation to the full. Constantly attempting to impress Roosevelt; -with pleas for American aid, armaments, ships, food and materials; all underwritten by the 'Lend-Lease' scheme, for which Britain would pay dearly. Unfortunately, Britain appeared to be about to collapse under powerful German assaults, Roosevelt remained apprehensive about entering into any commitment. It was not in his interest to be seen helping losers, in a flagging cause.

The Russian front was taking an enormous toll of casualties, from both adversaries. Russian and German tanks, guns, and troop movements, were ravaging the Russian countryside, towns and villages. German bombing of Britain, was on a scale never previously known. Roosevelt's concern was America; – not Britain, and Russian devastation. Britain, and America; allies and comrades in war, indeed? Ravenous America wanted its pound of flesh at all times. Roosevelt supplied arms to Russia, in order to maintain Russian men fighting on Russian soil, so long as they paid for the privilege, in gold.

British Battle Cruiser H.M.S. Edinburgh, carrying five tons of gold, from a Russian port, (Vladivostok?), to America, was sunk in the Barents Sea, in the Arctic Circle. It was a cold and desperate grave for the eighty-eight men, of His Majesty's British Navy, sailors whose families would never be told the truth of their ill-fated, and gallant mission: – Acting as debt collectors for Uncle Sam!

Observing Britain to be in a desperate state, and about to collapse with constant bombing, the French Government capitulated, in order to preserve Paris. Seeking friendship, fickle Mr Roosevelt did not want to be seen supporting the losing side, his sympathies tended towards Marshall Petain, and the Vichy French, now collaborating, looking very comfortable, in close cahoots with the Axis powers.

Axis powers looking firm favourites to complete an early victory, Roosevelt had problems of allegiance.

American security focused on official British personnel; correspondents, reporters, and consular staff were monitored as spies, movements and communications were checked, and recorded. Alistair Cooke, the most distinguished British foreign correspondent, and holder of dual U.S.-British nationality, was 'conveniently', considered a double agent. His offence was; 'making a request for petrol coupons', in order to travel extensively, and 'reporting the effects of the European war', within the U.S.A.

America was prepared to 'pull up the drawbridge', to retrench, and remain west of the Atlantic Ocean, dreading the notion of a Communist Russian conquest of Europe.

Information was released 50 years after the war, and reported in the *Yorkshire Post,* 23 December 1994. The article was headed, 'Expendable Europe': –

"The United States was prepared to drop radioactive poisons on Western Europe, in the late 1940s and early 1950s.

The radiation weapons were intended to paralyse industries in the event of a Soviet occupation, declassified documents from the U.S. National Archives show. But no radiation weapon is known to have been used, and they were not apparently put into the U.S. active arsenal".

Unaware that he might receive this treatment, – frantic to be in a position to report success, from whatever source, in order to bolster his flagging image, – both at home and overseas: – Churchill desperately needed a 'European cure'. He wanted failures of Singapore, Burma, and the Far East; 'put out of mind'.

In desperation, he hit upon the idea of launching an attack on a remote, and weakly defended, French Naval Base, on the island of Madagascar, to capture the island from the Vichy French. Roosevelt however, was a little peeved to hear of this rash act of aggression, disrupting his burgeoning romance with Marshall Petain, and he said so.

In the event, British forces overcame a weak resistance, and captured Madagascar Naval Base, ostensibly, in order to deny it to the Japanese,

– now in control of the Indian Ocean, and all seaways to the east, the Pacific, to West America.

Britain controlled Madagascar, the action completed in a couple of days, justified a Churchill philosophy: – He had, 'created a mass of manoeuvre'. In his war memoirs, Churchill magnified the minor conquest, 'as a major victory', and takes up several pages.

Throughout this same period: The Army in Burma was never to see, a day, or night end, without some form of action. Undertaking the longest withdrawal ever recorded in British military history; yet throughout thirty pages of Churchill memoirs, covering the early 1942 period of the war, there is not one mention of Burma, or his abandoned British Army. The sole concession to 1942 Far East activities, recorded in Churchill memoirs, is the comment; –

"The Japanese have not attacked Ceylon, or India".

To his death, there was never an apology for mistakes, or a word of praise, for the 1942 Burma campaign. Writers of Churchill autobiographies, find it convenient to ignore his embarrassments, mistakes, and downright incompetence!

29

JUNGLE WALK

On 7 May, it was as though the British Army was standing on its head, nobody giving orders. The rest day at an end, and every man being given the freedom of choice; there had to be a catch in it somewhere. Fed and rested, at Pyingaing village, located where the central plains meet the jungle of the north, it was late afternoon. Incapable of comprehending the diabolically base level of our existence: – Out of his depth in the realm of man management, in the squalid putridity of his existence; Chadwick, a diminished, frightened, dithering, Titular Commander, his age, and the crown on his shoulder being his sole saviours, called a meeting of all officers. He put forward a proposition for consideration, and sought a vote on the wishes of the meeting: -

> *"Gentlemen! We have a choice. Two villages in the jungle, located to the north of here, contain two small oil wells. Providing we are prepared to accompany them, a detachment of Indian Army sappers are equipped to destroy the installations. A march of about 85 miles is involved, and we have no guarantee of water, although the sappers are confident of finding a subterranean source on each day of the march. Men who feel they may not survive the jungle march, must be given the option of going to Kalewa, and ferried".*

> *"On reaching the Chindwin, it is up to us how we cross. Alternatively, we can continue along this track, the 40 or so miles to Kalewa, and take "pot luck" at crossing by the ferry. It's up to you. Shall we vote?"*

234

This was a British Army at war, in desperate strait, out of control, being invited to determine its own fate, in a free vote. There was no guidance, or speculation, regarding our possible survival. Were we a lost cause?

Unaware the Kalewa ferry was long destroyed, and sunk by Dacoits, we fortunately, selected the jungle march, in order to have the cover of foliage, for both camouflage and shade, from the heat of the sun.

Sadly, at Kalewa, although we did not know of this at the time, 42 tanks, of the 2/R.T.R. and 7th Hussars, had no hope of a ferry crossing, and remained, marooned on the east bank of the river; they could not negotiate jungle. With sad hearts, tank crews removed weapons, ammunition, and essential parts, hurling them into the water.

The jungle march vote was taken on the basis that there would be a log-jam queue, at the Kalewa crossing, with tanks, refugees, and itinerant groups of wounded and sick. Regardless of the destruction of the oil wells, we estimated an equal distance had to be covered, by whatever route. Crossing the Chindwin was a challenging task we officers were confident we could meet. As an engineer, I envisaged utilising available materials.

It was left to each officer to put the proposal to his men, emphasising, there could be no concessions for the weakened, or sick, of any rank. Any man feeling incapable of surviving the jungle trek, could take his chance on the more defined Kalewa road. I heard of no man opting for Kalewa.

Indian sappers were to accompany us, with mules carrying mechanical pumps, in order to extract water at prospective sites. Also, for this journey of an anticipated five or six days' march, for the first time in months, a doctor was attached. With itinerants, and the return of a few of our own men, – ones who had fallen behind, or gone missing in earlier skirmishes, – the total jungle contingent strength, was about 120 men.

8 May morning, produced a feeling of starting out on an expedition of exploration. A meal of sorts, and rest, on the previous day, had, once again, worked wonders on morale. Mules loaded with rations, pumps, wireless, and cooking gear. The battalion was travelling virtually alone. As mortar officer, I was ostensibly independent, and answerable to Chadwick. With no company ties; and I was detailed rearguard platoon, with the task of shepherding along stragglers.

Not the situation for faint-hearts. Every man knew, an accident, or sickness, could mean death. With no hope of aid once legs stopped walking. Each man would live, or die, according to his own efforts, and whatever stamina he might retain. In recent weeks, water, food, and marching, had been the same for every man, regardless of rank.

Of the battalion regular officers, apart from Chadwick, Douglas Wardleworth, returned from convalescence a day or two beforehand. Wounded in earlier conflict, east of Sittang, he had the added misfortune of accompanying his beautiful wife, as she was killed, when Japanese planes machine-gunned Myitkyina airfield. Other than Chadwick and Wardleworth, there was Throckmorton, I think he was from some army reserve list, and performed no function. The main officer strength was comprised of *Strathallan*'s intrepid emergency commissioned draft; we were in the majority.

Striking out from Pyingaing, instantly into jungle, with sweeter smelling air, and a striking contrast to the hotter, cultivated plains and farm-land of recent weeks, moving immediately into a series of high ridges, and deep valleys, running east to west, across the line of march. These were not small hillocks, but huge razorbacks, steep slopes of up to 2,000 feet, with trees and scrub cover, both up and down. This called for new energy, and new leg muscles, ones not used in the flat of the plains. Many soon realised, they had overestimated their capabilities, finding great difficulty in making the sheer climbs, and equally difficult descents.

Getting no further forward than ascending the first hill, before suffering our first casualty; it was the wireless set, which meant, instant goodbye, to possible communications. Renowned for sure-footedness though mules are, and their work rate, they are not equipped as mountain goats. The wireless mule, overbalanced by the weight of the set, went tumbling down, taking two or three men along with it. Men, mule, and wireless, all in one bundle, rolled many yards down the hill, causing havoc, and taking others with them. Most of the mules suffered similar fate, before it was realised they required help, on both ascent, and descent. slowing down the whole movement, placing extra work on tired men. The great blessing on this route was the natural camouflage and security from possible air attack; also, there were no villages in which nationalists and Dacoits could operate. Secure though the operation felt, all knew it was to be a very hard slog.

At the end of day one, in ten hours of marching, about 16 hard miles were covered. Significant, however, was the number of men finding it necessary to fall back, and to struggle into the nightfall perimeter. Lacking all normal facilities, no record was kept of individuals failing to catch up in the night; one or two men going amiss, remained just that; 'Missing Persons!' Search and recovery was not an option; no man had energy enough for additional effort. For months, there had been no pens, pencils, or paperwork; no records, documents, situation reports (SITREPS), or nominal rolls, and no means of recording jungle losses, except by word of mouth. Before moving off each day, with comings and goings of individuals, and disposition of companies, it was not possible to know, exactly, how many men remained with the unit.

The air of suspense at the end of day-one, as sappers tapped the dry watercourse, and waited for liquid to seep into the hole, was almost unbearable. It then seemed a further age, whilst mules had their priority fill; water was like wine after the hard march. There was consolation in knowing we carried meagre rations the tank boys had scraped together from food depots, before destroying sites, in order to deny them to the Japanese.

Marching on more level ground on the following morning was much easier, although progress was slower by far, as we hit dense pockets of jungle requiring cutting. As a maximum of only two or three men could operate at one time, it was difficult to maintain speeds, of even one mile an hour. The denser jungle was at all times, on the upward climb, as we mounted the south-facing hills and ridges. Foliage was sparser on the downward, northern-facing slopes. The scenery from the tops of higher ridges was spectacular, but nothing could surpass the infinite beauty in many of the valleys: – Where multi-coloured orchids sprouted from the trunks of giant teak trees. The whole base of many valleys were covered in a blanket of thousands upon thousands of cream, or blue, coloured butterflies: – Unfolding from one end, they would roll away like a huge whispering cloud, on our approach.

In spite of the slowed down progress, the 15 or so strenuous miles covered in the second day proved exhausting for some. The doctor; a tall, gaunt, pockmarked Eurasian; stayed behind with one man in extreme difficulty, and with no movement. It was some time later, we heard a shot, and as Dr Xavier rejoined, he commented, "I don't think that he will make it!"

There was no comment; many men had expressed the desire to take a, 'leaden tablet', rather than face capture by the Japanese, or suffer, and die in agony through dysentery or malaria. More than one man failed to make camp that night. Sadness was expressed amongst colleagues, only for it to be forgotten the following day, as each one considered his own increasing problem of survival.

Target destination for day three, was the first of the two oil wells at the isolated small village of Indaw, almost 20 'map' miles ahead, and considerably further in jungle trek. It would have been boring, had I not let my mind wander, and consider the prospect of such a trip in peacetime. To see such spectacular beauty, the grandeur of the hills, and smell of the tall trees, which few white men had seen, was compensation for the inconvenience. Not all could dwell on the scenery with such delight, to appreciate the spectacular orchids and butterflies. Splendid to behold, but not for all, as the doctor remained behind a couple of times to tend the faltering sick, and each time, we were to hear the thud of a shot, before his return some minutes later.

Arrival at Indaw required particular care of approach, even a small oil well might merit special attention from the Japanese; they could have sent an advanced raiding party up river by boat, as we undertook the long scenic walk through the woods. We need hardly have bothered, and the sappers did what was necessary to incapacitate the single well, and pump equipment. As a precautionary measure, the night was spent a few miles from Indaw.

The sapper water-diviners had performed magic; there was, however, no call for their skills on the final, 20-mile approach to the oil well at Pantha. Travelling in the eastern side of the Kadaw Valley, we followed the line of a fast flowing stream, with plenty of welcome clean water. Traversing the line of the stream meant climbing up and down rocky banks, crossing, and recrossing the stream over 50 times, following what appeared to be an indistinct animal track. Wading in and out of water, quite deep in places, was a novel experience after the hot, dry dust bowl of the plains.

This was strenuous in a different way, and the slight coolness was appreciated by the fitter men. It was in this stretch that a young Chinese boy, an itinerant travelling with the group, showed a skill that I had not seen before or since. He stopped, and bent down beside the stream, with one hand in the water, and in no more than a few seconds he withdrew the hand with a prime fifteen-inch trout in his grasp. It was eaten raw.

Day-by-day debilitation of each man had been a slow process, but was now speeding on by the hour, and all men were visibly disintegrating as we marched; there were no exceptions. Calf and leg muscles were bulging; shirts and shorts were hanging on withering bodies. Private Fish was very ill, a popular soldier, with friends throughout the unit, a sportsman, good for a song and a joke at any time. Like many others, he was suffering from dysentery, and almost every other illness.

Finding great difficulty in making camp on the previous two nights, Fish's shattered frame was clearly about to meet the ultimate. He fell back early on the following day, and all knew it would be a struggle for him to survive; he did, however, manage to rejoin at the halt. Fish was incapable of further movement at the restart, and after attempting a few yards, he stopped and slumped in the bushes. Xavier stayed with Fish, the familiar sound of a shot rang out, and the doctor rejoined us after about 15 minutes. No question was asked about which of the two had squeezed the trigger. Private Fish was the last, of the seven or eight men, lost on the jungle march east of the Chindwin River. Only superhuman effort was keeping many of the others fighting on, to stay with the unit.

Xavier had arrived, and joined the unit, in the guise of a doctor, with three pips on his shoulders, lacking equipment and medical aids. He was recognised, and identified by several soldiers, as a former 'Knob Doctor', at Mandalay pox hospital; a place known to its regulars: – Authentification indeed! Subsequent efforts to trace this man, through War Office records, failed, and there was no trace of such a person in the Royal Army Medical Corps. It appears that Xavier was a plausible impostor, although he did obviously have some nursing experience. *(As a result of publishing this book, I received remarkable news of the doctor).*

Travelling from Pantha, towards the bank of the Chindwin was the hardest part of this long and very tough march. In rough, rugged, wet jungle, or possible rain forest, with many steep climbs, and numerous diversions around inlets and tributaries, we had a growing impatience, and a feeling of uncertainty, as to exactly where we were, and how far we had to go in order to arrive opposite the small riverside village of Yu-a, situated on the far west bank. Our map did not have detail enough for tiny settlements, although we fully expected to come upon one on our side of the river, and establish a means of ferrying across; but there was none. Yu-a, an established village on the far western bank of the Chindwin, was the place we aimed to be opposite.

Clambering on in the semi-darkness, for many hard miles, we arrived at what was accepted to be the correct spot on the river bank, a rough and desolate place, with a peculiar mystic coldness, and damp all around; a breeding ground for mosquitoes and leeches. This was an inhospitable place in which to arrive, after more than 90 miles of a tough jungle march, of nine or ten days. To have trudged so far, through such beautifully scenic parts of the world, to have seen so many spectacular sights, and yet to lose en-route almost one man of every ten, with not one enemy bullet fired, was tragic.

My wish, is that those unfortunates left behind may be blanketed, and blessed by the spectacular butterflies, as they lie quietly and at peace, close by a beautiful orchid. As a man leaves his 'mucker' in distress, it is with an apologetic smile, and a shake of the head; as each one bows out, he knows it to be for the last time. For the first time since meeting at the regimental depot, they lie there in silence. There is the tender hug, and the soft kiss on the cheek, as the eyes glaze over; the words are spoken, "Goodbye pal. God bless! I'm proud to have known you!"

What mattered to every man, was that he be known, as a member of, 'The Regiment'; A KOYLI! 'The Regiment' jealously guards the brave deeds, and the failures; it honours the brave, and tolerates the coward, so long as he served with the regiment. Bravery is unpredictable, often coming from the humble, quiet, unassuming one; although mostly, 'it

W. W. Dawson

W. Abbot

Serjeant Thomas Benjamin (Benny) Mee as corporal,
aged 24 years at Sale Barracks, Rangoon, 1938

Jim Major, B.E.M.

Major V. L. Stevens (Steve)

J. Isaacs   G. Bareham

E. T. Hewitt   M. Mycock

W. Slee   W. Kibbler

TO THE VERY END

Gerald Lyster
1945

245

Gerald and Patricia Fitzpatrick

Gerald Fitzpatrick

248

just happens', and is not recognised by officialdom. The British 'Soldier of the Line', is a prince among men; he seeks nothing, other than good, trustworthy friends, and competent commanders. There were many princes in the 2nd Battalion, The King's Own Yorkshire Light Infantry. Not one of those men lost to the jungle would have considered taking the alternative choice, of travelling the uncertain track to Kalewa; a track which proved, in the end, to be equally treacherous as the jungle stroll.

No matter the cost, or discomfort, there was no question of parting from chums in the unit. Family and friends back at home were hardly a memory, and the long weeks of absence with no letter, created a dependency on the man, actually there, by one's side. Uncertainty of life itself, caused a bonding within a section, within a platoon, or within a company. As the hard months of endurance took their toll, there was pride in achieving day-by-day survival. No man would willingly part from his 'mucker', it is a deep and enduring bond, one that has no equivalent in civilian life; it is honoured forever by his comrades. It is the magic that a survivor savours in silence, for the remainder of his life, no matter how many years roll by. He knows exactly the spot where 'Chalky', or 'Nobby', or 'Dusty' fell, to lie at peace forever. He remembers the anniversaries, the date they joined, the moment they met, the days of embarkation, the landing, and so much more; and there, printed indelibly in his mind across all else, are his army number and, 'the last three', of every man in the platoon. He feels the ache and the pain, as he remembers the joy and the pride they shared together. The allegiance transcends all family ties and understanding; his family cannot see, or envisage, the picture of the young man, so vivid in his mind; 'His Mucker!'.

The bond was made for life, and it is for life. He sees clearly the young man, he has not aged one day over the last fifty years, he sees the smile, he hears the chat, and he remembers the mischief.

It is a deep pride, a private inner thing he alone knows; his eyes moisten, and the occasional tear runs down his wrinkled cheek. They were, 'Soldiers of the Line'. Together, They Served! 'Chalky', 'Nobby' and 'Dusty'! No, they don't change!

30

SWIM THE CHINDWIN

Being rearguard, I was positioned well back in the wet undergrowth, some distance from the leaders. With no sight of the river, the message arrived, 'Any swimmers? Go forward!'

Having trained as a swimmer, with the City of Leeds Olympic training squad, throughout my teens, and knowing that I had the ability, I went forward. Joining the army as a sapper recruit, I won the 1939, London Division Swimming Championships, with 501 Field Company, R.E. at Chelsea baths. With the R.E. Field Company, it was a 'nutter' of an adjutant, who became, in due course, Major 'Mad' Mike Calvert, who challenged me to a swim. I declined the offer to swim naked, when on a bridging exercise, across the freezing river at Royal Tunbridge Wells, in the bleak snow-bound winter of 1939.

Leaving Sergeant Mee in charge of the platoon, and taking batman Ted Hewitt forward, I was feeling a little apprehensive as to what was required. What I saw, initially, was the vast expanse of the massive, fast-flowing River Chindwin. The purpose of the swim was explained; I was to swim to the opposite bank, and persuade the men of the small village of Yu-a, to help in getting the column across, in boats. That is, providing they had boats with which to do this; it was as simple as that.

The opposite bank was a far distant horizon, three quarters of a mile distant, and, in the shimmering mist of heat haze, it looked much further than that. There was no chance of the column crossing the river without assistance, and boats. Any ideas of cutting trees and making rafts, were clearly 'pie in the sky'. The swim was a daunting challenge, that I knew I must accept.

"You're not swimming that bloody thing, are you?" asked Hewitt.

"Yes, I am"

"You must be bloody mad. You'll never make it."

"Yes, I will."

For the first time since sliding down the *nullah* at the Yin Chaung, and bursting my boil, I stripped and removed my underpants. For the last month, bugs had eaten bugs in my filthy underpants, there was no mark remaining, nothing to show where the congealed mess from the boil had been. Stripped off, Hewitt taking my clothes, I expressed surprise to see nine or ten men already swimming; they were a good distance out from the bank. It had obviously taken some little time for the message to reach me, at the tail end of the column. However, I was pleased, and encouraged, to see so many volunteers striking out for the far shore; if they felt they might do it, I was sure that I could.

Feeding from mountain snows, the cold, bubbling, gargantuan River Chindwin would soon become a raging and impassable torrent. The very predictable monsoons of North Burma were due to start in the next few days, about 24-26 May. As it was, rain already started further to the north, accounted for the present increase of flow. The formidable width, and the speed of current, were not the greatest of problems. I knew that when fit, I could swim, or float, all day if necessary, to hit some landfall. I did have some doubts, however, about my present strength and stamina, being so physically exhausted. I knew the dangers of stomach cramp with the loss of weight, so much marching, and the day-by-day strain of every muscle.

Resolving within myself, that I was going to 'give it a go', I was aware that it would give me 'free rein'; I did not have to rely on others for crossing the river. It would result in my being on the safer side of the river, wherever I landed. Although, thinking earnestly of the needs of the column, it was not a case of 100 per cent altruism. I wanted Me across!

I set forward to enter the water, and what a shock I got. The formidable width and flow of the river was one thing, but the next sight stopped me in my tracks, in sheer terror. In the water, four or five feet to my front, was passing a dreadful horror. From spawning grounds in up-river lakes, mammoth eels, or sea snakes, were making their way south to the Indian

Ocean, in the form of a huge solid tube. An inter-twining mass, no more than inches below the surface, and close by the shore. It was frightening just to be standing on the river bank. I was petrified to think of going into the water, joining with them.

This was no place for a nice Irish boy who had climbed Croagh Patrick, the mountain from which Saint Patrick banished snakes from Ireland; for to me, those things in the water were snakes. Twelve feet or more in length, and as many inches in diameter, they were passing downstream in their thousands, maybe hundreds of thousands. Cowardice was very near the surface in me; it was only the fact that others had entered the water ahead of me, and were swimming freely, that took me, shivering and shaking, into the river.

Aware of the energy-sapping task ahead, I started by striking out with a steady breaststroke. I was going along nicely when I got caught up in what felt like the bow wave of a speedboat; it was a sepoy of the sappers, overtaking me – using a crawl stroke, he sped by me. So powerful was this man's stroke, I thought he must have been tampered with by one of the snakes. He lifted out of the water, almost to the waist, by the power of his stroke, and he was expending so much energy, and travelling at such speed, that I thought myself to be motionless. Quite suddenly, 20 or 30 feet ahead of me, the sepoy vanished; he must have run out of steam, and been totally exhausted, as there was no signal of distress, and no struggle. Sure enough, he was gone, away with the snakes. He would float by Rangoon, as had the first dead man I saw from the deck of *Ellenga,* so many days ago, bloated, sun baked, and very dead.

Such was the width of the river, that from the centre, with eyes at water level, it was not possible to see either bank. I was swimming almost upstream, against the current, with the flow of the river striking my right shoulder, in order to maintain direction. It was energy-sapping to maintain even a modest breaststroke, and doubts began to grow. I had seen men, considering themselves fit, as they started out on the jungle walk, only to fail with little warning as they were overtaken by illness and fatigue. Of course, the thought of something similar happening to me crossed my mind; I knew that I was exhausted, and yet so much rested on my shoulders. There was no knowing how many of the forward bunch of swimmers would reach the far bank; – so, for the sake of those behind, I must keep going and succeed.

In midstream, away from the day-to-day running of the platoon, there was time to think over the situation of the men back on the east bank. With rations exhausted and no hope of supplies, they would be completely written off, standing by the banks of the Chindwin; there was no way out in the event of swimmers failing to obtain assistance. I was swimming for England, with my life on the line. Competing with the fast current of the river was taxing in the extreme, particularly in view of the privations suffered in recent weeks. How many of the swimmers, if any, would succeed in crossing safely? Certainly, I had no intention of being beaten, although it meant swimming against the flow, a distance equal to more than twice the river width. Exhausting though it was, there could be no turning back. In the early stages, the far bank appeared to be moving further away with every stroke, and I felt the strain as my body cooled, minute by minute, to a frightening and dangerous degree. After what seemed an eternity, the far skyline gradually became discernible through the lifting heat haze; the safe shore was ahead, and ever more inviting and invigorating, the strokes became easier as trees and sand came into view.

Not that it mattered, but there was no knowing how long it took to swim the river, and nobody asked about the number of starters who failed on the strenuous task. Emerging in ones and twos from many landing points on the far bank, naked to a man, I realised that Douglas Wardleworth had answered the call forward long before I did. He was already across; the only other person from the battalion to join in the swim.

There was an understandable feeling of trepidation, amongst ourselves and the villagers of Yu-a, as we approached one another along the sandy shore. We, a group of naked and unarmed swimmers, approached apprehensively, lest the villagers came armed with *dahs* with which to castrate us. The villagers were equally apprehensive at seeing such a gathering of naked men. It was some little time before the village headman appeared. He had been summoned, and there was a period of uncertainty. After an initial misunderstanding of our needs, a villager with a knowledge of English arrived, just in time to help put matters right, and explain that the daughters of the village would remain safe.

Eventually, several small, serviceable canoes, each capable of carrying between four and seven men, were recovered from being hidden in the jungle and scrub, some distance south from the village. Then began a day-long task for the excellent, experienced village fishermen, ferrying the remainder of the column across the river. Meanwhile, the kindly, friendly folk, brought the swimmers a red fruit juice drink, of true nectar, tasting of rich plum; it was so good that sixty years later, I recall that drink as most beautiful, and memorable.

One mule was the only casualty reported on the crossing; a handler lost balance, causing him to release the head harness. The man was distressed at the loss of so faithful an animal, one that had served the battalion so obediently on the long jungle march, and hoped that it might hit a landfall, or a sandbank, and survive. Hewitt eventually arrived to hand me my clothing, with no more than his usual look of disdain; not one word was spoken, but the look said a hell of a lot.

I had never thought it would be so, but the Chindwin crossing became a marker in my future years; a man who can swim a river of those proportions, in the condition I found myself, can do anything.

31

SALUTE OR SHOOT

A scrape of something to eat in the mess tin, and an assurance that there might be sufficient rations for one more similar 'banquet', before accepting the hard fact that the cupboard was bare: – No further rations, and no idea how we might survive in the event of our meeting with difficulties, and undue delays, such as rivers, hills and jungle.

There was of course, the 'fickle-factor' to consider; there was a danger that these friendly folk would be forced, or equally friendly, towards the Japanese, a prospect that we could not afford. Before departing our friends at Yu-a, and with assurances that King George would recompense them, apologies were made for putting holes in the boats of the good villagers.

The westward route out, was into virtually uncharted territory; we followed what there was of a most indistinct village track, uncertain of distance and difficulty. It meant following the line of the river Yu, through what transpired to be the most beautiful and spectacular of valleys, the western half of the Kabaw. A tranquil, small river flowed gently through lush grassland, interspersed with tall trees; the track crossed and re-crossed the river several times, like the one on the eastern side of the Chindwin. The terrain was rough in places, although mostly it was easy walking, and the short rest at Yu-a, helped resuscitate the men. Notable on this side of the river was the lack of sound in the jungle. It was almost silent compared with the hubbub on the eastern side, where we had the constant screaming of the 'woogle-woogle bird'; – (I had mistakenly thought the never-ending noise of monkeys, to be that of birds).

After a few miles of walking, I expected weaker members to falter and succumb to ailments, but here they found something that was to spur them on to survive, and override all ills and aches. The terrifying sight of dead refugees around the track, made it a case of; – 'There, but for the grace of God, go I'. Far worse was to come, however, with the vile smell and horrible choking taste of death. Into the Valley of Death marched The King's Own Yorkshire Light Infantry; the Kabaw Valley. Refugees, dead and dying in their hundreds, possibly thousands, were dispersed all around this most beautiful and tranquil setting. Bullocks and mules lay dead in the shafts of carts. Flies by the million swarmed throughout; one wondered if one could believe one's eyes in scenery so tranquil, it could be a setting for paradise.

Crossing the Irrawaddy further to the south, the unfortunate refugees had covered hundreds of miles up the west bank of the Rivers Irrawaddy and Chindwin. With rations exhausted, succumbing to the elements and ailments, the tired refugees had found water, the most precious of all commodities. Unable to move further, and without food or hope, they had abandoned all, and died in this place. It was horrifying; the sight, smell and taste, could never be forgotten. Our situation was little different to that of the refugees; aware that we might suffer a similar fate unless help came quickly. It was ironic that a British infantry battalion should be reduced, to being unable to offer the slightest help to even one of these doomed refugees. The impact of witnessing the possible vulturine disposal of unfortunates, on our sick and wounded men, was quite miraculous. It was like a Lourdes cure; the pace quickened, backs straightened, men simply dared not fall back to die in this place.

Leaving Kabaw Valley the following day, was a surprisingly well-defined track, which climbed steadily, hour after hour. Walking was now easier than trekking through jungle. I walked on, quite unaware of my own developing problem; open jungle sores were forming on my instep, and behind the knee joint of my right leg. Leeches must have taken their fill, and the puncture marks turned sceptic; it was as we stopped for a short halt, that I felt the pain, and became aware of the familiar open sores, already over one inch in diameter. A number of men with similar scabs were now walking with skin hanging from their legs.

Dwelling on the sores was no answer, as we continued up the long slope. I was tired and walking with lowered head. Arriving at the head of a steep pass, my eyes were cast down from the intense burning sun, and the never-ending sweat. I was surprised! No, I was shocked! To see, as I lifted my head slightly, a pair of highly polished brown boots, and above them, a pair of immaculately creased khaki drill trousers, and the smartest bush-jacket I had seen in more than three months.

There, standing on a mound to the right of the track, was General Alexander, Irish Guards, and General Officer Commanding Burma, with a less flashy officer perched alongside him. It was my first and last sighting of Alexander. Should I salute? Or should I not salute? It was a difficult decision.

I had long lost all respect for anything representing higher command; they had dismally failed me and my colleagues, and the good men within our care. The only things that Alexander and I had in common, were that we were both commissioned officers in, His Majesty's British Army, we both wore brown boots; his well-shined, mine dull, and well-worn. It was a question of; – "Do I Salute? Or do I Shoot?" My first reaction was, "You despicable sod! You represent everything that has got me into this state. Why the hell should I salute you?" It would have been an easy matter to shoot the two of them. No! I had pride in myself, and wanted my men to have pride and self-respect. The salute would be for the platoon, rather than for any general; it was not done out of respect for Alexander. I wanted Alexander to recognise, acknowledge, and for him to salute my men as I gave the order:

"Kings Own Yorkshire Light Infantry! Mortar Platoon! March to attention! Eyes-right!" I whipped up my first salute in weeks, and nine wonderful men did Alexander proud, turning eyes in unison.

We now knew that we were safe; one does not see a General Officer Commanding, in war territory. Alexander had early good fortune, when the Japanese were unaware that they had him 'in the bag' near Rangoon. He ensured that they did not get a second chance, by keeping well out of danger. At the time, I did not know the senior officer alongside Alexander, the quiet man, standing discreetly apart on the mound. I was to come to know and respect him later, as General Bill Slim. For almost twelve months, I was an instructor at Slim's tough Battle School for officers, at Ranchi. Bill Slim was, in due course, to command the 14th Army, and he was also a true judge of men; importantly, he was prepared not only to talk to them, but also to listen to them. In his book, 'Defeat into Victory', he writes; -

"On the last day of the 900 mile retreat, I stood on a bank beside the road and watched the rearguard march into India.

All of them, British, Indian, and Gurkha, were gaunt and ragged as scarecrows. Yet still they trudged behind their surviving officer. They still carried their arms. They might look like scarecrows, but they looked like soldiers too".

Slim never failed to issue the code discussed at the Battle School, the one KOYLI officers had honoured throughout the campaign:

"I tell you as officers, that you will neither eat, nor drink, nor smoke, nor sit down, nor lean against a tree, until you have personally seen that your men have first had the chance to do any of those things. If you will do this for them they will follow you to the ends of the earth".

When Mountbatten was appointed Supreme Commander, South East Asia Command, he was advised by Brooke, Chief of The Imperial General Staff, 'to get rid of all the useless senior officers. Except Slim.'

Having seen Alexander standing by the trackside, Mycock was so relieved, he spoke once again; – "We're out now. I've one round of ammo' left, sir". He had 'saved' one round, in case he needed it for himself. Where he came from, and where he went, I never knew. He was a very secretive man. Private Michael Mycock, never forgotten in more than sixty years. Passing Alexander, we were on Indian soil, and shortly, arrived at the small hill town of Tamu. Even at this late stage, part of the battalion was, once again, 'sent back', by Bruce Scott, to the head of the pass, in order to provide, quite unnecessarily, cover for the few straggling troops still arriving. There was no doubt, Japanese troops had been left well behind; – Alexander's presence indicated the ground was safe, otherwise he would not have been around.

Alexander was true to form, as a Guards' Officer. He had been, 'out of town', for over two months, London beckoned, and he certainly wanted no more of the east. He was to be rid of his accursed Burma Command, and on his way back to London within the next three days, with the patronising words, "The Burma rescue operation, as I have to regard it, is over": – What Rescue? And what standard of, 'Regard'?

When despatched on the Burma assignment, he asked Brooke, Chief of the Imperial General Staff; – "You will send me all you can?" Brooke sent Sweet F-all, in large lumps. Returned to England, Alexander remained quiet about the failure of Brooke to fulfil his promise of adequate supplies. Not one word of apology, or recrimination, is to be found.

Alexander was in great haste to depart. Making no effort whatsoever to approach any of the surviving units. There was not one word of appreciation, for effort.

It was cold on the Tamu, 5000-foot high plateau, where Steve eventually succumbed to his ailments. Shivering and shaking like a leaf, he asked, "Fitz, I'm so cold, can I share your blanket?"

"Get in Steve!"

The conflict was over; all that now remained, was making more than 80 miles, to the railhead, and survive for however long it took to arrive there. The prospect was four or five days of marching.

Many had good reason to thank the men and women of the Naga tribes, headhunters up to recent times, who, dressed in no more than a piece of string around the waist, with a small panel of leather front and rear. Using primitive tools, they had worked round the clock in their hundreds, hacking out a perilous twisting road through jungle hills. The road was completed in a few short weeks, and carried army transports, where only a short time before, no road was thought possible. It was a road that would almost certainly disintegrate in the imminent monsoon rains. Considering the time, the place, and equipment available, the mountain road was by far the most spectacular feat of civil engineering in the war; and to look back down the long, steep, twisting slope was an awe-inspiring sight.

The rough and twisting Manipur Road, from Tamu to Palel, crossed 40 or 50 miles of high mountain plateau, running from south to north, to the east of Assam, and dividing what are generally referred to as the East, and Far East. Conducting, 'march and ride', on this stretch, the last two unfortunates of the battalion were to die. Sergeant 'Ike' Oldcorn of Bradford, and Private F. P. Crabtree, of Shipley, both collapsed, dead, within less than six hours' march of Palel.

I was favoured, owing to rapid development of the jungle sores on my leg, and allowed early transportation over this beautiful sector. My transport was a three-tonner filled with sick Rajput soldiers, but they were not sick enough for my liking. Halfway across the high mountains, and at the top of a huge crevasse, lay a bullock, obviously in great pain, and screaming with a broken leg. Halting the truck, I got out and drew my pistol, with the intention of putting the unfortunate animal out of its misery, only to hear a shout from the truck. On looking round, I found myself gazing up the barrels of four rifles, pointing straight at me. The bullock was left on the roadside. The spectacular sight on that journey, was the silhouette looking line of the Himalayan Mountains, many hundred miles distant.

Monsoon rains began to fall as our trucks arrived at Palel. We had a quick meal before continuing on the remaining 30 or so miles across the sweeping plateau, to Imphal, where the rain was now torrential. The allocated assembly field, already marked out as the KOYLI reception area, was a morass, there were no huts and no tents. Happily enough, the same rains would be making torrents of the rivers, and *chaungs* of Burma, holding back advancing Japanese.

At Imphal, the first person to meet and greet me, as I dismounted from the transport, was an old mate and neighbour, one who had lived two doors away from me before the war, in another hole in the ground, a back-to-back house. Corporal Fred Thompson, of the West Yorkshire Regiment, was supervising unloading.

"Hello! Fiddlefart! What the hell are you doing here?" "Oh! Sorry, Sir!" – as he saw the black, one pip mark, on the epaulette of the well-worn, 'shirt cellular'.

Chadwick asked me to make a careful count of the battalion strength; all present within the saturated area of ground allocated for sleep that night, 19 May 1942. It totalled 9 officers,* and 70 other ranks, possibly one tenth of the operational strength of the battalion. Most of those present were sick, and due for months of hospitalisation. The figure would vary within minutes, as ones and twos arrived on later transports, and as others departed to report sick. Wardleworth, recently returned from convalescence, and four recently arrived T/A officers, were acting rearguard, for the glory of Bruce Scott. The figure of those present, was simply, those 'on site', at the time of count.

Following the early loss of Keegan, to the east of the River Sittang, there were four other Commanders during the period of withdrawal:

David Martin, in the period following the crossing of the Sittang, and later, after being missing in the five days of skirmishing around the Alexander ambush, until his arrival at Tharrawaddy.

Gerald Fitzpatrick, appointed by my peers at Tharrawaddy in the absence of seniors, including Martin; organised defences and nominated staff. I assumed control for more than three days, far longer than the unfortunate Tynte.

Tynte (ex-Cameronians), survived no more than two hours, killed attempting, single-handedly, to clear the north side of the Alexander roadblock; – I never met with the man.

Geoffrey Chadwick, assumed command of the unit from Martin, at Yenangyaung, and continued until the final extrication at Kohima.

Three commanders were lost, Keegan, Tynte, and Martin, all through unnecessary bravado. Keegan recovered following evacuation, and survived to a great age. Records indicate 8 officers, and 122 men were killed in action. 400 men were wounded, and about 400 evacuated, with at least 50 missing.

It was 96 days, from the battalion first joining battle with the Japanese, on 11 February 1942; – and 75 days, since our intrepid draft of junior officers parted from S.S. *Ellenga* at Rangoon, to meet Major Pip Moran and join with the battalion.

---

* The 9 officers were: G. Chadwick, N. Throckmorton, G. Fitzpatrick, A. Maclaren-Young, L. P. Wise, J. Marsh, J. A. Welbourne, V. L. Stevens, D.V. Oakley; two majors, and seven junior officers from, S.S.*Strathallan* draft.

Three weeks of incompetence, at the outset, by British generals, with Churchill interference; – completed the destruction of a front line infantry division. The cowardly destruction, by Smyth, of the Sittang River Bridge, spelt out termination.

Ten further weeks of withdrawal followed, with combat, humiliation, and neglect, but never retreat. In order to extricate ourselves, we held the enemy at every meeting, and when necessary, did it again. We were unaware that this was to be the longest, and certainly the loneliest, and hungriest, withdrawal action of any British Army. I had been no more than an interested observer as the Dunkirk survivors returned, to be fêted and to receive the glory. The Burma evacuation was somewhat different, it was so much further from home; such an embarrassment to the authorities that it was better forgotten. Members of 2/KOYLI knew, nothing mattered, other than their survival.

Seemingly, and feeling, no more than a boy? I was a proud man; my peers having appointed me to command: – I had planned, given orders, and been obeyed in all respects. At the hostile village of Taungtha, supervised the most difficult of orders, in front of the dithering Chadwick. Under fire, on the darkest of nights, emerging from a swamp, been ordered by Baxter to take over his company, or be shot in the worst of conditions. All action I had undertaken with confidence: -

Yes! I could soldier!

32

SCATTER

Heavy rain, and the mud on the ground, was therapeutic to sleep in, following the constant heat of past weeks. Reveille next morning meant food, as a first priority, after which all were required to undergo medical examination. Though far from feeling an invalid, I was declared sick, owing to the rapid spread of the jungle sores, and whisked off to Dinapore railhead, along with Steve, who was desperately ill; – dispatched to hospital at Gauhatti, where the screening process sorted sick and wounded categories.

Encountering civilisation, at Kalimpong rail station, close by the tea plantation, we knew that we were on safe ground. The long trestle tables were laid, with bright white tablecloths, and cups and saucers, alongside large steaming urns. Fine though this site was, it was the collection of ladies, in their beautiful, many-coloured pastel dresses, and newly pressed aprons, that were a tonic for the eyes. Their smiles, and the few cheerful words were uplifting. This was where a man knew exactly what those past testing weeks were all about.

On arrival at hospital, it was not surprising to find it overcrowded; wards and balconies overflowing, those less ill accommodated on lawns. One night at the hospital, and I was sent on my way, 70 or so miles to heaven, 6,500 feet up, to the beautiful hill station of Shillong, capital of Assam. It was a place of paradise from the first day of arrival, on 24 May.

Gerry Small, Director of Education, and his charming wife Beth, had made over part of their beautiful, large, thatch-roofed bungalow, 'La Chaumière', to accommodate convalescing officers, and the reception was beyond our wildest dreams. Large rooms, with beds nicely spaced along the walls, white sheets, red blankets, and pyjamas. There were showers, and huge warmed towels, followed by Scotch whisky, dispensed all round, and a never-ending supply of curried chicken. It was the dream I had fought for, and striven to arrive at, perfect in every way.

75 days in Burma? My weight reduced from 158 lbs (72 Kg), to 112 lbs (51 Kg), a loss of 46 lb (21 Kg). Feeling I had lived three lifetimes. The experience of those long, testing days ensured that henceforth, in any adversity, I knew true values and humility. Acquiring true judgement of man, his potentials and his failings. I would never be afraid.

The solitary infantryman, amongst thirteen officers accommodated at 'La Chaumiere', I was alone in a mix of engineers, signallers, and others, one of them a civilian. It was clear that not one of them had been hammered to the extent that I had in the last three months, and the active dozen were up and about within one or two days of arrival. I was the odd one out, and appreciating the luxury of the beautiful bed for a third day, when the angel of 'La Chaumière', nursing sister Constance May Bowen, became irritated.

"Mr Fitzpatrick! It's about time you were getting up and about like the others!"

"Go to hell! Leave me alone!"

I was instantly, full of remorse, and could have bitten off my tongue at the boorish retort. However, the words were spoken, and Connie stalked from the room. She could not know the extent of my debilitation throughout the last few weeks, and I felt as low as a man can feel.

Late that night; called for replacement dressings on my leg. I was embarrassed, humble, fearful, and dreading to face the one person that most certainly did not merit my rudery. Unaccustomed to such situations, apologies were not my strong point, and it was difficult to know, with what words of contrition to approach Connie.

"I'm sorry, Mrs Bowen, I'm terribly sorry about what I said this afternoon. It was very wrong of me, please forgive me?" The kiss; so timely, was the most beautiful and memorable of my life. Here was heaven.

Steve was evacuated to 17th British Military Hospital, at the pleasant Dehra Dun hill station, and spent many months convalescing. He did many jobs in India, precluding him rejoining the regiment. Steve and I were next to meet on board ship, when repatriated to England, in July 1945.

Although Steve and I both found ourselves leaving the battalion in more haste than we would have wished, hospitalised from the mud bath, there was one man well ahead of us; Major Nicholas Throckmorton, on his way before all others. Without anybody's knowledge, or authority, Nick was the first man away from the bed of mud, to the railhead of Dinapore. Here, he managed to wangle himself onto the train, and away to Calcutta.

The remainder of the battalion was evacuated, with almost 100 percent sick, scattered throughout India, in hospitals, transit camps, or attached to other units. Unfortunately, there was another tier of departures from the unit, a small band, the few deserters, those returned prematurely to India. Some amongst them caused pandemonium at reception organisations, with a series of deceptions, to gain benefit in pay and travel. It was easy to believe the truth, these men had received no pay for six months; once paid, however, a few of them managed to repeat the story, and receive pay on more than one occasion. In short, they managed to get the battalion a bad name amongst the military hierarchy. As is the way of things, the bad name travelled further, and faster, than any good name, to places where they would have been happiest to think the battalion no longer existed. In the eyes of some senior staff, the battalion had virtually vanished from the face of the earth, months beforehand.

It was as though the survival was an embarrassment, in places like Wavell's Delhi H.Q. and no doubt, Churchill's Whitehall den. We had for months been eliminated from their minds, and it would have been cosy, almost uplifting, to report; – 'The loss of our gallant Army in Burma'.

It was fortunate for Churchill that greater operations, in Africa, and Europe, brought about by the Churchillian tactic, 'Cause a mass of manoeuvre', masked the loss of Burma. With spectacular and well-publicised activity nearer home, it became easy to forget the distant fiasco. Had not the African and European campaigns flourished, Churchill would have assuredly been toppled in Parliament.

The stigma attached to the battalion, certainly influenced the newly arrived, Lord Louis Mountbatten. Reminded by his Generals of, 'the zone of active combat', Mountbatten found it expedient to transfer, from the luxury, comfort, and indifference, of the Hotel Suisse, in Kandy, Ceylon, with his S.E.A.C. Headquarters, to the more appropriate venue, at Delhi; 2/KOYLI were already resident at the nearby Cantonment Barracks. Mountbatten sought to be, 'Hail fellow, well met', popular with 'the Chaps', and 'the Girls'. He occasionally attended, the Saturday night 'All Ranks Dance', at the KOYLI drill hall; – mixed and talked with nurses from the various hospitals; – Navy girls, – and members of the Women's Auxiliary Corps (India), the lovely W.A.C.I.s.

Although nothing was ever said throughout his many visits, to which exception might be taken, Mountbatten never once engaged in conversation with KOYLI officers. On the contrary, he distanced himself: – Time and time again, he was invited to visit the Officers' Mess, the answer was always the same, cool appreciative negative. Mountbatten's refusals were at all times courteous, and his excuses believable, yet he would attend a Royal Air Force Mess, even the newly arrived American Messes. It was thought, had Indian politician, Nehru been invited, Nehru's 'close friend', Lady Edwina Mountbatten, may well have joined him. Not only was it Mountbatten avoided the unit; – at various camps and stations, throughout the two years since leaving Burma, not one senior rank General Officer had visited, to address officers, and men; certainly not Wavell!

The battalion was studiously disregarded, as though in disgrace, perhaps because generals could not face questioning on incompetence. General Staff remained remote; they did not wish to know about the struggles, and actions, during the long withdrawal, in which decisions were made completely outside their control.

In the aftermath of war, in the years of nostalgia and remembrance, it became prudent to recognise, glorify, and to honour the successes, and various campaigns. It was so in *Dekho!,* April 1995 magazine, for the 'Final Reunion' of The Burma Star Association.

Patron of the association, H.R.H. The Duke of Edinburgh, writes of the Burma campaign: -

"We may like to think of it as a war that was "forgotten" by many people in this country, but it will never be forgotten by history, and that is where it really matters. Generations from now will read the exploits, the failures, the successes and the sacrifices of those we knew who tried to defend, and then triumphantly restored freedom and hope to millions of people in South East Asia and the Pacific. If they read carefully, they will also become aware of the raw courage, dogged endurance and sheer determination of that gallant brotherhood of friends and allies."

Avoiding mention of the deplorable hiatus, of the 1942 withdrawal; Prince Phillip puts a nice gloss on the Burma campaign. Future generations might look for the glory in the writings of the world's premier historian; – Mr Winston Spencer Churchill. The words are brief! In his Memoirs, he dismisses the operation in few words: –

"Retreat without action, resulting in inglorious defeat".

And with no further comment!

WITH RESPECT TO MY E.C.O. COLLEAGUES

Reinforced with a draft of 350 conscript recruits, the battalion re-mustered at Shillong in July 1942. In this relaxing place, our E.C.O. contingent were reverted to subordinate roles. Established senior officers of the regiment, ones recovered from illness, and those who had played no part whatsoever in the Burma withdrawal, appeared, and assumed command. Lieutenant Colonels Bob Poole, and Brownie Wood, Major Ricky Valance, Captains Tony Hart, John Wood and Whitworth.

BIBLIOGRAPHY

Gilbert, Martin, *Winston S Churchill Vol II (1941–5) (Heinemann)*

Hudson, Lowenheim, *Roosevelt and Churchill, Their Secret Wartime Correspondence* from *Documents on Australian Foreign Policy, Vol 5* (1937-49) (Australian Government Publishing Service)

Kimball, Warren F, *Churchill and Roosevelt, The Complete Correspondence* (HarperCollins)

Woollcomb, Robert, *The Campaigns of Wavell, 1939—43* (Cassell)
Gilbert, Martin, *Churchill (1941-45) Road to Victory* (Heinemann)

Jackson, WGF, *Alex of Tunis* (B T Batsford Ltd)

Slim, William, *Defeat into Victory* (Corgi Books)

ADDENDA

Summary

Second Battalion, The King's Own Yorkshire Light Infantry was virtually on a war footing from August 1941. Moved and mobilised at Taungyi, in the Shan States, until eventually fighting their way out of Burma, at Kohima, in late May 1942, after a period of nine months. In deplorable conditions, emaciated, under-equipped and ill-armed, seeking battle with the enemy on every possible occasion, defeating them many times in direct conflict: – Inflicted casualties and hindered Japanese progress towards the Indian frontier, until the start of the long monsoon season. Lacking medical aid, struggled along with sick and wounded, leaving many dead and dying, over the many hundreds of miles, from Moulmein, in the South of Burma, to Kohima in the North. Sgt Ike Oldcorn, and Pte P.P. Crabtree, were the last two to collapse, and die of exhaustion or starvation, both within yards of reaching safety.

Resisting the advance, the battalion inflicted much damage, on Japanese, Burmese nationalists, and Dacoit bands, in atrocious conditions. The crossing of the rivers, Salween, Bilin, Sittang, Irrawaddy, and Chindwin, marked stages of progress. A desperate offensive action, by two small platoons at the Yenangyaung oilfield, was combined with action in the wide, dry, sandy beds of the Yin Chaung and Pin Chaung.

To inflict casualties, and harass a rapacious and well-equipped enemy, speaks volumes for the toughness and resilience of stubborn tough Yorkshiremen – 'plus one'. It would be ungracious not to mention the one 'Cockney', somehow escaped, from the Middlesex, Machine Gun Regiment, — Private Martin. Tough, loyal, and strong as an ox, he was involved in every action.

The Kohima Memorial, erected after the war in memory of the Burma dead, says simply; -

> When you go home,
> tell them of us, and say,
> for your tomorrow,
> we gave our today.

Whatever glory there may have been, throughout the first Burma campaign, was never adequately recognised, or claimed, by the battalion. Hospitalised, and convalescent survivers, were evacuated for months, or years, in an atmosphere not receptive to news of withdrawals. Churchill, with problems nearer home, did not wish to know; – 'The Forgotten Army'; – He discarded it!

Reluctantly, Wavell remained loyal to Churchill, and his Government, sending out this message to 'All Ranks', following the withdrawal from Burma: -

"I have been fully aware of the very difficult conditions in which you have been fighting in Burma for the last few months, against greatly superior numbers, with the enemy in control of the air, and with no relief or reinforcements. These conditions have been inevitable since the Japanese gained temporary command of the sea, which made the holding of Rangoon impossible. The enemy has been able to bring into Burma heavy reinforcements, while the absence of communications with India has prevented us from reinforcing or relieving you".

"Your main task during the months has been to occupy and delay large Japanese forces so as to give time for the defences of India to be reinforced and organised, and this you have most successfully and gallantly accomplished in spite of all difficulties.

I thank you for the great work you have done and for the fortitude with which you have borne your losses and hardships. You are now seasoned troops who, after a period of rest and refitting, will be of the greatest value for further operations in more favourable conditions against an enemy, whom you know you can defeat, given anything like equal terms".

A.P. WAVELL (Signed)

General

Commander-in-Chief in India

A Burma Star campaign medal, became a Victoria Cross to each recipient, as he sank into oblivion. Greater campaigns closer to Churchill's heart overtook the Burma war, attracting more publicity. Men of the 1942 Burma campaign realised, they were never to feature in the Churchillian plan; -'discarded', as an embarrassment. Appointing Wavell as Supreme Commander, was Churchill's 'value judgement' of the eastern theatre of the war. It was a lost cause.

At a later day, when Roosevelt began cracking his whip, Churchill's indifferent regard towards the eastern theatre changed. Pressed for action and success in Burma, Churchill renewed interest. Having never once been near the area, he joined the planning process and appointed Mountbatten, Supreme Allied Commander, South East Asia Command: – From a 'map study', Churchill was happy to advise Mountbatten on how he might conduct a successful campaign, to recapture Burma.

As Japanese forces attacked Imphal, and Kohima, on the Indo-Burma border, on 4 May 1944, Churchill's change of attitude, is shown in his message to Mountbatten. It read: -

"Let nothing go from the battle that you need for victory. I will not accept denial of this from any quarter and will back you to the full".

Remote and aloof as commander, Wavell was a quiet man and sought no public difference with Churchill. Silent to the end, he made no fuss, query or explanation. He simply did not attend Churchill's Victory Parade in London at the end of the war.

Mountbatten subsequently adopted Wavell's 1942 scheme, one prepared for the re-conquest of Burma, almost verbatim. He received, troops, ships, tanks, planes, supplies, and equipment. Provisions that were no more than a dream for Wavell.

American main objectives, were achieved at the end of the war: – With the British Empire disintegrated, the American dollar was established, as the world's leading currency. Hostility had been contained outside mainland America: – In the Pacific, Atlantic, Europe, Middle East, and Far East. American losses throughout the war were 292,131 servicemen, and no city bombed or town devastated. Apart from 400,000 British Forces, and Merchant Navy killed; – Britain suffered 60,000 civilian, men, women, and children killed. Towns and cities devastated, withstanding the brunt of Luftwaffer bombing.

Russia lost 100 men, to every one American; at least 25,000,000 Russians were killed. Her principal cities were bombed and ruined to devastation. Stalin never forgot this appalling death toll, or the American reluctance to enter or assist in the war against Hitler, until kicked in the arse by Japan. The Russians were never to forget the phoney American 'aid', in their hour of need.

It was 50 years before Russia yielded an inch of territory gained in the conflict. It was not going to become secondary to, or dependent upon any other power, in arms, or in the state of preparedness for war. The lessons learned had been hard, at the cost of millions of lives; there was never again to be compromise.

Wavell's values and priorities

Acknowledgement of The King's Own Yorkshire Light Infantry contribution in Burma is reflected in the miserly distribution of military decorations, bestowed upon the battalion, in recognition of months of virtually, non-stop action:

Geoffrey Chadwick, O.B.E. (Order of the British Empire)
Douglas Wardleworth, M.C. (Military Cross)
John Howson, M.M. (Military Medal)

Day-by-day acts of valour and gallantry, as a way of life and over a four month period, were taken for granted. It was as though the struggling Burma Force were of no consequence.

Wavell becoming Viceroy of India, showed the same insensitivity to military priorities. In 1945, presenting five well-deserved Victoria Crosses, for gallantry in action, to Gurkha and Indian troops, he wanted a showpiece parade outside the Red Fort at Delhi, in order to excite the Indian press. He ordered KOYLI, in a parade of 'white faces', as a form of theatre decoration.

At the time of preparation for the parade, my company and I were several hundred miles away at Bikaner, a small desert town, 200 miles out in the Sind desert. We were on a sensitive operation of special security, involving prisoners at the one and only Japanese prisoner of war camp. The danger of the operation was overridden, and the security of prison camp staff, became a secondary consideration. Important! Was the ceremony of Wavell's carnival.

Being recalled, and on hearing the news of our impending departure, the Prime Minister of the State had to be dissuaded from sending a telegram to General Auchinleck, Commander in Chief, India, saying; – "Imperative, KOYLI detachment remain and meet Maharajah!" There was no consideration given to which should be given priority, Wavell's carnival, or the prisoner of war camp, or who would benefit by leaving the company, to complete the sensitive Bikaner duty? Wavell wanted! and Wavell got!

I stood on Wavell's parade, sick at heart, aware that behind me on the parade were many men deserving the same recognition as the medal recipients. The few medals handed out to KOYLI were an insult. Here were men who had earned recognition several times over, men like Benny Mee, Geordie Bareham, Joss Isaacs, Michael Mycock, Bill Kibbler, 'Jacko' of Bamsley, Danny Lobben, and so many others.

The battalion Wavell discarded in Burma, was stationed in Delhi Cantonment barracks, four miles away from his residence at Viceregal Lodge. He never once saw fit to visit the unit, or invite members to visit him.

Unforgiving of government and military indifference over the years, I made sure I visited both Bladon churchyard, and the small harbour of Bundoran, in County Sligo, in order to see the places where both, Churchill, and Mountbatten, lie dead. Maybe I wanted to see them both beneath me.

'Princes' in peace

On leaving the army, nothing was ever going to be the same for 'Jacko' Jackson, and Danny Lobben. Starting as privates, finishing as privates, within a few short months, they had lived the equivalent of several lifetimes, as with innumerable private soldiers throughout the British Army. Humour, mixed with true endeavour, was their hallmark, and nothing was too much for them; they showed initiative at all times, never waiting to be told, or ordered to do things, they were the men who made the proud rank of Private, in a British infantry battalion, have significance.

Following release from the army, Jacko returned to mining at Barnsley Main Colliery; he died far too young to appreciate his growing family. Danny lost his wife at an early age; he himself died a tragic early death, in unfortunate circumstances. Like many giving so much, gods amongst men in war, they were never to achieve the same status or recognition in peace.

Private Jim Major, the butcher/cook to the battalion, returned to his small village of Owston Ferry, in Lincolnshire. For more than 40 years, he became both, postmaster, and butcher. He was rewarded in 1982, in recognition of, – 'His many services to the community', by the presentation of the British Empire Medal.

Bill Dawson, the first man to be wounded, completed almost 50 years employment at Askern 'Coalite' works, near Doncaster. A qualified football referee, he maintained a lifelong interest and involvement in the sport. He made no issue of the fact that he had no left shoulder, other than to say, that he would dearly have loved to fulfil his early potential, and play soccer in the big leagues.

Benny Mee was a breeder of canaries; judging at numerous competitive shows. Joss Isaacs became a decorator in his own right, and also competed in bicycle racing, until turned seventy years of age.

I mention but two of the Junior Officers, two gentle and quietly-spoken men, neither of them outstanding in physique, although within themselves men of steel, guts and sheer determination, to trust and follow to the ends of the earth. Both ceaselessly led patrols, by day and by night, trusted by their men who knew they would never let them down. Speaking with a soft Scottish burr, Andrew Maclaren Young returned to his career in fine arts at the Tate Gallery. Douglas Haig returned to qualify, and distinguish himself, as a fine veterinary officer, serving in Africa, and Barbados. Like Jacko and Danny, they also died far too young; they had so much to do, and so much to give.

Premature deaths were seldom attributable to war service, or to the privations imposed by the government, and those appointed to command. Many men spent a lifetime seeking justice, and compensation, for the blunders of government-appointed incompetents.

First contact—Private Bill Dawson

> *W.W. Dawson*
> *'Forest Glade'*
> *West End Road*
> *Norton, Doncaster*

> *June 26, 1994*

Dear Sir,

It is with regret I have not been able to answer your letter until now. I have been away from home on holiday and your letter was one of several to be answered when I returned. I also had to catch up with the gardening. Hope you will accept my apology.

I don't know if I can help you but my war started at Martaban across the river from Moulmein. I can't remember the dates when the Battalion moved from the Shan States to Thaton, it must have been late January. I know we detrained at Thaton. 'A'-Coy. was sent to Martaban and I think the Battalion were in reserve at Thaton. Before 'A'-Coy. moved, could have been the day before or maybe 2 days, Sgt. Major Housley sent for D. Oates and myself and gave us orders to go to Martaban with a Captain from the Madras Sappers and Miners. We were to take his orders until we reported back to A.Coy.

We went to Martaban to assist the Captain in blowing two Barges which had been left FULL of PETROL at Martaban Station. On the station approaches we were shelled from Moulmein. The Officer and Derek Oates went to blow the Barges while I was told to look after the jeep, and shoot anyone who came near. There was chaos in the empty station which was being shelled. Wagons on their sides, fires all over the place. Large fires in Moulmein too on the other side of the river. Only thing I could find any good to me was a tin of Ovaltine which came in handy for Oates and I later.

The Barges went up and the Captain drove the jeep down the road like S. Moss. Japs threw everything at us from Moulmein but we arrived at a bungalow in a Rubber Plantation where we were given dinner with orders from the Captain to eat as much as we could because it could be the last for some time. He got it right! Ashamed I can't remember the Captain's name, hope he got through O.K. Anyway I know that Derek Oates from Batley and Bill Dawson were the first men from a British Battalion to be fired on in Burma. Oates was killed in the bayonet charge at Bilin two or three yards on my right (Burst in the Chest) 17 February 1942.

'A' Coy. went to Martaban a few days later, can't remember the date, we stayed a few days. I remember being Bombed by the Japs, we were in slit-trenches and only one man was hit. We withdrew from Martaban on the night of 9-10 February. Only thing I can remember about it was chaos. At daylight the order was 'Everyman for himself', we were in the open and in swamps. I arrived at Thaton along with Sgt. Lawman and two men. Can't remember their names. The Battalion withdrew from Thaton some time later. I received a small wound on the back of my right hand.

Next stop Bilin River. Two slices of Bread and Jam, Tea. I don't drink Tea. D. Oates and Tom Richardson always shared my tea.

In the bayonet charge at Bilin I was on the left of the road and got a bullet through the left Shoulder. Unable to fire my Tommy-Gun a Cpl. Clayton? took the Gun and left me with 3 hand grenades. The only thing I can remember after seeing a lot of my mates being killed was Japs using bayonets to kill wounded men. When they were near enough to me I pulled the pins out with my teeth and let them have all three, 8 -10-12 Japs, I don't know. Held my left arm as tight as I could and walked passed them in the partial darkness or dusk. In about 100 yds I came across Sgt. Lawman, he had been hit in the left arm and side but we were able to walk down the road together.

Cpl. Rowley came down from a tree and made bandages for our wounds. When he saw my shoulder he said two words 'God Christ', did the best he could for us and went to get help. I never saw him again. I think a dirty stinking vest saved my life and Lawman's. Sgt. Rowley stepped on a mine in Holland in 1944 and was killed. Sgt. Lawman died in Doncaster about 12 years ago. Last time I saw him was at Doncaster Rovers Ground, while the game was on we had a good old natter.

After Bilin we were picked up and our war was over. Spent the next 14 months in hospital at Poona after being flown out of Burma on 23 April 1942.

Keeping well now although the old shoulder gives me a bit of stick now and then. I know Jim Major is at home although he had a spell in hospital in Sheffield, he lives not far from Jim Skin. You may know him, he joined the Battalion at Yenangyaung.

Hope the above is of some use to you and your work is a success.

Best Regards

Bill Dawson

Australian messages/signals – (sic).

FROM HUDSON – *Documentation on Australian Foreign Policy 1937-1949*

Sir Earle Page, Special Representative in the   365
United Kingdom,
to Mr John Curtin, Prime Minister
Cablegram 1613   London, 22 February 1942
Most Immediate   Most Secret   Himself Alone

1. Have just received copy of Churchill's cablegram (a) some hours after its despatch.

2. The statement regarding diversion convoy Northwards and inability of some ships to reach Australia with their fuel conflicts with information regarding movement of ships conveyed to me and communicated to you in my P.47 and P.48.

3. I am Seeing Churchill who tonight is away from London first thing Monday morning to secure an explanation of the alteration of the previous instructions, of which alteration I was unaware.

4. Notwithstanding the natural resentment that your Government may feel in the absence of some satisfactory explanation that such a vital alteration has been made without prior reference I strongly urge that recriminations should be avoided as they can only do harm to our getting the maximum co-operative effort in the Allied cause.

Mr John Curtin, Prime Minister   366
to Mr Clement Attlee, U.K. Secretary of State
for Dominion Affairs
Cablegram 139   Canberra, 23 February 1942
Most Immediate   Most Secret

Prime Minister to – Prime Minister Winston Churchill Reference your 241 (2)

1. In your 233 (3) it was clearly implied that the convoy was not proceeding to the northward. From 241 it appears that you have diverted the convoy towards Rangoon and had treated our approval to this vital diversion as merely a matter of form. By doing so you have established a physical situation which adds to the dangers of the convoy and the responsibility of the consequences of such diversion rests upon you.

2. We have already informed the President (Franklin D. Roosevelt) of the reasons for our decision and, having regard to the terms of his communications to me, we are quite satisfied from his sympathetic reply that he fully understands and appreciates the reasons for our decision.

3. Wavell's message considered by Pacific War Council on Saturday reveals that Java faces imminent invasion. Australia's outer defences are now quickly vanishing and our vulnerability is completely exposed.

4. With A.I.F. troops we sought to save Malaya and Singapore, falling back on Netherlands East Indies. All these northern defences are gone or going. Now you contemplate using the A.I.F. to save Burma. All this has been done as in Greece without adequate air support.

5. We feel a primary obligation to save Australia not only for itself but to preserve it as a base for the development of the war against Japan. In the circumstances it is quite impossible to reverse a decision which we made with the utmost care and which we have affirmed and re-affirmed.

6. Our Chief of General Staff (Lt. Gen. V. A. H. Sturdee) advises although your 241 refers to the leading division only the fact is that owing to the loading of the flights it is impossible at the present time to separate the two divisions and the destination of all the flights will be governed by that of the first flight. This fact re-inforces us in our decision.

Mr Clement Attlee, U.K. Secretary of State   367
for Dominion Affairs,
to Mr John Curtin, Prime Minister
Cablegram 249 London,   23 February 1942, 9.23 p.m.
                                                Received 24 February 1942

Your telegram 23rd February, 139(1) Following for Prime Minister from
Prime Minister (Winston Churchill) Begins:

1.   Your convoy is now proceeding to re-fuel at Colombo. It will then
      proceed to Australia in accordance with your wishes.

2.   My decision to move it northward during the few hours required
      to receive your final answer was necessary because otherwise your
      help, if given, might not have arrived in time.

3.   As soon as the convoy was turned north, arrangements were made
      to increase its escort and this increased escort will be maintained
      during its voyage to Colombo and on leaving Colombo again for as
      long as practicable.

4.   Of course, I take full responsibility for my action.

Sir Earle Page, Special Representative   368
in the United Kingdom,
to Mr John Curtin, Prime Minister
Cablegram 1637   London, 24 February 1942, 12.52 a.m.
                                                Received 24 February 1942
Most Immediate   Most Secret   Himself Alone

1   Further to my telegram 1613 the Prime Minister (Winston
      Churchill) has informed me that he is very sorry that I was not kept
      more closely informed of the movements of the convoy and is sure
      that I will understand how this happened in the very disturbed
      position of the war. As well, you will realise how involved has been
      the United Kingdom political situation. During these few days there
      has been a complete re-casting of British Cabinet and Saturday
      particularly was a day of exceptional preoccupation for the Prime

Minister and Officers most concerned.

2   The Responsible Officer has reported to the Prime Minister that when he gave me the information on Thursday which was telegraphed to you in my telegram P.48(3) that the convoy was steaming on its course to Australia, it was absolutely correct. It was not till late Friday evening after despatch of the Prime Minister's cable 233 that he, confident of an affirmative answer to his appeal to divert the convoy, instructed the Admiralty to order the convoy to proceed northwards.

3   The Admiralty, anticipating that your reply to 233 would be received in time for the convoy either to go to Rangoon or proceed to Australia without any complication, issued the necessary instructions. Meanwhile the Admiralty had got anxious about the fuel position and telegraphed to the Commander-in-Chief Eastern Fleet (Vice-Admiral Sir James Somerville) as to how far north the fleet could go and still have enough fuel if your reply was unfavourable. The reply received indicated that some ships had by that time not got enough fuel to proceed direct to Australia and on the recommendation of the Chiefs of Staff the Prime Minister despatched his telegram 241.

4   I was pleased to note the restrained tone of your reply 139 which undoubtedly will assist future relations between our Governments. Since establishment of the new system of consultation I have been kept very fully and promptly informed of all matters of concern to Australia and am satisfied that the delay in informing you and me in this instance while most unfortunate in the circumstances was due to inadvertence.

Endorsement-Mr J.E. Major B.E.M.

Owston Ferry
28 April 2000

I served in Burma throughout the long withdrawal, from December 1941 to May 1942, with the 2nd Battalion The Kings

Own Yorkshire Light Infantry, and never once parted from the regiment.

Four days after arriving on the Indian border at Kohima, having starved and thirsted for many weeks, I was evacuated to Brielly with malaria and dysentery.

I have read the galley proof of the book No Mandalay No Maymyo (79 Survive), by Captain Gerald Fitzpatrick and, not before time, the book records all action as I remember it precisely.

I was proud to be one of those to survive and am amazed to see revealed subsequently the influences of the government, particularly the indifference shown to those in command by the British Prime Minister. Also, the shabby treatment by the British of the governments of Australia and China, including the excellent Chinese army, the one which relieved us in a desperate situation, was deplorable in the extreme.

I am now aged 84 and throughout my life I have regretted the loss of so many of my good friends and colleagues in this action, undertaken as members of the British armed forces.

J.E. Major, BEM

Letter from Wallace Abbott

Mon 29 May 2000

Dear Mr Fitzpatrick,

I enclose the draft document which you gave me at the Leeds meeting. The amendments which I have made do not materially alter the story but in the interests of accuracy, are perhaps relevant.

The only addition I would suggest is my reason for volunteering. To reiterate what I told you when we talked at Leeds. Regimental History mentions only one shooting incident at the Bilin position. There were in fact two, the first of which was directly responsible for my volunteering. It occured at dusk on the second day when a sentry, Pte Slide, fired a Thompson Gun at one of our own patrols returning to the position. He killed Pte Allsop and wounded Sgt Edwards and L/C Steel. Slide himself was badly wounded in the chest when the patrol returned fire. That night I was in charge of a party of six who carried Slide the eight miles back to Battalion HQ. We brought an ambulance* back to Bilin for the other wounded, arriving at 'B' Coy just at dawn (I understand that Slide died the following day in the Casualty Clearing Station).

Two days later, again at dusk, a second incident occured when Pte Hazelgrave fired a rifle shot at the cooks when they returned to the cook house area after distributing the evening meal. The shot struck the first man's rifle and ricocheted, slightly wounding two men who were next in line. Hazelgrave, whose nerve had broken, had been taken out of the line and put to work helping the cooks.

Later (maybe two days), when it became obvious that we were cut off from the battalion, with no contact and rations exhausted, also much firing from the direction of the Battalion, I considered that, as I was probably the only man who had been to HQ from the Bilin position, it was up to me to try again. I did not take the decision lightly, I knew I would be pushing my luck, having twice travelled that road already. There seemed to be no other way and this was the only logical conclusion.

When I suggested to Capt. Baxter that I try again to get through to HQ he asked me to take along the two wounded men. Fortunately he agreed when I told him I was going through the jungle, not along the road, and that the journey would probably be too much for them.

The rest of my story you know already. After a long detour I got back to the road at a road junction and saw the two trucks. I thought I was back in friendly territory and foolishly broke cover?

Yours sincerely

W. Abbott

P.S. Reading through my letter I should explain that when the ambulances returned to HQ after the first shooting incident the other five people of the stretcher party went back with it to HQ as escort, or so I was told. They did not return to the Bilin position. WA